Economic Crisis and Political Economy

Palgrave Studies in the History of Economic Thought Series

Palgrave Studies in the History of Economic Thought publishes contributions by leading scholars, illuminating key events, theories and individuals that have had a lasting impact on the development of modern-day economics. The topics covered include the development of economies, institutions and theories.

Titles include:

Jan Toporowski (*author*)
MICHAŁ KALECKI AN INTELLECTUAL BIOGRAPHY
Volume 1 Rondezvous in Cambridge 1899–1939

Timothy Shenk (*author*)
MAURICE DOBB: Political Economist

Riccardo Bellofiore, Ewa Karwowski and Jan Toporowski (*edited by*)
THE LEGACY OF ROSA LUXEMBURG, OSKAR LANGE AND MICHAŁ KALECKI
Volume 1 of Essays in Honour of Tadeusz Kowalik

Riccardo Bellofiore, Ewa Karwowski and Jan Toporowski (*edited by*)
ECONOMIC CRISIS AND POLITICAL ECONOMY
Volume 2 of Essays in Honour of Tadeusz Kowalik

The full list of titles available is on the website:
www.palgrave.com/economics

Palgrave Studies in the History of Economic Thought Series
Series Standing Order ISBN 978–1–137–35018–3
(*outside North America only*)

You can receive future titles in this series as they are published by placing a standing order. Please contact your bookseller or, in case of difficulty, write to us at the address below with your name and address, the title of the series and the ISBN quoted above.

Customer Services Department, Macmillan Distribution Ltd, Houndmills, Basingstoke, Hampshire RG21 6XS, England.

Economic Crisis and Political Economy

Volume 2 of Essays in Honour of Tadeusz Kowalik

Edited by

Riccardo Bellofiore
University of Bergamo, Italy

Ewa Karwowski
School of Oriental and African Studies, University of London

and

Jan Toporowski
School of Oriental and African Studies, University of London

palgrave
macmillan

Softcover reprint of the hardcover 1st edition 2013 978-1-137-33574-6

First published 2014 by
PALGRAVE MACMILLAN

Palgrave Macmillan in the UK is an imprint of Macmillan Publishers Limited, registered in England, company number 785998, of Houndmills, Basingstoke, Hampshire RG21 6XS.

Palgrave Macmillan in the US is a division of St Martin's Press LLC, 175 Fifth Avenue, New York, NY 10010.

Palgrave Macmillan is the global academic imprint of the above companies and has companies and representatives throughout the world.

Palgrave® and Macmillan® are registered trademarks in the United States, the United Kingdom, Europe and other countries

ISBN 978-1-349-46322-0 ISBN 978-1-137-33575-3 (eBook)
DOI 10.1057/9781137335753

A catalogue record for this book is available from the British Library.

A catalog record for this book is available from the Library of Congress.

Transferred to Digital Printing in 2013

Contents

List of Illustrations

Figures

Tables

Acknowledgements

The editors of these volumes wish to thank Irena Kowalik and Mateusz Kowalik for their generous support; Taiba Batool and Ania Wroński at Palgrave Macmillan for their encouragement and understanding; Hanna Szymborska for research assistance; Anita Prażmowska and Giovanna Vertova for their patience; and, above all, Tadeusz Kowalik for his untiring inspiration. The kindness and the generosity of the contributors have made these volumes the outstanding tribute that Tadeusz Kowalik deserves, and leaves the editors with sole responsibility for remaining errors.

Notes on Contributors

Paul Auerbach is Reader in Economics in the Department of Economics, Kingston University, London.

Riccardo Bellofiore is Professor of Economics at the University of Bergamo, Italy.

Alberto Chilosi is Professor of Economic Policy at the University of Pisa, Italy.

Pat Devine is an Honorary Research Fellow at the University of Manchester, UK, and Convenor of the Red Green Study Group.

Gary A. Dymski is Professor of Applied Economics at Leeds University Business School, University of Leeds, UK.

Ewa Karwowski is a researcher at the School of Oriental and African Studies, University of London.

John E. King has recently retired from La Trobe University, Australia.

Kazimierz Łaski is Emeritus Professor of Economics at the University of Linz, Austria, and the Vienna Institute for International Economic Studies.

Marc Lavoie is a professor in the Department of Economics at the University of Ottawa, Canada, and IMK Research Fellow at the Institut für Makroökonomie in Düsseldorf, Germany.

Edwin Le Heron is Associate Professor in Economics at the Bordeaux Institute of Political Science, France, and researcher at the GREThA of University of Bordeaux.

Paul Mattick has recently retired as Professor of Philosophy at Adelphi University, USA.

D. Mario Nuti has recently retired as Professor of Comparative Economic Systems at the University of Roma 'La Sapienza'.

Leon Podkaminer is Professor of Economics, Institute of Economic Sciences of the Polish Academy of Sciences; Vienna Institute for International Economic Studies and Wyższa Szkoła Administracji, Bielsko-Biała, Poland.

Malcolm Sawyer is Emeritus Professor of Economics, Leeds University Business School, University of Leeds, UK.

Dimitris P. Sotiropoulos is Senior Lecturer at the Business School of the Open University, UK.

Janusz J. Tomidajewicz is Professor of Economic Policy in the Department of Economic and Local Government Policy of Poznań University of Economics, Poland.

Jan Toporowski is Professor of Economics and Finance at the School of Oriental and African Studies, University of London.

Alessandro Vercelli is Professor of Economics at the University of Siena, Italy.The editors of these volumes wish to thank Irena Kowalik and Mateusz Kowalik for their generous support; Taiba Batool and Gemma Shields at Palgrave for their encouragement and understanding; Hanna Szymborska for research assistance; Anita Prażmowska and Giovanna Vertova for their patience; and, above all, Tadeusz Kowalik for his untiring inspiration. Their kindness, and the generosity of the contributors, has made these volumes the outstanding tribute that Tadeusz Kowalik deserves, and leaves the editors with sole responsibility for remaining errors.

Introduction: Tadeusz Kowalik and the Political Economy of the 20th Century

Riccardo Bellofiore, Ewa Karwowski and Jan Toporowski

Tadeusz Kowalik (1926–2012) is best known as the editor of the two great Polish political economists, Michał Kalecki (1899–1970) and Oskar Lange (1904–1965), an advisor to the Polish trades union movement *Solidarity* during the 1980s, when it played a key part in bringing down the Communist Government in Poland, and subsequently a fierce critic of the capitalism established in his country. In his work Kowalik challenged both the commonly accepted view of the 'Keynesian Revolution' and the inability of Polish communists to come to terms with their revolutionary past and find a place for themselves in the modern world.

Tadeusz Kowalik was born on 19 November 1926 in the village of Kajetanówka outside the city of Lublin in Eastern Poland, traditionally the poorer, more backward part of the country. He completed his undergraduate studies in law at Warsaw University with outstanding results in 1951. Supervised by Oskar Lange, he studied for a doctorate in Economics on the work of the Polish sociologist and economist Ludwik Krzywicki; this was awarded to Kowalik in 1958. By then he was already editor of the weekly newspaper *Życie Gospodarcze* (*Economic Life*), where he promoted reform of the over-centralised state economic system. He lasted only two years in this position before being removed when the ruling party started to close down the discussion on reform. However, under the patronage of his supervisor he kept his position as Lecturer in Political Economy at the social science university run for activists in the ruling party, and commenced research for his post-doctoral degree, the *habilitacja*.

During his first visit to the UK, in the early 1960s, Kowalik defended a version of the then fashionable Convergence Thesis, that the communist and the capitalist worlds were both gradually becoming welfare technocracies tempered by democracy. In London, Kowalik met Isaac Deutscher, the distinguished Marxist historian and member of the pre-war Communist Party of Poland (KPP). The KPP had been disbanded in 1938 and its leaders executed by Stalin.

In October 1965, Lange died. By then Kowalik was working with Kalecki in criticising the economic policy failures of the government and distortions in economic planning. He was also collaborating with the philosopher Leszek Kołakowski and the economist Włodzimierz Brus, using their party positions to protect dissidents within and outside the ruling party. In the crackdown on Jews and 'revisionists' in 1968, Kowalik was expelled from the Party. The meeting with Deutscher was put forward as evidence of the ideological laxity that needed to be purged, despite the formal rehabilitation of the KPP in 1956. However, Kowalik retained his position at the Polish Academy of Sciences. Much of his output for the next two decades appeared under the name of friendly associates who were not subject to the ban on publication, most notably Edward Lipiński, at that time the oldest and most distinguished Polish economist, who had given Kalecki his first job in 1929. After Kalecki's death in 1970, Kowalik took on the additional responsibility of supervising the editing by Jerzy Osiatyński of the Kalecki *Collected Works*.

From 1968, Tadeusz Kowalik was active in unofficial, dissident, university discussions; wage austerity was reimposed in Poland after 1976, leading to a resumption of strikes. These culminated in the emergence of the *Solidarity* trade union. In 1980 Kowalik travelled to Gdańsk to assist the workers in their negotiations with the Polish government. He wrote and edited prolifically in the underground press in support of Solidarity and its principles of democratic syndicalism. Here he drew on the political programmes and critiques of Soviet industrial organisation put forward in Poland in the 1920s and 1930s by non-Communist Marxists, among them his mentor Oskar Lange. There were also the themes of reformed socialism that Kowalik had been advocating since the 1950s.

1 Revising Keynesian political economy

Tadeusz Kowalik's political economy was inspired by his political activism. He had been radicalised by the poverty he experienced in his youth and the struggle against the Nazi occupation of Poland, becoming a member of the Polish Workers' Party in 1948. His economic ideas were formed initially by Oskar Lange, who had encouraged

Kowalik to read Marx and take seriously all schools of thought in economics. Lange bequeathed to Kowalik something of the characteristic Lange approach to Marxism, according to which economics was losing its ideological character, and 'bourgeois' economics differed only in not being conscious of its socialist potential. Kowalik therefore shared with Lange an openness and non-dogmatic approach to economic analysis that made them both liked and respected by economists of all persuasions.

But whereas Lange formed the style of Tadeusz Kowalik's political ideas, the originality of those ideas came from Kowalik's collaboration with Kalecki and his research on Rosa Luxemburg, which gave Kowalik a radical new approach to the theory of Kalecki –and in turn caused Kalecki himself to review his own work. After the death of John Maynard Keynes in 1946, Joan Robinson advanced the view that Kalecki was the 'more consistent' Keynesian (Robinson, 1969). Among Marxists (with certain notable exceptions, such as Maurice Dobb in Cambridge and Paul Sweezy in the US) Kalecki came to be regarded as a 'Left Keynesian', using essentially Keynesian ideas about the importance of fiscal policy in maintaining a level of aggregate demand appropriate to full employment to argue for socialism (for example, King, 2002). Tadeusz Kowalik was a key figure in challenging the framing of Kalecki within a Keynesian theoretical and policy agenda.

In the early 1960s, Kowalik was asked to contribute a biographical chapter to the *festschrift* that was to celebrate Kalecki's 65th birthday in 1964. As part of his preparation for this, Kowalik undertook a series of interviews with Kalecki about his work and his ideas. It is now apparent that these interviews are more than just a record of Kalecki's key publications and his discussions with Keynes; Kowalik took Kalecki back to the debates among radical socialists in Poland during the 1920s and early 1930s, centred on the instability of capitalism, mass unemployment and economic depression. The central ideas in these debates were those of the Austrian Marxist Rudolf Hilferding, Rosa Luxemburg and the Russian Marxist Mikhail Tugan-Baranowski. Following his interviews with Kowalik, Kalecki returned to these authors and went on to publish a paper recording his understanding that Luxemburg and Tugan-Baranowski had both addressed the key issue of aggregate demand in capitalism. However, aggregate demand was not important in just the Keynesian sense that it directly determined the levels of employment; in a capitalist economy the key function of demand is that it is necessary to allow capitalists to realise profits. It is in this context that the problem of aggregate demand is found in Tugan-

Baranowski and Rosa Luxemburg; according to Kalecki, both had identified the effective constraint on capitalist development. Their theories pointed to the key role of external markets (including armaments) and the absurdity of an antagonistic system in which employment and worker consumption depend on the production of machines for the production of machines (or, worse, production as a means of destruction), both so apparent in post-War US capitalism. But, as Kowalik argued, Kalecki, together with Steindl, presented a more convincing and comprehensive explanation of the failure of capitalism to realise its dynamic prospectus.

Kowalik and Kalecki returned to these ideas after 1968, both of them now disgraced following the anti-semitic, anti-revisionist purges of that year. The outcome was their joint paper *The 'Crucial Reform'* in capitalism, an attempt to make sense of the Keynesian Revolution in economic policy within the framework of those early Marxist discussions about whether free market capitalism could maintain full employment without resorting to fascism or war (Kalecki and Kowalik, 1971). The paper was published in Italy just as workers' strikes in Poland forced a change of government, but without rehabilitating those who had been purged in 1968. But by the time the paper came out, Kalecki was dead. Kowalik retained his position in the Polish Academy of Sciences as editor of the Lange Collected Works; the Academy had an autonomous position among Polish institutions dominated by the communist authorities, and the Lange project was considered of national and international importance. In 1973 the project was expanded to include the publication of a collected edition of Kalecki's writings, under Kowalik's general supervision.

2 The political economy of Rosa Luxemburg

A rare exception to the ban on publishing under his own name was made in 1971, when Tadeusz Kowalik's book *Róża Luksemburg Teoria Akumulacji i Imperializmu* was published (Kowalik, 1971). This book is Tadeusz Kowalik's masterpiece. In it he tried to reconstruct the political economy of the first half of the 20th century, a task that Karl Marx had set out to achieve for mid-19th century political economy but never completed.

To understand the true significance of Tadeusz Kowalik's achievement, it is necessary to understand the circumstances under which the book arose and (as in Marx) the political economy of his time. The political conditions that give significance to Tadeusz Kowalik's political economy started in 1938, with the dissolution by the Communist International of the Polish Communist Party, the KPP, on grounds that the Party had fallen too much under the influence of Rosa Luxemburg and Leon Trotsky. In 1956 the KPP was formally rehabilitated, and in 1963 the first post-war Polish edition of Rosa Luxemburg's *The Accumulation of Capital* appeared (Luxemburg, 1913a). In that same year, Tadeusz Kowalik completed the post-doctoral thesis that was to become *Róża Luksemburg Teoria Akumulacji i Imperializmu*. The starting point for Kowalik's analysis was the Russian Narodniks' explanations as to why, in their view, capitalism could not develop in Russia with the limited markets that the country provided at the end of the 19th century. This led to Tugan-Baranowski's response: his rejection of the underconsumptionist argument on the grounds that capitalism could continue producing machines for the sake of production, irrespective of the state of consumer demand. Almost by stealth, Tugan-Baranowski became a central and deeply ambiguous figure in 20th-century political economy. This was not for his solution of an abstract problem of capitalist accumulation, but for his study of English banking crises (Tugan-Baranowski, 1905). Despite the fact that his work was never translated into English, Tugan-Baranowski's study became a key text on the business cycle and was an important influence on British exponents of the monetary business cycle, among them John Maynard Keynes and Dennis Robertson.[1]

Tadeusz Kowalik thus found the roots of 20th-century political economy in Marx's critique of Say's law and his argument, in Volumes II and III of *Capital*, that capitalist reproduction or growth cannot take place in a way that is stable or crisis-free. The question of external markets then opens the door for Keynesian political economy, constructed around demand deficiency and the state as an external market. For Tadeusz Kowalik, the central figure through whose work all these very different writers are connected is Michał Kalecki. In his *Essays in the Theory of Economic Fluctuations*, published on the eve of the Second World War, Kalecki had expressed the connection as follows: Rosa Luxemburg's 'theory cannot be accepted as a whole, but the necessity of covering the "gap of saving" by home investment or exports was outlined by her perhaps more clearly than anywhere else before the publication of Mr. Keynes's *General Theory*' (Kalecki, 1939b: p. 46, Osiatyński, 1990: p. 446). Inspired by his discussions with Tadeusz Kowalik, Kalecki was to develop this point further in his 1967 paper on Rosa Luxemburg and Tugan-Baranowski. Kowalik worked with Kalecki on his last paper on the 'Crucial Reform' of capitalism, which sets the 'Keynesian Revolution' in the context of those debates around capitalist reproduction (Kalecki, 1967; Kalecki and Kowalik, 1971). The 'revolution' in policy was the more effective use of government expenditure as a means of assisting in the realisation of capitalists' surplus.

Kalecki's pioneering work in 20th-century macroeconomics was therefore a recurrent theme in Tadeusz Kowalik's ideas, and he considered Kalecki's business cycle theory as the medium through which Keynesian ideas are linked to those late-19th-century debates on capitalist reproduction. This theme recurs from the Kalecki biographical essay through to Kowalik's last essays on Rosa Luxemburg (Kowalik, 1964a and 2009).[2]

Shortly after publication of his book on Rosa Luxemburg, in two very long entries published only in Italian in the *Enciclopedia Einaudi* ('Capitale', Capital and 'Crisi', Crisis), which in fact form a book together, Kowalik proposed his own broader perspective on capitalism and its development through structural crises. In 'Capitale' he connected the notion of capital to that of socio-economic formation, showing how primary accumulation and the formation of the (national and world) market produced capitalist social relations, thanks to the hegemony that bourgeoisie exercised by various means, including State intervention. The key authors addressed by Kowalik were Marx (stressing the role of alienation in his thought) and Max Weber. The notion that capitalism is a system of rational economic calculation by firms' management is, in Kowalik's view, reductive. It is discredited by the ubiquitous waste in contemporary capitalism, but also by the systematic recurrence of crises. His conclusion, drawn from Kalecki and Lange, is similar to that drawn by the *Monthly Review*, partially from Kalecki, but also from Thorstein Veblen.

In the entry 'Crisi' the discourse is put forward on a larger scale than that of Kowalik's book on Luxemburg, though the key reference (together with Schumpeter) is once again Kalecki. After an historic survey of the (exogenous) crises affecting economies and societies before capitalism, and of the (endogenous) periodic alternation of prosperity and depression in capitalism, he confronted the contradictions and limitations of Keynes and the Keynesian tradition. Business cycles and crises were primarily due to the dual and ambiguous role of investment (the least stable component of effective demand and, along with capitalist consumption, the main autonomous component). Investment is also an activity that adds to productive capacity and must therefore look for ever-expanding markets. A contributing factor to instability is the time discrepancy between the manifestation of the crisis and the delayed effects of the decisions taken to overcome it. The solution to the effective demand problem cannot but lead to the cycle, and the cycle to periodic structural crises.

In this outlook, neomercantilist export-led growth and Keynesian economic policies are insufficient, and it is understandable why they have led to paradoxical results. The expansion of foreign trade shifted the crises to underdeveloped countries, while deficit spending materialised in armaments and militarism. The key reason for the difficulties, however, has to do with the same nature of capitalism, that is with the intrinsic instability of a system driven by capitalists' investment demand: so much so that capitalist crises cannot be overcome without overcoming capitalism. Full employment can only be temporary, and is regularly reversed. In this way, Kowalik took Kalecki out of left Keynesianism, and located his work firmly within an original development of the Marxian tradition.

3 Volumes in honour of Tadeusz Kowalik

The eighth and final volume of the Lange *Collected Works* was published in 1986. But then in 1990, a further two volumes were published, containing selected papers that had been previously edited for political reasons (Hagemejer and Kowalik, 1986). The Lange *Works*, along with his collaboration with Kalecki and his studies of Rosa Luxemburg, remain Kowalik's most monumental achievement. At the time of his death, Kowalik was working on an edition of Lange's voluminous correspondence and an intellectual biography of Lange. Kowalik's last book, *From Solidarity to Sellout: The Restoration of Capitalism in Poland*, was published by New York's Monthly Review Press only days before he died.

In 2010 Tadeusz Kowalik was approached with a proposal for a *festschrift* in his honour. His response was, characteristically, to decline the honour with thanks under the pretext that 'this is not my style'. He requested instead a volume commemorating the thinkers who had so influenced him: Rosa Luxemburg, Oskar Lange and Michał Kalecki. We have been overwhelmed by the generosity of the response to our invitation to contribute. One volume has grown to two full volumes, reflecting the very rich intellectual legacy that Tadeusz Kowalik had inherited from his teachers, and to which he himself contributed.

The chapters in the volumes fall more or less naturally into two categories. The first consists of chapters that examine the ideas of

Luxemburg, Lange and Kalecki as they developed them. Key themes in this group of chapters are the theories of Kalecki and Luxemburg as developing the schemes of reproduction that appear in Volume II of Marx's *Capital* (chapters by G.C. Harcourt and Peter Kriesler, Noemi Levy-Orlik, Gabriele Pastrello, Riccardo Bellofiore, John Bellamy Foster and Andrew Trigg), Marxian political economy and the methodology of Oskar Lange (Roberto Lampa, Paul Zarembka and Meghnad Desai), the political economy of developing countries (Marcin Kula), and the relationship between the ideas of Lange and Kalecki and the dominating figure of 20th-century macroeconomics, John Maynard Keynes (Jo Michell and Jan Toporowski). The second group of chapters brings the ideas of Luxemburg, Lange and Kalecki up to date by examining how those ideas illuminate the financial crisis of the 21st century (chapters by Paul Auerbach and Dimitris Sotiropoulos, Edwin Le Heron, Malcolm Sawyer, Kazimierz Łaski and Leon Podkaminer, Alberto Chilosi, Janusz J. Tomidajewicz and Pat Devine), and how that crisis illuminates those ideas (John King, Gary Dymski, D. Mario Nuti, Alessandro Vercelli, Ewa Karwowski, Paul Mattick and Marc Lavoie).

In sum these chapters cover the political economy of Tadeusz Kowalik, whose purpose was not to interpret the world but to change it with an honest, unsentimental understanding of capitalism and socialism that is shared by the authors and the editors.

Ewa Karwowski, Riccardo Bellofiore and Jan Toporowski

We are grateful to Tadeusz Kowalik for his generous discussion of his scholarship and ideas with us. We thank Alessandro Roncaglia, Julio Lopez, John Bellamy Foster, Hanna Szymborska, Kazimierz Łaski, Geoff Harcourt, John King, Mario Nuti, Leon Podkaminer and Tracy Mott for comments on earlier drafts of this Introduction.

Notes

1. 'I find myself in strong sympathy with the school of writers – Tugan-Baranovski, Hull, Spiethoff and Schumpeter – of which Tugan-Baranovski was the first and the most original' (Keynes, 1971: pp. 89–90).
2. Some idea of the influence of Michał Kalecki on Tadeusz Kowalik's thinking about Rosa Luxemburg is provided by the paper which Kowalik contributed to the Kalecki festschrift, entitled *R. Luxemburg's Theory of Accumulation and Imperialism (An Attempted Interpretation)*. Kowalik refers to this paper in this book as containing the essential conclusions of his *habilitacja* thesis (see note 14 at the end of the Introduction). But in the earlier paper, Kowalik merely states that Kalecki had resolved the problems in Rosa Luxemburg's analysis, and the paper itself makes much more of Oskar Lange's criticisms of Luxemburg's theory. By the time Kowalik's book came out in 1971, Kalecki had been given a

much more central role as the link between the Marxian political economy of Luxemburg, Tugan-Baranowski, Hilferding and so on, and mid-20th-century Keynesian political economy; and Lange himself is reduced to expressing his view that realisation problems are purely monetary phenomena (see note 99 at the end of ch. 4 of Kowalik, 1971).

1

The Economic System as an End or as a Means, and the Future of Socialism: An Evolutionary Viewpoint

Alberto Chilosi

1.1 The economic system as an end or as a means

A criterion for the choice between different (economic, political or social) systems may be the capability of a system to pursue the ends that correspond to one's interests and values (that is to a system of preferences over alternative social states)('The higher the level of social development, the stronger the tendency towards variety and differentiation, i.e., enrichment of the forms of social and economic life' Kowalik, 2003: p. 206). The adoption of specific varieties of the institutions that make up a system can be calibrated to the pursuit of those aims, given the initial historical and institutional setup. Thus, the system and the institutions that make it up and qualify its specific variety can be seen as a means, an empirically adaptable instrument, rather than an end in itself. An alternative viewpoint attributes an intrinsic value to the choice of a system as such. The choice of the system becomes a choice of intrinsic, epochal or ethical, value, a choice of civilisation, independent of the actual results that such a choice may bring about in the immediate or in the middle run (historically speaking). This remark applies to both economic and political systems. For instance, the second viewpoint is often applied to democracy, seen as a value in itself rather than, à la Churchill, as the least obnoxious political system that has been invented up to now, since it renders relatively more probable social states that are valued higher relative to widely (albeit not unanimously) shared social values.

1.2 The fetishism of systems

The fetishism of socialism or capitalism leads to the persuasion that the choice of a system has an intrinsic emancipator or transformational value, for two possible reasons. The first is the millenarian viewpoint of the realisation of the ultimate bliss in an indefinite future which is sometimes perceived as imminent. The second is the ethical viewpoint. Historically the first viewpoint applied in particular to socialism; the millenarian force of 'real' socialism rested in the official doctrine that the system was a transition towards a qualitatively superior stage, where the intrinsic imperfections of the intermediate stage would be overcome. In the Marxist tradition this was supposed to apply in particular to the limitation of resources in relation to needs, nullifying the relevance of the distributional issue (Marx, 1875b).

It is more difficult, if not impossible, to attribute millenarian properties to an existing and long-established system, whose characteristics are well known and apparent, that has already fulfilled its potentialities and manifested its intrinsic flaws and imperfections. In the case of transition economies, the starting point was characterised by much lower average living standards in comparison to the advanced market economies, and the attainment of the living standards of the advanced liberal democracies was seen as some kind of relative bliss which could be brought about by the institutional transformation towards a capitalist market economy. In this context, systemic transformation becomes a pre-eminent objective to be pursued by every possible means and as fast as possible, without adequately considering the specificities of the historical and institutional context and the extent of the transition costs associated with its speed and modalities. In another context the relative well-being achieved in the framework of the capitalist system can be defended through an idealisation of the latter, which, being the most natural system is considered to be, à la Pangloss, the best of all possible systems – not artificially constructed along a pre-determined model, such as socialism, which, unlike capitalism and market, is seen as an unnatural constructivist deviation. At the same time the ideology may assume an ethical connotation, and the market may be seen as intrinsically just, because through the market everybody receives according to their merits and so on.

As far as socialism is concerned, the fetishism may, even independent of any millenarian view, be based on the moral foundation of the ethical illegitimacy of profit. This view may be based on ad-hoc theories (such as the Marxian theory of labour value and exploitation), on simplistic viewpoints (such as the idea that the wealth of somebody must perforce originate from the poverty of somebody else), and on erroneous perceptions of the functioning of the real world. Or, more simply, it can derive from the consideration that private capital and entrepreneurial incomes lead to wide income differentials that can be perceived as ethically unjustified.

1.3 The intrinsic imperfection of economic systems and their comparison

In reality, the institutions of both 'real' capitalism and 'real' socialism are largely imperfect, and are characterised by an unavoidable set of shortcomings and inefficiencies on which there is no need to dwell because they are well known.[1] The contest between 'real' capitalism and 'real' socialism during the 20th century has eventually seen the former prevail. The experiment has been of enormous value in deepening our understanding of social facts and possibilities. Meanwhile, the costs have been sustained on their very flesh by the citizens of the former socialist bloc, who have since then served as guinea pigs for another original experiment, of lesser, but still great, social significance – that of the post-communist transition, aiming (according to the late Branko Horvat's preferred terminology) at the restoration of capitalism, or rather to the construction, or reconstruction, of modern capitalist institutions.

Does all this mean that socialism is doomed not only for the present, but also for the indefinite future? Will it be worthwhile to try again? In the name of what? Certainly the simple consideration that the capitalist system, in all its variations, leads to questionable results, with respect to both ethics and efficiency, in comparison with some abstract benchmark is not enough to justify a new, however partial, experiment in socialism. The view that the proven imperfection of a system is a sufficient reason for the establishment of a new system, after the removal (be it forcible or peaceful) of the first, is a fallacy which has led to tragic consequences, but which continues to find new supporters (such as recently the so-called anti-globalisers and other radical groups).

Owing to the inevitable shortcomings of actual systems and the experience of the 20th century, the only reasonable perspective may consist in an instrumental and pragmatic approach towards systems and institutions whereby the latter are not considered to have intrinsic value, and their merit lies exclusively in the societal objectives they allow to be reached in a limited time horizon rather than in what they are alleged to bring about in an indefinite future. Moreover, one must be aware that the consequences of introducing new institutions depend on the specific historical circumstances, as has been shown by the different impact of the introduction of analogous institutions in different countries. In particular, the introduction, or restoration, of market institutions has in general produced better results in the countries where a functioning market economy was present in a not too distant past.

1.4 Socialism of the means and socialism of the aims

From this perspective we can make a distinction between socialism of the means and socialism of the aims. The means consist, on the negative side, in the prohibition of private entrepreneurial activity and of private ownership of productive assets. The positive part is the substitution of public, or 'social', ownership and entrepreneurship for private ('capitalist') ownership and entrepreneurship.

But socialism can also be seen as a set of aims such as equality, or social security, the same as those that would usually be advocated for justifying the adoption of a variety of socialism of the means, apart from the discredited Marxist justification of socialism as being an historically inevitable and much more productive, economic system. Theoretically speaking, these aims translate into preferences over social states. More precisely, one may characterise as 'socialist' a subset of the possible preference sets, the set of those preference sets that are relatively better shaped by socialist values. Thus, one may conceive a socialism of aims that is in principle independent of the choice of a particular social system through which socialist aims can be pursued. In this case the socialism of aims, not being constrained to a particular choice of means, acquires in theory an additional degree of freedom, and its pursuit may bring about outcomes that are not inferior to those that can be achieved through the constrained pursuit of socialism, given a 'socialist' preference system. From this perspective, what is left of socialism is the specificity of the aims that are pursued. This is so even in a context where capitalist institutions prevail, if the latter are seen as more suitable to achieve preferred social outcomes on the basis of the given 'socialist' preference system in which socialist aims, such as equality or social security, cannot be exclusive but must be traded off with relevant alternative aims, such as material affluence or the range of choice. Summing up, from this perspective socialism is characterised by the nature and the weighting of its objectives, independent of the institutional means used for their pursuit. The qualification of President Obama as a socialist by the 'tea party' republicans could be seen from the viewpoint of socialism of the aims not as absurd as it is from that of the socialism of means.

1.5 Is there socialism in the future of capitalism?

The fact that in the 20th century the socialism of means (or organisational socialism) failed in the contest with capitalism does not mean that in the future a different setup could not reveal itself as superior. In a very long-run perspective the failing could turn out to be only temporary; in Schumpeter's words a simple 'surface' in relation to 'the tendency toward another civilization that slowly works deep down below'.[2] Moreover some institutions that are usually considered as socialist could be usefully imported into capitalism (or rather, into the mixed economy), as has been the case in the past, such as with the social security systems. The reverse could also be successful, for instance the insertion of capitalist institutions into Soviet socialism under Lenin's New Economic Policy, or the transformation of the Chinese economy since 1978, amounting to a gradual evolution into a capitalist mixed market economy where the capitalist element gradually increases its relative weight in time, and the power of private (or at any rate decentralised) entrepreneurship is harnessed to achieve exceptional rates of growth in a context of still strong State ownership and control.

As far as the public[3] ownership and management of economic activities goes, this has been shown in the past to be on the whole less efficient in the case of the former socialist countries in dynamic terms, with respect to the generation and absorption of technical progress in consumer satisfaction, more in general in terms of factor dynamic efficiency (growth in the value of production deriving from total factor growth) – and also, more trivially, in terms of X-efficiency.[4] At the same time, the relative organisational slack that in general characterises public sector activities, which theoretically speaking could be compatible with Pareto-efficiency, may well be inefficient from the point of view of the principle of compensation, and thus from the unconstrained Paretian viewpoint as well (that is, its advantage for public employees could be less than its cost for taxpayers). In practice, up to now whenever State and private enterprises have coexisted, the former have proved to be on the whole less efficient.[5] But the actual consequences of State ownership and control can be different in the different social and political contexts, and not always so disastrous such as, for instance, in the Italian case, where the accumulated past losses of State enterprises account for about half of the present huge public debt.[6] As a matter of principle there is no fundamental reason why the performance of State-owned enterprises should be worse than that of privately owned enterprises. For efficiency, what matters more than ownership are probably the extent of competition and the enforcement of hard budget constraints (here lies the problem with State-owned enterprises: they are often established in non-competitive environments, and instead of the objective of profitability they are assigned by politicians a variety of different other commitments, Stiglitz, 1994: pp. 80–81). But in the future things may change for the reasons considered below, and public ownership and management may become relatively more efficient than private ownership and management.

1.6 Public goods, collective goods, and the socialisation of consumption

But let us consider first of all the process of change in the nature of consumer goods leading to a progressive increase, as a consequence of changes in technology and tastes, in the relative importance of public goods. Among the possible characteristics of a socialist system there is the tendency towards socialisation of consumption; this means an allocation of consumer goods independent of individual budget constraints. In Marx's *Critique of the Gotha Programme*, the part of social product 'which is intended for the common satisfaction of needs [...] from the outset [...] grows considerably in comparison with present-day society and it grows in proportion as the new society develops'.[7]

There are three types of consumption that can be of relevance here:

(1) collective consumption proper, which may be made up of private, public or semi-public goods in an economic sense, whose production and distribution is decided collectively through the political process and are not rationed through private budget constraints (such as public provision of health, education, social services, defence, law and order, national broadcasting, even private consumer goods under the future hypothetical abundance of Full Communism and saturation of needs).

(2) purely public goods (at least in the sense of non-rivalry), which are privately or publicly produced (such as radio and TV broadcasting or the Internet)[8] and are freely available, financed by the State (such as in the case of national broadcasting services), by private volunteers and benefactors (as in the case of Wikipedia)[9] or advertising. In the latter case, production of public goods is strictly derivative of the existence of a large market for private goods in which the rewards from advertising

can be reaped. Since the production of public goods is the main reason for the existence of the State, there are some obvious theoretical reasons in favour of pushing the limits of private provision forward through public financing or direct public production.

(3) Non-rival but excludable goods for the consumption of which a royalty is charged. There is a clear market failure here that may (but need not) constitute a reason for public provision. If the barriers to entry are low (as in the case of the setting up of Internet sites), and no conditions of natural monopoly apply, or monopolistic positions are contestable by newcomers anyway, competition tends to bring the fees down towards the point where they only just cover costs, and the fees may be quite disproportionately low relative to the consumer surplus that is created. Moreover, in order to have the provider of the good (say, the Internet site or the broadcasting site) and the good itself (say, a computer programme) known to the public, some initial losses would be incurred and the good made available, as may often be the case, for a very low fee or nothing. Since this is an ongoing process (as the dynamics of Internet sites may show) those whose opportunity cost of time is lower may look for the newcomers rather than pay the incumbent sites for their services. This opportunity can benefit the worse off, who by spending some of their time could avoid paying for goods that others are enjoying for a fee. These may still be public goods as far as non-rivalrous allocation of consumption is concerned. In other words, in the case when dominant positions are realised through sunk costs and network economies of scale, because of significant dynamic contestability and the degree of the economies of scale the fees often tend to be very low in relation to the substantial nature of the goods and to the consumer surplus that may be created, and consumers with low opportunity cost of time can avoid paying altogether.

Of the above three categories of goods, only the first makes up collective consumption in the sense that provision is collectively decided through political representation, and allocated irrespective of budget constraints. Moreover, public non-profit production, such as in the areas mentioned by Marx (1875b), health and education, may be preferable whenever the nature of the product cannot be sufficiently appreciated by the public, and there is need for strict quality control.[10] This may mitigate the potential impact of some types of medical services that are increasingly costly and are intrinsically mostly private goods. There could be good reasons, owing to their specific nature, for public provision and an allocation through assignment rather than through the market.

All in all, we may have entered a period when the nature of consumption is quite different from those times when, even in relatively more prosperous countries, the great bulk of consumption was made up by the predominantly private goods (primarily food, but also clothing, shelter, transportation and personal services) that were unequally distributed.[11] This implies an involuntary, but important, element of socialism, because of the socialisation of a growing part of consumption which is basically not rationed through purchasing power. (There is a kind of paradox here. In most cases the new goods are enjoyed individually, in the intimacy of the home, even if through access to a virtual agora, while some of the kinds of consumption that the new goods are displacing – theatres, cinemas, concerts, conferences – represent forms of collective enjoyment, even if their prevailing character is, economically speaking, private or semi-private.) This could also contribute to explaining why the Internet revolution has not brought about the increase of the growth rate of productivity that some had expected.[12] Part of the 'output' of the Internet is made up by public goods that directly enter into the consumer utility function, and could in theory be measured in terms of the value of private goods that are displaced in the formation of real income, but in practice may be not adequately accounted for in national income accounting. The incentive problem of a society where an ever-increasing part of consumption is made up of public goods for the enjoyment of which the only relevant constraint is the availability of free time is obvious; the relative utility of leisure increases, with increasingly negative effects on the labour supply and the creation of the tax base needed to finance, among others, the production of the public goods themselves.[13] In the end, the only way out could be the re-introduction of such outdated revenue sources as capitation, wealth taxes or State monopolies. An obvious additional second best measure could be, whenever possible and if not too costly, to tax the time used for accessing public goods such as the Internet (Anderberg et al., 2000). But such a measure would be very unpopular and could have intrinsic negative costs in terms of efficiency, given the quasi-public-good nature of Internet access. In the end, given the contradiction between the efficiency objective pointing towards encouraging, and possibly subsidising, the production of Internet contents, given their nature of public (or quasi-public) goods, and the financial considerations leading to the taxation of the time spent on the Internet, the actual situation where the Internet is basically neither taxed nor subsidised may appear as a reasonable compromise, resulting in the minimisation of transaction costs.

1.7 Will public production ever become more efficient than private production?

Let us turn now to the consideration of the relative efficiency of public vs. private production, both of public and of private goods. As long as the sentiment of individual responsibility and respect for the public interest grows, with civil and economic progress, through the accumulation of human and social capital, one cannot exclude the possibility that public management of production could eventually become as efficient as private capitalist management – even more so if people prefer to work in a public rather than a private organisation. For instance, the number of those who dislike the specific business culture of private firms in general, and of corporations in particular, and would rather work, even at lower wages, in organisations with a different culture, aiming at the satisfaction of social needs or with a public principal, may increase in time. This kind of attitude could also prove itself more compatible than the selfishness of some types of narrow business culture with building those relations of trusts and cooperation that are of fundamental importance for a successful market economy: employees could be better motivated, and so more productive, if the purpose of the enterprise is seen as the creation of some social value rather than the creation of shareholder value. In the process the profitability of the firm could also be enhanced. The same kind of psychological attitude can also express itself in the private but communal production of public (in the sense of non-rival) goods, of which excludability is not sought, even if concretely possible, and where a motivation which can be appreciated as 'socialist' is to be part of a community of producers and consumers without the pursuit of private economic gain. This obviously applies to the Linux–Thornvald open-source model, as opposite to the rival Bill Gates–Microsoft, and in particular to that remarkable great social and cultural endeavour of our times, the production and diffusion of Wikipedia. We have here private production for the generation of public goods, where the individualistic profit motive is moderated by a communitarian philosophy aiming, partly at least, at the disinterested (and anonymous!) pursuit of communitarian objectives.[14] A kind of partial 'transition from a civilization based on money and competition to one based on cooperation and participation' (Brus and Kowalik, 1983: p. 245).

If the higher potential future efficiency of public production leads, as it should in a market economy, to higher profitability, so that public enterprises, or mixed enterprises with public control, are more profitable in equitable competition without bending rules or budget constraints in favour of anybody, then public production could grow more rapidly than private, and in a contest of the two systems some sort of the socialism of the means could appear anew, partially at least, as a viable alternative.[15]

As we have already mentioned, in the experience of Western economies in general the public sector has been characterised by lower efficiency. In the countries of the old Soviet bloc the socialist system did not arise from the factual demonstration of the superiority of public towards private production, but from the prohibition of private ownership and entrepreneurship, implemented through repression, requisition, and the introduction of radical limitations to the freedom of contract.[16] This has forestalled competition between different forms of ownership and organisation and deprived the economy of the innovative contribution of private and decentralised entrepreneurship. As a matter of fact the supporters of socialist transformation had a reductive view of the role of private entrepreneurship and of capitalist forms of production. For them, the role of capitalists was essentially to reap the benefits of ownership of the means of production and exploitation of the proletariat. Nationalisation was the process through which those benefits were to be transferred to society at large and the exploitation of the proletariat ended. But nationalisation of private means of production was not really at the heart of the socialist system since, without prohibition and suppression of markets for productive resources, the competition of private entrepreneurship would have been able to reassert itself: so prohibition and suppression of systems competition was really at the heart of Soviet-style socialism. No consideration was given to the creative and innovative powers of private entrepreneurship that were lost through its prohibition.[17] But the contest continued outside the borders of the socialist bloc. One must consider here that while in Western economies competition to capitalist firms remained open in principle to firms privately organised on alternative principles (such as cooperatives or non-profit of any sort) as well as, in a number of countries, to State-owned enterprises, this kind of competition between different forms of entrepreneurship was not allowed in the East: non-socialist firms were either completely outlawed or severely restricted. Hence, when real socialism eventually collapsed, this meant the defeat of a comprehensive system of production, with no ready available alternatives. This may partly explain the severity of the consequences of the fall and why transition was much easier in countries where a limited private production sector had been allowed. The forcible suppression of organisational competition and of the tools of progress given by rival competition, independent of the type of ownership, has led in the end to the demise of the socialist regimes, since they could not bring about those higher living standards that their citizens were able to observe in the West. However, if competition between different types of entrepreneurship is maintained in case non-capitalist entrepreneurship were one day to prove more efficient, at least in some sectors of the economy, the process of privatisation of the economy could be reversed. In this evolutionary perspective every artificial intervention to alter the equality in the rules of competition between enterprises characterised by different ownership structures should be rejected.

1.8 Public production, private production, efficiency and egalitarianism

For those who have an intrinsic preference for socialism of the means, the greater, or even equal, efficiency of public enterprises could be a sufficient condition for the choice of a socialist system, since in this way their preference could be satisfied without sacrificing efficiency.[18] It would not be a necessary for those with an intrinsic preference for a socialist system to sacrifice efficiency in order to bring about socialism. But if preferences were socialist in aims only (for instance, if greater weight were given to equality) and a socialist system were able to attain greater equality at every efficiency level, the attainment of that efficiency level would be a sufficient condition for bringing about a socialist system.

So much in theory. In practice, however, the divergence in efficiency that has been shown in history is such that only a clear demonstration of a change in the nature and functioning of public enterprises could bring back onto the political agenda socialism of the means. Everything depends, however, on the structure of social preferences. If socialism of the means were acknowledged as the most suitable instrument to bring about egalitarian outcomes, and the social preference system is directed very much toward equality, this could lead to the re-introduction of classical socialist solutions. However, what we have learned of income inequality under capitalism and socialism suggests that with suitable redistributive policies a distribution of income no less unequal than in the countries of real socialism could be brought about even in capitalist economies.[19]

But the issue is far from simple. In different economic systems, independent of preferences, the effective trade-off between efficiency (however defined) and equality can be different. This trade-off may also be different today because of changes in the international and technological context. Thus, even if preferences are unchanged, the choice between efficiency and equality could in practice lead to a different mix today, with an increased weight given to efficiency, bringing about higher income levels and higher levels of social preferences – but at the cost of higher inequality, as expounded below:

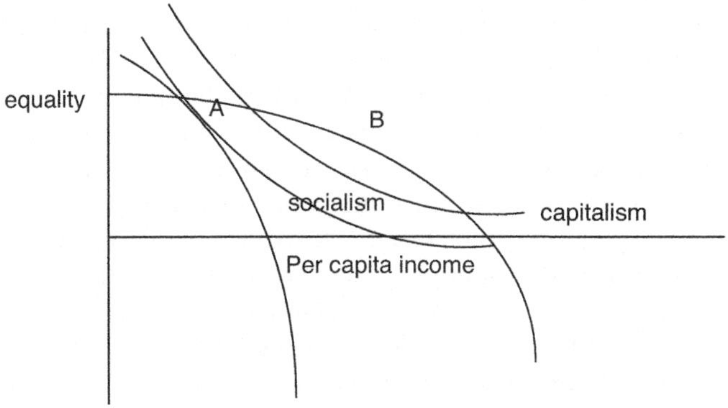

Figure 1.1 Alternative choices between equality and per capita income above subsistence level (as an efficiency index), with given preferences, but in two different systems or contexts, that variously favour equality or efficiency

Notes: It must be noted that the preferences that are represented are relatively egalitarian, as the indifference curves are relatively flat, even if not to the point of being lexicographic.) As to the shape of the frontiers, which can be assumed as deriving from the effective specific characteristics of the functioning of the two systems, there is no pretension to realism, and they can be drawn making the most wide-ranging assumptions. For the sake of the argument it is enough to assume that within the map of indifference curves the tangency point in capitalism is placed to the southeast of that of socialism and corresponds to a higher indifference curve. One may note that the degree of 'socialism' of preferences is given by the flatness of the indifference curves. In the case that they were more 'socialist', and thus flatter, than those drawn here, the tangency point corresponding to the highest indifference curve could correspond to the choice of a socialist system. But according to the experience of socialist countries, even there the degree of socialism of preferences has not been strong enough to compensate for the reduction in the average living standards and in the scope of consumer choices, in relation to those believed to be possible in the long run with a different system. Of course there are a lot of further questions concerning political institutions, but these are out of the scope of the present paper.

Obviously, the preference structure can be system-dependent, but it is far from obvious in what sense it would be so. It is not obvious that the inauguration of a socialist system, for instance, would alter the preferences in favour of equality, even more if the public understands that, as in the case of the figure, the choice in favour of equality is to the detriment of average living standards. The preference structure itself could in fact be altered by the effective outcomes. For instance, the awareness of the stronger inequalities in a market economy could determine a flattening of the indifference curves, as a consequence of the moral indignation that this fact may generate.[20]

1.9 The relevance of the third sector

The evolutionary argument can also apply to specific non-capitalist entrepreneurial forms that are normally considered to have a socialist character, such as cooperatives. These have a role to play, aside from a marginal existence, artificially fostered by ad hoc policy measures, as long as they are able to compete successfully on equal terms with traditional capitalist firms. Moreover, the problem of how to organise non-capitalist entrepreneurial competition with capitalist entrepreneurship arising from collective initiatives in civil society is trivial, since the basic organisational principle on which this competition can be based is the fundamental principle of the freedom of contract. More complex issues are implied by the organisation of the competition by State entrepreneurship; enterprises owned mainly by the State could be free to organise themselves, provided they could pay their way and not depend on public subsidies for their survival. Their growth should be dependent on their ability to self-finance, and to draw resources from the financial markets and, thus, in the end, their ability to generate profits. One could also avoid active privatisation of existing State-owned firms, while also avoiding subsidies from the public purse, leaving to the market the decision whether their relative importance in the economy should grow or shrink, or whether in order to survive they should change their ownership structure, turning to privately owned capital.[21] For those firms that enjoy monopoly rents the solution is not privatisation as such, but the elimination of monopoly power. Private monopolies are no better, even with respect to efficiency, than public monopolies. A difficult issue is how to organise publicly owned enterprises, in the interests of pluralism and of competition between different entrepreneurial forms. One could, for instance, allow local authorities to establish them in the framework of the general freedom of economic initiative; but obviously there should be some kind of limitation on their financing by their founders instead of, say, from retained profits. Similar considerations could be made with respect to mixed-ownership enterprises.

1.10 The argument of systemic externalities

For the supporters of socialism of the means, there remains the countervailing argument of systemic externalities, according to which success in bringing about socialism could follow only after the complete suppression of capitalist institutions. A motive could refer to the dynamics of organised interests and pressure groups altering the conditions of competition, possibly 'capturing' those in charge of determining and enforcing these conditions. But in reality every existing organisation enters into this kind of dynamics. Non-capitalist types of firms, such as cooperatives or non-profit, not to speak of State-owned enterprises, may succeed in building forms of social representation and defensive lobbying that are clearly no less effective than those of capitalist firms. An additional motive could be the possible relationship between economic institutions and social preferences, whose nature however is neither obvious nor of simple determination (Bowles, 1998). The same applies to possible changes in individual values and personality induced by the nature of the social and economic system.

On the whole, the argument of systemic externalities is rather worn. The suspicion is that in practice its true justification is to suppress the terms of comparison for judging success or failure. Suspicions can also be raised relating to arguments for special support to be given to certain types of organisation of economic activity (such as cooperatives with elements of industrial democracy, small firms vs. big firms etc.) drawn from political and social externalities. Often these arguments and the ensuing subvention of 'non-profit' enterprise reflect a preconceived ideological aversion towards entrepreneurial profit, derogatorily identified as 'speculation' – as can even be found, shamefully, in the Italian Constitution (art. 45). The argument is dangerous because it justifies every possible intervention altering the competition between alternative forms of productive organisations.

In reality, measures of this kind do not help the alternative organisational forms to develop all their supposed potential, instead favouring their lingering within a protective niche whose extent depends on the actual transfers of resources (possibly in the indirect form of fiscal exemptions) from the more productive organisational forms. If in the development of non-capitalist forms of entrepreneurship there arises an opportunity for an eventual transformation of the overall organisation of productive processes, their survival cannot be made conditional on the existence of other organisational forms from which they are able to draw resources. In the long term, their financial losses can jeopardise their legitimacy. Special concessions for given organisational forms induce distortion of entrepreneurial activities, with the purpose of taking advantage of those concessions. A host of specific limitations are then required in order to exclude those who should not be entitled to those concessions, unless controls and verifications of a bureaucratic nature are introduced. But this would hinder the development and expansion of those entrepreneurial forms that in the first instance one would like to favour and promote. Specific automatic support for non profit would however remain: as much as profit taxes apply to *distributed* profits, a non-profit organisation by definition does not distribute profits, and the surplus it is able to create is not diminished by the tax.

Thus non-profit growth could be encouraged by two factors:

(1) profits are not distributed (even if the negative side of the coin of course is that this prevents them from being financed through equity);
(2) profits are not subject to the taxation on distributed profits, since no profit is distributed.

1.11 Institutional experiments and transition

Even if the basic institutional foundations of a system (currently capitalist) have turned out as winners in the systemic contest, we are still left with the issue of what kind of specific institutional varieties and combinations of them would bring about the best results. That a system can gradually and successfully be transformed through experiments and the insertion of original elements deriving from another system, until, possibly, changing into a fundamentally different one is shown by the lesson of the progressive Chinese transformation after 1978. Similarly, in the future the capitalist economies could well undergo a gradual transformation in the opposite direction, whenever the conditions that have been discussed above for a successful transition towards non-capitalist forms of entrepreneurship are met. This approach, of gradual and empirically founded institutional transformation would hardly have been able to solve the problem of institutional transformation in the countries of Central and Eastern Europe after the demise of the Soviet model. In the case of China we have institutional experiments that with favourable results can be expanded, yet could be restricted initially to just a part of this country with its huge population and territory, because of the territorial rather than sectorial basis of socialist planning in the framework of a political and social system that has stability and internal consistency (Roland, 2000: p. 57).[22] This took place in a context of serious economic backwardness, where the basic productive unit of the economic system, after the liquidation of the communes, was the peasant family.[23] But whenever the legitimation of the previous system collapses abruptly, gradual processes of transformation are much more difficult to sustain, and a natural tendency to engender a great leap forward arises, sometimes in the same vein as the old voluntaristic fallacy.[24]

1.12 The future of capitalism and socialism

In the end, considering the future of capitalism and socialism we must exercise caution. Everybody can see clearly with hindsight, but nobody can foretell the future, and many false predictions have been made, even by prominent authorities. The only comfort is that posterity is unlikely to read our speculations here, and even in the improbable case that people do, we will not be there to bear the brunt of their possibly well-founded criticism. Speculation about the immediate future may be risky. But speculation about the distant future has the advantage in the end that it is harmless for the speculator at least.

Notes

1. For a extensive non-technical consideration, see Berliner (1999). As Stiglitz (1994: p. 243) puts it, 'we live in an imperfect world, in which often we face nothing but the choice of the lesser of two evils!'
2. 'From the standpoint of immediate practice as well as for the purposes of short-run forecasting – and in these things, a century is a "short run" – all this surface may be more important than the tendency toward another civilization that slowly works deep down below' (Schumpeter, 1976[1942]: p. 163).
3. Here and below, by 'public' ownership or entrepreneurship we broadly intend 'non-private'.
4. For the comparative efficiency of real socialism and capitalism, see in particular Bergson, (1987 and 1992); Gomułka and Rostowski (1988).
5. For the relative worse performance of State-owned in relation to private owned enterprises in mixed economies, see the empirical analyses reviewed in Megginson and Netter (2001, section 3: pp. 328–338).
6. For the role of State-owned enterprises in emerging economies see the special report by *The Economist*, 2012.
7. This statement inspired the 1961 Programme of the Communist Party of the USSR, according to which 'as the country advances towards communism, personal needs will be increasingly met by public consumption funds, whose rate of growth will exceed the rate of growth of payments for labour' (Chilosi, 1978).
8. Here we are referring not to access to the Internet as such, but to the contents of the Internet.
9. On the exceptionally interesting case of Wikipedia see below.
10. For instance an inquiry has established that in the USA the mortality rates in for-profit hospitals are higher than in non-profit hospitals. Source: BBC News Bulletin 27 May 2002.

11. It should be noted, however, that a specific type of public goods consumption, such as the satisfaction deriving from the power and prestige and the territorial conquests of one's country, which could be achieved through investments in armies and wars, seems to play a lesser role happily enough in the present world than in a not too distant past.
12. For these kinds of issues one may refer to Gordon (2000). Unlike other authors (in particular those whose contributions are contained in the same issue of the *Journal of Economic Perspectives*) Gordon does have a reductive consideration of the potential impact of the Internet and IT on productivity.
13. See however Corneo (2001), according to whom there is a positive correlation in OECD countries between hours of work and hours of television viewing. This is explained by the existence of an inefficient equilibrium, which is dominated by another possible one in which work hours are shorter and agents spend more time socialising; the welfare-dominant equilibrium is blocked by the externality implicit in socialisation (the availability of others to socialise increases the advantages of socialisation). Another relevant consideration (introduced by Gordon (2000)) is that free time spent using new technologies is an alternative not so much to work time and consumption of private good and services as to other kinds of uses of free time (playing cards for instance).
14. There is nothing essentially new in it (aside from anonymity), since it is akin to the motivation for political or philanthropic activity at its best, or even to possible motivation for entrepreneurial activity as such.
15. But is the ideology of public service compatible with that of profit making? They are not necessarily mutually exclusive, once profits are seen as a measure of economic efficiency and the source of the means through which the pursuit of public service can be increased. Obviously there are many reasons to deny the significance of profit as an adequate measure of entrepreneurial efficiency. Unfortunately, it seems that no better rule of thumb for measuring efficiency exists.
16. In general, mutually agreed contracts should be in the interest of the parties involved, provided the information on the object of the contract is adequate. Prohibition may be justified in order to defend the interest of one of the parties in case of deceit, or because of the externalities it produces (such as on societal values or the political system) or because of ethical motives. In the case of real socialism the main reason to outlaw employment by private entrepreneurs (and so private entrepreneurship itself) appears to be the last, as private employment leads to exploitation, according to the Marxian viewpoint.
17. See for instance Lange's viewpoint in his writings on socialist transformation (Lange, 1973a; and in particular Lange, 1973b); this does not detract from Lange's great achievements, among others, in the socialist calculation debate. But that debate itself was alien to the basic considerations of the opportunities for grassroots innovation and above all of the incentives for entrepreneurship (both public and private). The consequence was that 'Socialist countries have been relatively successful in developing traditional industries [...] but they have failed to show even a single case of leap-frogging into a comparatively new and promising field. [...] The only widely known new product originating in a socialist country is probably the Rubik cube'

(Brus and Kowalik, 1983: p. 250). Obviously the above excludes military production: the T34 in World War II was considered a better tank than its German counterparts, and Kalashnikov is a household name for an assault rifle in many parts of the world. The employee self-managed companies that sprung out of the Polish privatisation, according to Kowalik (2001b: pp. 233–237), 'performed so [...] surprisingly efficiently: their rate of gross return and net profitability was on average considerably higher than those seen on other privatization paths' (p. 233). On this, more in what follows.

18. Obviously, other non-economic factors enter into the choice between public and private, in particular those relating to the economic conditions for political and cultural pluralism. Generally speaking the latter is associated with the existence of a private market economy, also because historically under a socialist system public control of information and cultural production and strict censorship did apply. On the other hand this is no automatic guarantee of effective pluralism, as clearly demonstrated by the overwhelming control of the mass media in Italy by a single business tycoon, concurrently leader of the most powerful political party.
19. This is not entirely certain, however. For one, socialist countries were at lower development levels. Therefore the significance of the comparison is affected by the long-drawn question of the relationship between development and distribution. Moreover there are a host of statistical problems that derive from some fundamental differences in the two systems to be compared, which are usually disregarded, in particular how to make allowance for the different structure of the prices of consumer goods, and the limitations to the availability of the latter under real socialism. On these issues see Chilosi (1994). For the data concerning the comparisons in income distribution between western market economies and the countries of real socialism, see Atkinson and Micklewright (1992); Chilosi (1990a and 1990b) and the literature quoted there.
20. An ample empirical inquiry has shown a marked orientation in favour of equality in the economies in transition, much more than in Western Europe (Shrcke, 2001). Thus, it seems that persistence of the distributional values of the previous system did continue to prevail there.
21. This was the Darwinian solution that I proposed at the beginning of the transition process for the transformation of the socialist economies, obviously accompanied by the abolition of the prohibition on private entrepreneurial activities (Chilosi, 1990a and 1990b).
22. The great advantage of territorially limited reform is that it can pay due attention to a set of interrelations that could, although with more difficulty, be managed in a national framework without introducing strong elements of irreversibility. The costs (not only economic, but political and social as well) associated with reform reversal are much lower in a limited territory than when the reform applies to the entire economy.
23. Moreover, one should not downplay the relevance of the tradition of the autonomous role of the peasant village (Krug, 2000a: p. 12). This tradition of autonomy has allowed the local communities to develop its economic and organisational potentialities, stimulating the institutional innovations that lie at the basis of the Township and Village Enterprises. The nature of the latter is somewhat controversial. Under the appearance of the formal

municipal ownership, complex contractual relationships could mask forms of private or mixed entrepreneurship, remedying the institutional restrictions on the market in those capital goods whose ownership remains public (Krug, 2000b; Oxford Analytica, 2001) and the absence of adequate legal guarantees against the predatory tendencies of public authorities (Sun, 2002: p. 252).

24. A problem with gradual reform lies in the institutional compatibilities that it can engender. For instance, in the case of liberalisation of private entrepreneurship in an economic system with price control and unbalanced markets, private activity can profitably focus on arbitrage alone. In the case of China this issue is solved through liberalisation at the margin, without suddenly and radically destroying the old system of compulsory consignments and price controls as has happened in various Eastern European countries that have adopted the big bang strategy with adverse social and economic effects. For more on these issues, see Roland (2000, ch. 6: pp. 131–152).

2
Whatever Happened to the 'Crucial Reform'?

John E. King

2.1 Introduction[1]

'The owl of Minerva spreads its wings at dusk.' Or so Hegel believed. In plain English: you only find out what's going on when it's about to stop. Thus Michał Kalecki and Tadeusz Kowalik wrote their influential 'Observations on the "Crucial Reform"' between September 1969 and January 1970.[2] It was published in 1971, just as the fundamental reforms that the capitalist system had undergone in the immediate post-war years were about to unravel, and the Golden Age that they had helped to generate was coming to an end. Kalecki and Kowalik were in very good company. Almost no-one predicted the rise of neoliberalism (Howard and King, 2008). To take one particularly striking example, this is the final sentence of Michel Aglietta's *A Theory of Capitalist Regulation*, published in French in 1976 and in English three years later, in the year that Margaret Thatcher came to power in the United Kingdom: 'The coming massive socialisation of the conditions of life will destroy free enterprise as the pillar of liberal ideology' (Aglietta, 1979: p. 385). The owl of Minerva seems to have taken a long time on its way to France.

2.2 What was the 'crucial reform'?

'Let us imagine', Kalecki and Kowalik begin

> that the strong pressure of the masses leads to such a radical reform of the system, in spite of the opposition of the ruling class, that, without abolishing existing relations of production, a new valve is opened for the development of the forces of production. There will then be a paradoxical situation: a 'crucial reform' imposed on the ruling class

> may stabilize the system, temporarily at least. As we argue below, we have to do with just such a situation in contemporary capitalism. (Kalecki and Kowalik, 1971: p. 467)

There is almost a taste of Hayek in their account of 'the unintended effects of the pressure of the working masses on the bourgeois state' (ibid: p. 614), and clear parallels, explicitly recognised by the authors themselves, with earlier socialist theorists like Rudolf Hilferding and Rosa Luxemburg. Hilferding had suggested that a 'general cartel' of capitalists might institute a new phase of 'organised capitalism' in which the contradictions of competitive capitalism would lose much of their force,[3] while Luxemburg had placed special emphasis on the conquest of 'non-capitalist markets' in the colonies and semi-colonies. Both raised the possibility in principle that government purchases, if applied on a sufficient scale, 'can overcome the discrepancy between production potential and the capacity of markets' (ibid: p. 470). In the aftermath of the Great Depression, this was precisely what had been done in both Germany and the United States. 'With initially fairly strong opposition from the *grande bourgeoisie*', Kalecki and Kowalik wrote, 'capitalist governments set about protecting the foundations of their system from the threat of mass unemployment.' This did not involve planned control over the economy but rather 'government intervention to fill the gap of insufficient demand and to organise additional employment' (ibid: p. 472). Then, after 1945, the centrally controlled capitalism' of the war years gave way to

> a capitalist system of large corporations with supplementary markets guaranteed by government purchases, mainly of armaments, which allowed the realization of accumulated profits. The share of government expenditure in the total demand for goods and services increased considerably in comparison with the inter-war period. (ibid: p. 472)

And this had important political effects. Full employment, together with 'a considerable expansion of social security', gave rise to

> a certain transformation of the working class, which on the whole became radically reformist in its attitude towards capitalism. Preserving high employment rates in the leading capitalist countries generally gives the workers a satisfactory level of real income. With high and steady employment, real wages, at least over the long term, rise along with increases in labour productivity [...] As a result, anti-capitalist attitudes have weakened considerably. (ibid: pp. 472–473)

Something similar had occurred also in those post-colonial countries that Kalecki had earlier characterised as 'intermediate regimes': 'these countries have also passed through a "crucial reform", although it took different forms, and although there is considerably less stability than in the "neo-capitalist" countries' (ibid: p. 474). In addition, the Cold War had suppressed imperialist rivalries between the leading capitalist states, giving rise to a situation very similar to the 'ultra-imperialism' that Karl Kautsky had foreshadowed in 1914 and making the prospect of war between them very remote (ibid: p. 615).

The article concludes with some reservations. 'The relative stability of reformed capitalism depends on a high degree of social conformity', Kalecki and Kowalik note. 'One can express the cautious opinion that recent student movements seem to be an omen of the declining ability of the bourgeois power apparatus to manipulate new generations entering the historical scene' (ibid: p. 476), and perhaps had the potential to link up with renewed working class protests. But this did not lead them to deny the historical significance of the 'crucial reform'.

These were not new arguments. Something similar had formed the basis of both the 'revisionist' position in post-1945 European social democracy (for example, Crosland, 1956) and the somewhat later 'Eurocommunist' movement, which was reformist in everything but name and was especially influential in Italy and Spain (Sassoon, 1996: chs 20–21). The political economy of reformism had been debated in Marxist circles since the late 1950s, with the conference volume *Has Capitalism Changed?* (Tsuru, 1961) representing an important milestone (see also Howard and King, 1992: ch. 4). The revisionists were still stubbornly resisted by more orthodox Communists, as can be seen from the reaction of the Italian Marxist Antonio Pesenti to Kalecki and Kowalik:

'there is an underestimation here of internal contradictions, especially economic ones, which are continually developing in every stage of capitalism', and also an underestimation of the revolutionary potential of the workers. 'It is this faith in the creative possibilities of the class struggle', Pesenti wrote, 'and its capacity to take advantage of the continually reappearing contradictions of capitalism, that allows me to exclude the possibility of speaking about some "crucial reform" leading to a "stabilization of the system"' Pesenti, 1971: pp. 612–613).

Nevertheless, this is precisely what had happened in the quarter-century after 1945, which represented a real 'Golden Age' for the advanced capitalist countries (Hobsbawm, 1994: ch. 9; Marglin and Schor, 1990). The 'crucial reform', which was admittedly implemented more thoroughly in Western Europe than in North America, involved all five principles of post-war reformist democratic socialism: a firm government commitment to full employment; a unionised and tightly regulated labour market; highly progressive taxation; a substantial and comprehensive welfare state; and the public ownership of public utilities and other important natural monopolies (King, 2003). A sixth principle should perhaps be added: cheap money, and with it the taming of the financial sector.

The first four principles ensured that in every advanced capitalist country consumer expenditure rose at least as fast as productive capacity, eliminating the tendency towards underconsumption that had been identified as the chief economic contradiction of early 20th-century capitalism by many Marxists, from Otto Bauer to Paul Sweezy, and also by dissenting bourgeois economists like J.A. Hobson and John Kenneth Galbraith. The fifth and sixth principles made it possible to stabilise both private and public investment expenditure, making a real step forwards towards the 'socially controlled rate of investment' that John Maynard Keynes had called for in the *General Theory* (Keynes, 1936: p. 325). And there was, indeed, a pronounced and continuing weakening of anti-capitalist attitudes within the Western working class.

2.3 How did it all come to an end?

Ironically, by 1971 the crucial reform was already beginning to unravel. We can distinguish five aspects of this process; I shall not refer to them as 'stages', as the chronology is rather complicated (Glyn, 2006, provides a definitive history). The first and perhaps the most important aspect was the collapse of the Bretton Woods system of fixed exchange rates, which led to greatly increased financial instability and also to much greater scope for financial speculation, higher profits and greater political influence for financial interests – although the latter did not become apparent for a long time. It also contributed to the acceleration of inflation throughout the capitalist world, since the constraints formerly imposed on the domestic price level by the need to defend the exchange rate had been removed. This created an atmosphere of greater uncertainty, which resulted in lower investment, slower growth and higher unemployment than had prevailed during the Golden Age (Davidson, 1982). The international monetary system was more robust than it had been in 1929, however, so that there was no repeat of the

Great Depression. In the title of Hyman Minsky's best-known book, 'It' did not happen again, because the capitalist state was much larger, and its influence over the economy much greater, than had been the case in 1929. Big Government had both flow and stock effects: built-in fiscal stabilisers were more effective when taxation accounted for 30 to 40 per cent of GDP than when it had taken 10 to 15 per cent, and the huge build-up of government debt in the Second World War provided private financial companies with a correspondingly immense stock of risk-free securities, reducing financial fragility (Minsky, 1982).

The second element in the reversal of the crucial reform was financialisation: an ugly name for a very ugly phenomenon (Hein, 2012a). It had economic, political and ideological dimensions. High interest rates saw not just the end of cheap money but also a large increase in the share of GDP and an even greater increase in the share of total profits accruing to the so-called FIRE sector (finance, insurance and real estate). Non-financial corporations were increasingly driven by 'shareholder value', emphasising short-run profit maximisation at the expense of all other goals. The supposed interests of financial capital came also to dominate government policy, leading in microeconomic terms to the comprehensive (and extremely dangerous) deregulation of financial market activities, and in macroeconomics to a fixation on inflation targeting and an abandonment of any attempt to maintain full employment. Ideologically, the increasing involvement of all but the very poor in financial markets, through mortgage finance and occupational pension schemes, contributed powerfully to the dominance of neoliberal ideas among working people whose parents and grandparents had thought like Social Democrats. The cultural and symbolic power of finance must not be overlooked: 'a power that seems answerable to no other power' (LiPuma and Lee, 2004: p. 189).

Third, there was a slow but relentless unwinding of the first five principles of post-war social democracy that have been discussed earlier. The commitment to full employment was the first to go, as already noted, with inflation becoming the only target for monetary policy (and the revival of the pre-Keynesian belief in 'sound finance' emasculating fiscal policy).[4] Mass unemployment greatly weakened the unions, and it was given a helping hand by repressive legislation, especially in the Anglo-Saxon countries (Fernie and Metcalfe, 2005). Tax systems became much less progressive, with the rise of tax havens, the remorseless shift from direct to indirect taxation, reductions in the higher marginal rates of income tax, concessions on the taxation of capital gains and – very important in England – the abolition of local government rates, a progressive and hard-to-evade wealth tax that was replaced by a quasi-poll tax. Welfare benefits were reduced, especially for the unemployed, and harsh eligibility conditions were imposed. This process has gone further in some countries than in others (Tanzi, 2011), but the tendency towards a contraction of the welfare state is pretty well universal. Last but by no means least, there was privatisation mania initiated by Margaret Thatcher and soon imitated all over the world.

Fourth, there was a tendency for the various 'varieties of capitalism' to approach the Anglo-Saxon model. This was most obvious in the case of the former state socialist countries of Eastern Europe after the fall of the Berlin Wall and the collapse of the Soviet Union. It can also be clearly seen in the 'intermediate regimes' identified by Kalecki, which were tamed by the imposition of neoliberalism upon them by the international institutions that implemented the Washington Consensus. Even South Korea suffered this fate after the 1996–1997 East Asian financial crisis left it at the mercy of the IMF. The 'co-ordinated market economies' of North-West Europe have come to look more and more like the Anglo-Saxon 'liberal market economies', with weaker unions, widening income differentials, reduced welfare benefits and an increase in the influence of financial markets over the policies of companies and governments alike.[5] Even in Japan, the impact of global financialisation and the long period of near-stagnation that began in 1990 may have similar consequences, though in this case the eventual outcome (at the time of writing, in October 2013) is not yet clear. Only China is a clear exception to the general rule; I shall return to the Chinese variety of capitalism at the end of this chapter.

Fifth, and finally, the so-called 'Great Moderation' after 1992 appeared to demonstrate the advantages of neoliberal capitalism and to confirm the case against the 'crucial reform'. For the next 15 years there was a genuinely 'long boom', in the course of which growth resumed, unemployment fell and inflation almost disappeared. The benefits of the Great Moderation were, of course, grossly overstated at the time: on every measure except inflation the performance of the advanced capitalist economies was inferior to that of the Golden Age (Rothschild, 2009), and as became apparent in 2007, the reversal of the 'crucial reform' had in fact made the system very much *less* stable in the longer term.

2.4 Why was the 'crucial reform' reversed?

There were well-known ideological factors at play in the reversal of the 'crucial reform'. The revival of classical liberalism after 1980 took many by surprise, but it had never entirely died out, least of all in the United States, where hostility to Big Government had very deep roots. It was reinforced by developments in mainstream academic economics, where there was a very clear contrast between the broadly social democratic position of the generation that had grown up in the 1930s and the succeeding generation, which was predominantly neoliberal (Backhouse, 2005). This ideological transformation was most evident in the counter-revolution in macroeconomics that challenged and very soon destroyed the neoclassical-Keynesian synthesis. By the end of the 20th century a New Neoclassical Synthesis had emerged, involving a return to Say's Law and the elimination of the problem of effective demand (Dullien, 2011). This was reflected in the emasculation of fiscal policy; the restriction of monetary policy to containing inflation, via the Taylor rule; and the adoption of the methodological dogma of 'microfoundations', which claimed that macroeconomics could and should be reduced to microeconomics (King, 2012a). In this way the economists provided a powerful ideological justification for abandoning the 'crucial reform'.

But ideas do not exist in a vacuum. Marx was basically correct when he wrote that '[i]t is not the consciousness of men that determines their existence, but their social existence that determines their consciousness' (Marx, 1857a[1971]: p. 21). There were three distinct, but closely related, changes in material reality that lay behind the changes in ideology. First, and most obvious, was the onset of stagflation in the 1970s, and the end of the Golden Age. Employers had never been happy with the persistence of full employment after 1945.[6] The eventual acceleration of inflation proved to be the final straw which discredited Keynesian macroeconomics and made monetarist and 'New Classical' ideas much more readily acceptable than they would otherwise have been. Second, and also very familiar, were the powerful forces unleashed by globalisation – especially financial globalisation – and the consequent undermining of the power of the nation-state and the greatly increased power of footloose capital relative to internationally immobile labour. Third, and less immediately apparent, there were deeper underlying long-run changes in both the forces and the social relations of production that increased the power of the market (Howard and King, 2008).

By the 1980s ideology and material reality had come together to generate a profound political and institutional transformation in almost all advanced capitalist countries. There was a clear shift from 'wage-led' to 'profit-led regimes' and, no less important, in the *beliefs* of capitalists, their governments and their economists in this shift (Hein, 2012b). Holding down real wages and reducing the labour share in national income was now seen as necessary for the promotion of economic growth, and not (as it had been in the Golden Age) as detrimental to it. This had very important implications for economic policy; in particular, it encouraged the 'de-regulation' of the labour market (actually a *re*-regulation in the interests of capital) and deep cuts in social welfare benefits, especially for the unemployed).

No less important was financialisation, and with it the return of what Robert Skidelsky (2011) has termed the 'Money Power'. A former Conservative peer, Skidelsky was (perhaps unknowingly) echoing the words of an old-style Social Democrat. In 1952 Aneurin Bevan had distinguished three conflicting social forces: private property, poverty and democracy. 'The issue therefore in a capitalist democracy resolves itself into this: either poverty will use democracy to win the struggle against property, or property, in fear of poverty, will destroy democracy [...] poverty, great wealth and democracy are ultimately incompatible elements in any society' (Bevan, 1952: p. 3).[7] The capitulation of all European governments to 'the markets' in the continuing Eurozone crisis of 2011–2013 has confirmed that Bevan was right (see Streeck, 2011).

I have a personal anecdote to illustrate his point. In November 2011, when I was living in Graz, the Austrian government announced its intention to amend the federal constitution to include a clause imposing strict limits on government borrowing. No attempt had been made at even a pretence of consulting the electorate, or the membership of the two parties that made up the coalition government (Christian Democrats and so-called Social Democrats), or even the leadership of those parties. That night I watched an extended interview on the evening television news with the chief minister of Salzburg province, the Social Democrat Gabi Burgstaller. It was clear that she had only very recently learned of the government's decision, probably from the journalist who had arranged the interview. 'What are the principal benefits of this proposal?' she was asked. There was a long pause, and for a moment I thought she might reply 'Damned if I know'. Her actual answer was even more shocking: 'Well', she said, 'it will get the ratings agencies off our backs, and that will be a good thing, won't it?' Such is liberal democracy in the early 21st century.[8]

2.5 And the future?

In his 95th year, the great Austrian heterodox economist Kurt Rothschild was interviewed by the journalist Renate Graber. A very modest man, he had always erred on the side of caution when attempting to make economic or political forecasts. Almost at the end of his life (he died in the following year), Rothschild was even more insistent on the difficulty of prediction. 'Are you optimistic or pessimistic for the future?' Graber asked him. 'Every scientist,' he replied, 'assuming that economists are scientists, says that you have to be sceptical. Normally we construct scenarios that are more or less probable. But right now we are in an entirely new situation, for which we have only inadequate economic theories and models' (Rothschild and Graber, 2009).

There are, indeed, many possible scenarios for the future of global capitalism, other than 'business as usual'. I shall focus on three.[9] The first is a renewed Global Financial Crisis that cannot be controlled (unlike that of 2008), but instead leads to economic collapse on the scale of the Great Depression. This will result either in a revival of Fascism or in a second 'crucial reform', in which a revitalised social democracy restores the central features of the post-1945 settlement. It may take something as extreme as this to clear the brains of the European elites of what the Austrian Keynesian, Stephan Schulmeister, has described as the 'neoliberal smog' that has engulfed them, damaging the health of the capitalist system in the long term and blinding its apologists to the true causes of their immediate problems. To switch metaphors: socialists would once again find themselves 'sitting at the sick-bed of capitalism, not only as doctors who want to cure the patient, but as prospective heirs who cannot wait for the end and would like to hasten it by administering poison', as Fritz Tarnow had told the Leipzig conference of the Social Democrat Party in 1931 (cited by Sturmthal, 1944: p. 71).[10] In this scenario the capitalist patient has been unable to diagnose his illness and is completely unable to prescribe the necessary treatment; his attempts at self-medication have only made things worse. The socialist doctor can diagnose and treat the patient, but she has a moral dilemma: she would very much like the patient to die, so that she can inherit the fortune, but she is bound by the Hippocratic oath (and by her obligation to the patient's proletarian dependents, who would suffer greatly during any transition to a new and better regime). Thus she administers the cure, and the patient recovers.

There are, of course, less competent medical practitioners. To take one particularly dreadful recent example: neoliberal macroeconomic surgery was performed on Latvia in 2007, before the full onset of the Global Financial Crisis. The patient survived, but it was a very near thing: GDP fell by 24.1 per cent between late 2007 and late 2009, and 10 per cent of the working population left the country (Weisbrot and Ray, 2011). This was suffering on a scale comparable to that of the Great Depression – actually more severe, by comparison with any European country. The largest peak-to-trough fall in real GDP in any European country between 1922 and 1935 was in Austria, at 22.5 per cent;[11] only Canada (at a 30.1 per cent decline) and the United States (29.5 per cent) fared worse (Mann, 2004, table 2.1: p. 50). At the time of writing (October 2013), similar treatment is being inflicted on the hapless PIIGS at the behest of the 'Money Power'.[12]

De-financialisation would have to be at the heart of any new 'crucial reform' of the capitalist system; 'tough on finance, tough on the causes of finance', so to speak. In principle, this would be entirely consistent with the healthy functioning of a reformed capitalism. As Dean Baker reminds us:

> The [US] economy thrived in the three decades following World War II with a financial sector that was proportionately one-fourth of its current size. There is no reason that the financial sector should use up a larger share of the economy's resources today than it did three decades ago. Effective regulation will restore the financial sector to its proper role in the economy. (Baker, 2010: p. 79)

Regulation, though, is only part of the story. De-financialisation would have to go hand in hand with de-privatisation (or re-socialisation) of housing and pensions. This would be desirable on other grounds, since it would allow risks to be transferred from individuals back to society, where they belong (Quiggin, 2010: ch. 5). The re-socialisation of retirement incomes, in particular, would greatly reduce the amount of money available to be managed by financial companies (Nersisyan, 2012), and the large-scale provision of subsidised public housing would make a new housing bubble that relied upon sub-prime mortgages much less likely to occur. Even this might not be sufficient to curb the power of finance. It would probably be necessary to eliminate currency speculation, for example by adopting the improved version of the Bretton Woods system that Paul Davidson has been advocating for decades, with an international clearing union supporting a regime of fixed (but adjustable) exchange rates (see, for example, Davidson, 2002).[13]

Simply listing the requirements for a 21st-century version of the 'crucial reform' is sufficient to demonstrate how unlikely it is to occur, unless there is a global depression of 1930s proportions. There is an alternative scenario, which Kalecki might very well have found convincing: growing imperialist rivalry between the United States and China leads to a new rearmament boom and the return of 'military Keynesianism', restoring something like full employment but at a greatly increased risk of war. There is evidence that the Pentagon is coming to see China as the only significant threat to United States world dominance, with the Iraq and Afghanistan wars having been dangerous distractions from the real challenge to American global hegemony that already exists in the Asia-Pacific. The prospect of increasing tension between the US and China is causing concern to mainstream theorists in strategic studies and international relations. In the medium term there is a real possibility of war breaking out between them, much as it did between Britain and Germany in 1914, as a result of mistakes and misconceptions made in a climate of mutual suspicion and nationalistic hostility fuelled by deep economic rivalry and coming after a protracted arms race (White, 2012). This 'military Keynesian' scenario is not necessarily inconsistent with a second 'crucial reform', though it would limit the scope for improvements in living standards for the civilian population. In fact something like it might be needed to strengthen nationalist consciousness and dispel the 'neoliberal fog', at least in the West.

The third scenario is precisely 'the decline of the West' and the emergence of China as the mid-21st-century global hegemon, with the United States accepting its relatively humble position with good grace and the strategic issues between the two nations being managed peacefully along the lines of Kautsky's 'ultra-imperialism'. 'Capitalism with Chinese characteristics' would certainly not be neoliberal, and there is no reason to suppose that it would be social democratic, but it might well serve as a model for many other nations of the global South. In this case a new 'crucial reform' of the type identified by Kalecki and Kowalik would have distinct Chinese characteristics. It may not be too far away, given the general recognition that the current 'profit-led' regime in China is unsustainable.[14]

Notes

1. I am grateful to Geoff Harcourt and Peter Kriesler for comments on an earlier draft. The usual disclaimer applies.
2. See Kowalik (1991) for the circumstances under which the article was written, and Besomi (2006) for a perceptive discussion of the broader intellectual background, in the context of Kalecki's work on business cycles, capital accumulation and the principles of historical materialism.

3. Hilferding had been anticipated by 'the Polish sociologist Ludwik Krzywicki, who noticed strong tendencies toward "industrial feudalism". This was the vision of a "nation-estate" – a kind of feudal estate embracing the whole country – with a hierarchical social structure governed by a financial oligarchy' (Kalecki and Kowalik, 1971: p. 469). Something similar was described by Oskar Lange in his *Democratic Program of Full Employment* (Lange, 1941: p. 268). I am grateful to Jan Toporowski for this reference. For an assessment of Krzywicki's work, see Kolakowski (1978: ch. IX).
4. Kalecki had predicted something like this back in 1943: 'The workers would "get out of hand" and the captains of industry would be anxious to "teach them a lesson" [...] In this situation a powerful alliance is likely to be formed between big business and rentier interests, and they would probably find more than one economist to declare that the situation was manifestly unsound' (Kalecki, 1943[1990]: p. 355).
5. This possibility was recognised by the founders of the 'varieties of capitalism' school: 'If the financial markets of a coordinated market economy are deregulated, for instance, it may become more difficult for firms to offer long-term employment. That could make it harder for them to recruit skilled labour or sustain worker loyalty, ultimately inspiring major changes in production regimes [...] Financial deregulation could be the string that unravels coordinated market economies' (Hall and Soskice, 2001: p. 64, cited by Streeck, 2009: p. 18). And so it proved.
6. This is very clear from Eric Wigham's authorised history of the Engineering Employers' Federation in the UK, where chapter 8 has the revealing title, 'Inflation and Frustration 1948–1957' (Wigham, 1973: pp. 160–188).
7. I am grateful to Tony Beddow for this reference.
8. The attempt failed, since the government was unable to get the required three-quarters majority in Parliament (the minority parties, the Greens on the left and the two neo-Fascist parties on the right, were both opposed to it).
9. See King (2012b) for an extended discussion.
10. The trade unionist and Social Democrat politician Fritz Tarnow (1880–1951) believed underconsumption to be at the heart of the economic problems of capitalism, and deflationary policies to be making the economic situation in Germany even worse. He was a supporter of the Woytinski Plan to devalue the mark and increase the general price level (Sturmthal, 1944: p. 77), and he also advocated deficit-funded increases in public expenditure aimed at restoring consumer demand and reducing mass unemployment. In many ways this was a precursor of the 'crucial reform', but although it won support from many trade unionists it was rejected not only by the Right but also by Social Democrats like Hilferding, who were intellectual prisoners of 'sound finance' (see Garvy, 1975). I am grateful to several subscribers to the SHOE email list for information about Tarnow.
11. Unfortunately no interwar GDP data are provided for Latvia itself.
12. PIIGS = Portugal, Italy, Ireland, Greece and Spain: the five Eurozone nations that suffered the worst from the financial crisis. Perhaps it should now be PIIGSS, with Slovenia having joined the ranks of the victims.
13. Davidson's rationale for a far-reaching reform of the international monetary system is quite different. I personally think that he exaggerates the contribution of exchange rate uncertainty to the poor performance of the world

economy since the end of Bretton Woods, but I accept that removing this source of uncertainty would be an additional, if rather minor, benefit of his proposal.

14. See Xu (2011) for a discussion of some of the recent literature. Astonishingly, the authoritative reader on the 'varieties of capitalism' literature edited by Bob Hancké (2009) has no index entry for China.

3

'Crucial Reform' in Post-War Socialism and Capitalism: Kowalik's Analysis and the Polish Transition

Gary A. Dymski

3.1 Introduction

Tadeusz Kowalik's writings include meditations on the 'crucial reform' of capitalism in the middle of the 20th century, and on the possibilities for the 'crucial reform' of Poland's 'real socialism' in the 1980s (for example, 'In one of his earlier works Lange wrote that socialism is more concerned with objectives than with the means to achieve them. Achievement of social welfare is the central issue.' Kowalik, 1986: p. 41). Kalecki and Kowalik wrote in 1969–1970 that capitalist society survived the middle of the 20th century via an unintended 'crucial reform' that dampened the anti-capitalist momentum of the working class. This chapter builds on Kalecki's own model of capitalist accumulation and crisis, and on his pessimistic assessment of the prospects for sustained prosperity under capitalist systems with democratically elected governments. While this 'crucial reform' had avoided the clash between democratic politics and capitalist accumulation foreseen by Kalecki (1943, 1944b) in the midst of World War II, the Kalecki–Kowalik paper of 1969–1970 exposes a continuing concern with the fragility of capitalist economies.

Kowalik then spent some years editing Lange's collected papers (Lange, 1994). This close encounter with one of Lange's defining themes – the economic theory of the socialist economy – together with Kowalik's own familiarity with Kalecki's approach to this topic (Kowalik, 1992a) provided a point of departure for a series of essays on Poland's transition after 1988 from 'real socialism' to post-socialist quasi-capitalism.

While both authors had participated in the largely technical 'socialist calculation' debate, what Kowalik emphasised, during the rising ferment of the Solidarność years, was a less apparent theme in that debate: the role of the workers' voice in allocating resources and making social decisions. Kowalik criticised the abandonment of the democratic impulse that had fuelled the uprising against the Stalinist regime, in favour of an International Monetary Fund (IMF) 'shock therapy' programme that obliterated the popular voice in economic decision-making.

This chapter develops a comparative analysis of Kowalik's writings on the problem of 'crucial reform' in Western capitalism and in Poland's socialist transition. In that process, two themes emerge. First, Kowalik's writings on the trajectories of capitalist and socialist development, like those of Kalecki and Lange, reject any notion that the ultimate triumph of capitalism or socialism as such – as an ideal form of economic organisation – is inevitable, much less imminent. Instead, his dispassionate and profoundly sceptical analyses led him to the view that both capitalism and socialism are riddled with contradictory impulses.

This perspective on capitalist and socialist transition, in turn, suggests a second implicit theme: that continuous prosperity via either a capitalist or a socialist path is blocked by a contradiction involving democratic voice. If political elites (in the case of real socialism) or capitalist elites (in the case of real capitalism) are forced by empowered citizens and workers to create space for widespread prosperity and participation, then either path can generate stable, secure incomes, along with some degree of consumer choice. But such empowerment is destabilising for the capitalists or the bureaucratic elites that have control over investment, the volume and nature of public goods, and other crucial societal resources. These elites' willingness to structure social and political relations so as to make sustained long-term prosperity feasible for the majority of the populations whose resources they control is offset by their fear of losing their prerogatives of control as well as their privileges. In sum, sustained prosperity thus both requires democratic empowerment of workers and is undercut by it. The way this contradiction plays out differs in real socialism and real capitalism. Kowalik's parallel reflections on both systems provide the key for exposing this shared dilemma.

Sections 3.2–3.5 explore Kowalik's writing in approximate chronological order. Section 3.2 summarises the Kowalik/Kalecki essay on the 'crucial reform' of capitalism in the context of Kalecki's concern with capitalism's future. Section 3.3 then examines Kowalik's interventions into the debate over the economics of socialism as framed by the work of Lange and Kalecki. Section 3.4 then provides an extensive summary of a 1986 working paper by Kowalik that examined the problem of the crucial reform for socialist economies in the context of the intense debate that accompanied socialist nations' transitions. We then turn, in Section 3.5, to Kowalik's essays on the Polish transition. This work repeatedly stresses that 'shock therapy', which seeks to cure economic 'maladies' by cold-turkey market liberalisation and privatisation, will bring chaos and undercut democratic guidance of both economy and society.

Section 3.6 concludes by setting out a hypothesis suggested by Kalecki's and Kowalik's extensive analyses – as noted above, the contradiction of democratic voice in both capitalist and socialist economies. This dilemma may arise in any system of economic allocation; once it emerges as a contradiction, it must be managed, not negated or denied.

3.2 Kalecki and Kowalik on the 'crucial reform' of capitalism

The co-authored paper by Kalecki and Kowalik (1971) on capitalism, written in 1969 and 1970, introduces the phrase 'crucial reform'. The motivations for and implications of this concept can be fully seen only in the context of two essays Kalecki had written a quarter-century earlier about the challenges of sustaining full employment in the capitalist economy.[1]

'The Political Economy of Full Employment' (Kalecki, 1943) argued that sustained full employment is impossible in advanced capitalist societies because of the dependence of capitalist accumulation on Marxian exploitation. If unemployment falls too low, workers' effort in production will decline, reducing the profit rate. So, as unemployment falls, worker effort may diminish, and capitalists may feel coerced into providing jobs under terms and conditions that compromise profitability. In effect, profit levels are subject to a labour-effort/output tradeoff. Low labour effort can be avoided by operating the economy at sub-full-employment levels, but such stagnation also diminishes profits. Continued capitalist accumulation is especially threatened if workers unite in social democratic parties that demand full employment through the political process. For then the very legitimacy of *de facto* control over the economy by owners of the means of production is challenged. When so threatened, capitalists will engage in capital strike and/or reduced investment, restoring some *de minimus* level of unemployment.

This upper limit to capital accumulation is paralleled by a lower limit, again due to both economic and political considerations. While high unemployment levels benefit capitalists, since they assure high labour effort and little upward pressure on wages, they entail low rates of capacity utilisation, which may be problematic for firms with significant financial leverage. In the political sphere, a high-enough rate of unemployment could lead to working-class political agitation and government countercyclical action. This leads to the idea of a political business cycle wherein macroeconomic growth fluctuates between these upper and lower limit points. As unemployment falls during the expansion, capitalists will use their power to withhold investment to regain control over government policies. In turn, the downturn is checked when unemployment leads to government countercyclical action and low wages lead capitalists to reinstate investment expenditures.

In 1944, Kalecki stated his argument more bluntly. There are, he wrote, three ways to achieve and maintain full employment in a capitalist society: government spending on public investment or on subsidies to mass consumption; stimulating private investment; and redistribution of income from higher- to lower-income classes. The second method 'is not satisfactory' but the first and third 'provide adequate means to maintain full employment' (Kalecki, 1944: p. 357).

We fast-forward 25 years to the paper that Kalecki and Kowalik began in 1969 and finished in 1970. This chapter starts by reflecting on a question that was uppermost in the minds of those observing the unresolved clash between socialist and capitalist systems that had been paused amidst the carnage of World War II; that is, would not struggles to reform capitalism in favour of working-class interests ultimately lead to the overthrow of capitalism, since success in reforms would lead to bolder reforms that would eventually unhinge a system founded on the pursuit of profit? This question was latent in the Eurocommunism movement which was challenging the rigid historical materialism preferred by the USSR, and raising the possibility of post-capitalist hybrid economic models informed by radical popular movements.[2] Kalecki and Kowalik answered this question in the negative. They proposed the possibility that

> the strong pressure of the masses leads to such a radical reform of the system, in spite of the opposition of the ruling class, that, without abolishing existing relations of production, a new value is opened for the development of forces of production. There will then be a

> paradoxical situation: a 'crucial reform' imposed on the ruling class may stabilize the system, temporarily at least. (Kalecki and Kowalik, 1991: p. 467)

Kalecki and Kowalik contrasted their perspective with that of several authors who thought that reform could transform capitalism into socialism; they began by criticising Edward Bernstein's 1909 *Evolutionary Socialism*, according to which (in these authors' summary) 'economic development and gradual social reforms would change mature capitalist societies into socialist ones' (Kalecki and Kowalik, 1971: p. 467). This and similar analyses, in their view, miss two intertwined points: capitalists will not submit meekly to the gradual diminution of the rate of profit, and thus the key question regarding any reform of capitalism is whether it addresses the realisation problem. They interpreted war and armaments expenditures (including World War II) from this viewpoint, but acknowledged the broader effort of governments in capitalist nations to 'limit unemployment to a few percent' (ibid: p. 470) via the expansion of social security and other measures. These led to an acceptance of 'something similar to the "right to work" slogan advanced by the revolution of 1848' and also led to a 'transformation of the working class, which [...] became radically reformist in its attitude toward capitalism' (ibid: p. 470). In a few sentences, the authors sketched out the essence of what Gordon, Edwards, and Reich (1982), among others, later called the 'capital–labour accord'.

Kalecki and Kowalik warned, however, that this situation is unstable. On the one hand, workers will accept even the buildup of military spending if this appears to maintain high rates of employment. On the other hand, the means used to avoid realisation problems are *ad hoc* not centrally controlled (as they could be in a socialist state), and workers will react adversely if the rules of the game – the exchange of loyalty to the capitalist system for low unemployment – are violated. Thus, 'relative stability [...] depends on a high degree of social conformity' (ibid: p. 476). The authors acknowledge that civil unrest such as student movements could unbalance such a state of stasis, but make no promises or predictions that this is likely.

In effect, this 1969–1970 paper adds a third alternative to the two prospects identified in Kalecki's 1943 and 1944 articles. That is, capitalists can avoid the labour-effort/output tradeoff and a profit squeeze due to the exhaustion of the reserve army of the unemployed if they support adequate safety-net provisions and obtain workers' acquiescence in supporting the expansion of the military-industrial complex (and the associated project of national military dominance).

3.3 The workers' voice and the debate over economics of socialism

Kowalik's writings about Poland are informed by his long study of the economics of socialism; and that study, in turn, is rooted in his work with Lange and Kalecki. Lange's writings pose the recurrent question of what constitutes the *differentia specifica* of the socialist economy. Our journey through Kowalik's scholarship on the socialist economy thus begins with Oskar Lange, whose collected works he edited; we then turn briefly to Kalecki's ideas on this subject before turning to Kowalik's own writings on this topic.

Kowalik (1987: pp. 1–2) noted that Lange, in advocating a mixed and not centralised approach to the economy, saw no need for a distinct theory of the socialist economy. But then what, for Lange, is a socialist economy? Lange's 1936 essay on this question begins by refuting claims that a rational use of economic resources under socialism is impossible. Lange first dismissed Mises' objection that the absence of private ownership of the means of production simply makes rational analysis of alternative uses of resources impossible. He then considered the Robbins/Hayek argument that the 'trial and error' process by which supply and demand can be equated – a bootstrap version of a Walrasian *tatonnement* process – is impossible in socialism, but feasible and even normal in capitalism. Lange acknowledged that since socialist economies have consumer goods and labour services markets but no markets for capital goods and other productive resources, the decisions of firm managers must be guided not by profit-maximisation but by a planning ministry which sets output and resource-use requirements and minimises average production cost. This said, Lange argued that the 'parametric function of prices' (Lange, 1994. p. 258) – price discovery – does have an analogue under socialist planning; he suggested that a process of 'trial and error' like that in the capitalist economy is feasible.

Lange went on to turn his interlocutors' arguments on their heads, questioning whether *'the further maintenance of the capitalist system is compatible with economic progress'* (ibid: p. 276, italics in original). He argued that capitalist firms will tend to become large and inflexible, and thus will have incentives to deter and not hasten technical progress, so as to protect their returns. The private owners of these firms will then make decisions that maximise their returns, including monopolistic rents. So, he asserted, in a transition from capitalism to socialism, public control over the banks and leading industries is crucial to insure socially optimal income flows and resource allocation patterns. Lange then argued that in the presence of effective governmental guidance, a mixed economy – in which small-scale private ownership and private enterprise exist side by side with a broadly socialist economy is feasible.

> To avoid the growth of an atmosphere of panic in the sector of private property and private enterprise the socialist government may have to prove the seriousness of its intentions by some immediate deeds in favour of the small entrepreneurs and small property holders (including holders of saving deposits and small stock and bondholders). It has to make it absolutely clear to everybody that socialism is not directed against private property as such, but only against that special type of private property which creates social privileges to the detriment of the great majority of the people or creates obstacles to economic progress, and that, consequently, all private property in the means of production and private enterprise which does have a *useful social function* will enjoy the full protection and support of the socialist State. (Lange, 1994: p. 283)

Lange then both pointed out the parallel between his argument and that of Keynes, and asserted the possible superiority of a socialist government in combatting depression. Since 'the marginal efficiency of capital (as defined by Mr. Keynes) is very low and the liquidity preference of the capitalists is very high' in a depression, 'a bold programme of public investments is needed to restore employment to a higher level' (Lange, 1994: p. 284). A capitalist government may be unable to carry out such a programme because of a pre-commitment to the idea that investment is socially beneficial only if it is profitable. 'Thus it may take a socialist government (p. 284) free from the ballast of bourgeois prejudices about economic policies, to restore the capitalist economy' (Lange, 1994: pp. 284–285).

This led Lange to recognise an 'inescapable dilemma' for a socialist government in a mixed economy: 'a Labour Plan is either a start for the wholesale attack on the capitalist system, or it must end in a betrayal of socialism'. Regarding the socialist enterprise itself, Lange asserted that it must satisfy two conditions: 'It must act as the trustee of the general social interest, and it must be a self-governing body' (Lange, 1994: p. 339).

Like Lange, Kalecki emphasised the challenge in a mixed economy of managing investment in the private sector. He augmented Lange's concern with overemphasis on a profit motive by observing that investment may be insufficient in areas of social priority, and excessive in areas serving less pressing social needs (such as luxury housing). Further, he pointed out that since public investment in a mixed economy must be financed from tax revenues, it is quite likely that rich and foreign capitalists can use political influence to avoid paying their fair share (ibid: pp. 88–89).[3]

Turning to the question of the socialist enterprise, Kalecki himself was firmly in favour of workers' councils and worker self-management, which he regarded as means for aligning societal goals with participants in production processes. However, enterprise autonomy was problematic, in Kalecki's eyes, for several reasons: it raised the possibility that incentive-based pay in some industries would lead to unemployment in society at large; any changes to prices or output would require complex calculations to re-equilibrate demand and supply with planned outcomes; and it would de-emphasise the focus in the socialist economy on satisfying the material needs of society as a whole (Osiatyński, 1988: ch. 2).

Lange's view of the economics of socialism came in for substantial criticism both because of the eminence of the author and the audacity of his view – in the context of the post-War 'Cold War' – that capitalist and socialist means of organising economic activity could be viewed along a continuum. One important counter was registered by Kornai (1986). We consider it here, since we will take up Kowalik's critical comments (1992b) on Kornai's essay below.

Kornai (1986) argued that Lange's model of socialism is erroneous on two central points. One concerns the possibility of benevolent central planning. For Kornai, 'The people at his Central Planning Board are reincarnations of Plato's philosophers, embodiments of unity, unselfishness, and wisdom. [...] strictly enforcing the "Rule", adjusting prices to excess demand. Such an unworldly bureaucracy never existed in the past and will never exist in the future. [...] They pursue their own individual and group interests .[...] Power creates an irresistible temptation to make use of it' (Kornai, 1986: p. 1726). Kornai's substitution of the self-aggrandisement of an empowered elite for a government committed to social welfare represents the first of two steps in his effort to undercut the logic of Lange's general-equilibrium parallelism.

The second step in this demolition-by-displacement comes with Kornai's assertion of Lange's second error: his failure to appreciate chronic disequilibrium in socialism. Specifically, whereas 'The Mises-Hayek-Schumpeter market implies a hard budget constraint and a buyers' market' in the capitalist economy, in the socialist economy, 'the system [...] do[es] not assure the prevalence of these two conditions, [and] there is no genuine market. The great shortcoming of the Lange model is that it does not even contemplate these conditions'. In Kornai's account, socialist firms' rivalry is not disciplined by the market, but instead is resolved by bureaucratic competition. Thus, 'The total potential of all rivals normally exceeds actual demand. Some win and some lose' (Kornai, 1986: p. 1727). So oversupply on the side of firms and shortage on the side of consumers coexist in a perfect mismatch.

Kornai's rejection of Lange's socialist model is rooted simultaneously in his acceptance of neoclassical supply–demand analysis and in his view that a general-equilibrium approach to such analysis – as embodied in Lange's model – should be categorically rejected. This deserves a comment. General equilibrium theory is commonly understood as an abstract framework which depicts the conditions for achieving decentralised equilibria via market competition. Its distance from real world conditions is clear. In effect, Kornai's critique uses over-faithful adherence to Walrasian equilibrium conditions against a model of socialist planning without considering which elements of those conditions might be violated in actually existing capitalist economies – and what the implications of those violations are. To assert that Lange's depiction of the principles of socialist planning as a failure because it treats real-world planning as equivalent to implementation of a timeless equilibrium is to make a category mistake.[4]

For Kornai to undercut Lange's approach required the detection of both errors. In particular, the problem of perverse managerial behaviour under socialist planning had been identified years earlier by Balassa (1973), who wrote that 'managers' objective was to obtain bonuses as large as permitted by the constraints imposed on the firm but not so large as to result in a subsequent tightening of the conditions for their attainment by the supervising ministry' (Balassa, 1973: p. 347). Balassa went on to argue for reforms that would permit profit maximisation for firms, and greater freedom over investment and other decisions, in accordance with what he termed the 'Lange–Lerner model' of the socialist economy. Kornai eliminates this possibility via his assertion that 'honest-broker' public oversight is impossible. The parallel with Karl Popper's views of market and state in *The Open Society and its Enemies* is very close: like Popper, Kornai views state intervention of any kind in economic processes as an impediment to the emergence of outcomes reflecting citizens' – consumers' – demands.

Kornai's rejection of socialist planning on the basis of its economic deficiencies was challenged by several commentators. Włodzimierz Brus (1990) wrote sceptically about Kornai's analysis of the actions of the 'revolutionaries from above', and called for gradualism in policies so as to maintain continuity in institutions. Branco Horvat wrote acerbically in the *Journal of Economic Behavior and Organization*:

> In short, Janos Kornai *believes* that (unconstrained?) private ownership is a panacea for all Hungarian troubles. That view is characteristic of the general mood in Eastern Europe and the book is likely to be popular there. The mood is also understandable as a psychological reaction to repressive regimes which lasted several decades. In 1945 everybody was nationalizing, in 1990 everybody is privatizing. In either case serious argument played a tertiary role. What one finds disturbing is that the road advocated does not lead to a free economy but to a new disappointment. (Horvat, 1991: p. 410)

In his 1990 commentary, Kowalik distinguished between the 'Bolshevik program and tactics' and the views of the 'overwhelming majority of the socialist party leaders' (Kowalik, 1990: p. 39).

> The case of Poland seems to indicate that the large industrial working class, the product of that conservative modernization, is indeed digging the grave of the system. This is not because, living in the 'socialist welfare state,' the workers will no longer stand for a lack of democracy, but because a communist system is incapable of creating such a welfare state. The communist economies [...] cannot succeed without a thorough [...] reconstruction. Yet there is so far no evidence that a reconstruction will work and not lead to a simple repudiation of the system.
>
> I personally hope that there is a 'third road' between the monocentric communism and the all-out development of a private market economy [...T]his third road is, I am deeply convinced, not only a valued choice but also the least costly of all roads out of the present crisis. (Kowalik, 1990: pp. 41–42)

Kowalik expressed concern over neoliberals in Poland, for whom 'to move the nation toward capitalism is the surest way to economic revival' (ibid: p. 44), and asserted his view that 'workers' self-management bodies are the most promising social movement for reform, for they are institutions that fight both statism and laissez-faire concepts' (ibid: p. 45).

3.4 Kowalik's 1986 'On Crucial Reform in the Socialist Economy'

Kowalik's advocacy of a 'third way' in a 1990 working paper, written in the year that saw Lech Wałęsa elected President of Poland, resulted from his careful study of the transition problem. He laid out his thinking in 'On Crucial Reform in Socialist Economy', an unpublished 1986 working paper for a Vienna think-tank. This chapter, a comprehensive rendering of Kowalik's thinking on the future of socialism, is summarised in depth in this section.

Kowalik's central concern in this 1986 essay is with the possibility of a 'crucial reform' of the socialist economy – that is, 'the transition from the "command economy" to an economy with a regulated market, but still within the framework of "real socialism"', which means, *inter alia*, 'abandonment of central planning' (Kowalik, 1986: p. 3) and the independence of the enterprises regarding the three main problems of production: what to produce, how much, and how.

Kowalik made it clear immediately that he saw socio-institutional and political change as the critical steps in achieving 'crucial reform'. As in Yugoslavia and Hungary, 'the deficiencies of the economic reform initiated already during the Solidarność period and implemented under the umbrella of martial law can be attributed to the political deadlock.' (ibid: p. 5) The arguments for economic decentralisation in the 1950s already recognised the need to challenge the 'power of the party and state elite' (ibid: p. 7). Kornai's work ignores 'the role of the party and other political institutions in regulating the economy' (ibid: p. 9). Kowalik drew an analogy between Keynes' ideas in the interwar period and the idea of political reform in the current moment. Keynes' ideas about large-scale government intervention (and the welfare state) provided the crucial reform that sustained capitalism even while it 'appeared to undermine the whole capitalist system' (ibid: p. 13). In the socialist economies at present, then, the crucial reform that is apparently unthinkable involves a displacement of the central role of the party.

Kowalik then considered why the chance for radical reform was lost in the earlier historical period. He recalled Polish sociologist Jan Szczepański's insight that the destabilisation of society leads to a 'defensive reaction of the power apparatus' (ibid: p. 15). He went on to assert 'extra-party pluralism to be an indispensable component of the "crucial reform" [...because the] sound functioning of the economy with a regulated market requires the articulation and defence of the different social groups' interests' (ibid: p. 31).

Kowalik argues that 'a clear distinction should be made between an option for capitalism as a social system and allowing for the co-existence of capitalist enterprises with the socialised sector, and the restoration of the private sector, that is, of private handicrafts and trade, small-scale industrial production units and family farms' (ibid: p. 35). State socialism involves one-party political rule and overemphasises concentration on production. Kowalik advocates 'democratic socialism', which must be pluralistic in three respects:

> there should be a variety of forms of ownership, but state ownership should not be dominant (other forms include self-management ownership, co-operatives, municipal and private forms of ownership);
> autonomy of the economic units;
> unrestricted opportunities for self-organisation of various groups for the protection of their interests. (ibid: p. 40)

In Kowalik's vision, democratic socialism involves self-organisation and advocacy in two spheres, the economic and the political. One key is '[p]luralism of ownership, [...which] widens the scope for [...] social activity [...and] constitutes a barrier to bureaucratization and "leviathanization" of the state' (ibid: p. 42). And while state overreach must be arrested, a strong state presence is needed to protect what might be termed the public interest. In the economic realm, this would involve ensuring that the goods needed for basic living standards are available, and that core infrastructure and investment in strategically important industries – is protected.

> There exists an economic, social and political rationale behind the pluralism of the forms of ownership. To put it in a nutshell, I see the scope for different forms of ownership in the following way: state ownership seems to be most justified in the key industries, such as mining and energy. Part of the infrastructure can be based on municipal ownership (local transport). Manufacturing industry can be an area of competition between different types of enterprises: [...] self-management [...] co-operatives, joint stock companies, [...] individualized private capital or on mixed capital. (ibid: p. 41)

The civil realm would need to be protected against socially harmful developments in the market and looking after public welfare. This would be done by planning – not by command central planning, which would be ruled out, but by other forms of planning 'based on broad participation in the decision-making process [...] mediating contradictory interests of different social groups'. This leads directly to a wider scope for self-organisation in the political sphere, as the 'social planning' envisioned by Kowalik 'presupposes [...] politically independent organizations [and] freedom of speech, publications and meetings. For economic life [...] political pluralism is of paramount importance' (ibid: p. 42).

These ideas, of course, pose the problem of how to achieve this political broadening. Kowalik's hopes for real socialism rested on the commitment to 'crucial reform' of 'the ruling elite', its willingness to 'implant a different type of logic' in which 'the language of dialogue, agreement, consensus and social contract has to be used' (ibid: p. 44). He then further developed the comparison between crucial reform of capitalism and of socialism. He argued that both 'aim at a greater stability and rationality of the respective systems by means of institutionalized mediation between social interest and individual or group interest' (ibid: p. 47). In the former case:

> The mainstay of the capitalist system – private ownership – [was] limited and [...] the economic rules of the game were altered. The logic of this change contradicted [...] traditional liberal doctrine [...] But it was precisely the radical reform which secured stability of the Western world for over a quarter of a century. (ibid: p. 48)

Crucial reform in real socialism must 'take an opposite character and direction' (ibid: p. 47), permitting: enterprises to operate on the basis of self-management and self-financing with minimal state control; a reduction in the decision-making prerogatives of the state, and its embrace of differentiated forms of ownership, control, and competition in the provision of public services; and finally, 'accepting social pluralism and institutionalizing it in a diversity of non-party forms' (ibid: p. 48). The state, in shifting from a command to a coordination function, 'would then more closely resemble its counterpart in the contemporary Western economies than in the majority of the communist countries before the reform' (ibid: p. 50).

Kowalik hastened to add that he is not calling for 'a turn from omnipresent collectivism to individualism'; but he notes that his call for crucial reform could easily be misinterpreted and manipulated, both by 'people in power [in the current socialist state], capable of mobilizing big collectives to serve the interests of that narrow group, [...and by] the ruled ones, who do not identify themselves with big, anonymous collectives that they frequently joined against their own will' (ibid: pp. 48–49).

In other words, a 'restitution of conditions to real collectivism' (ibid: p. 49) requires the ruling elite to set aside some of its own privileges and prerogatives, thereby salvaging real socialist society by embracing its democratisation.

3.5 Kowalik on the Polish transition from socialism to capitalism

Kowalik's reflections on how real socialism worthy of the name could emerge through internal reforms have an urgency derived from the quickening pace of conflict and change in the Poland of the 1980s. Solidarność was founded in 1980; it became the basis of an anti-bureaucratic social movement even while the government was attempting to suppress it. In 1989, Poland went through a political transition from a centrally coordinated Communist Party-led regime to a democratically elected government. Lech Wałęsa was elected President in 1990, and free parliamentary elections completed the transition in 1991. In November 1995, Wałęsa was defeated by Aleksander Kwaśniewski in Poland's second post-war free presidential election. Debate raged during those years over how the transition from social protest to government should be handled, given that the production model inherited from the Soviet-dominated past was not suited for the post-Communist future.

The remarkable actions of the 1989–1995 period led to considerable disagreement among analysts about how to react to the dramatic choices at hand. We can see this by contrasting a 1994 paper by Zygmunt Bauman with a 1996 rejoinder by Kowalik (1996) – that is, between two authors who both stood against state patronage and for democracy. Bauman characterised the dilemma as follows: the striking workers of Solidarność, 'least capable of entering the dreams of Europe and marked for extinction, were the very force that brought down communism [...] and are likely to be the first to experience the severest hardships of the economic transformation, such as the intensification of labour, the sharpening of work discipline, the loss of job security, and unemployment'. (Bauman, 1994: p. 19). Bauman concluded that it is 'too early for conclusions: the revolutionary process has started, but its destination and the direction it will take are uncertain.' (ibid: p. 22)

While sociologist Bauman is not explicit on this point, Kowalik read him as viewing this transition as a problem of industrial modernisation which will require the suppression of popular desires to gratify long-frustrated desires for up-to-date consumption in favour of a rational planning process that sets the stage for long-run growth. He saw Bauman as viewing workers subject to a 'post-modern narcissistic culture', so that the necessary re-invention of the productive apparatus – which he terms 'primary capital accumulation' – must be accomplished by State enforcement of a new social structure. What this leaves unspecified, however, is how this transition can be achieved. This in turn opens the door for the sort of conclusion reached by Balassa (1974) and Kornai (1986) – that the State managers are incapable of thinking beyond their own gratification and gain. Thus what is needed is a stern external force bringing about large-scale engineering. This was, in these analysts' eyes, the critical flaw in real socialism.[5]

Kowalik opposed both parts of this implicit program, which was implemented via Balcerowicz's 'Shock Therapy' plan in October 1989. The plan was based on the view of some – including its chief proponent – that centrally planned economies would invariably fail.[6] This view was based on an overly rosy assessment of the superiority of market incentives in allocating resources.[7] It was also based on the view of Kornai (1986) and others that proofs of the plausibility of central planning – chief among them, Lange (1936) – required the existence of omniscient, benevolent planners who could never be found in any real world. Kowalik (1992b) criticised Kornai (1986) on several grounds: first, he noted that Lange did consider the problem of bureaucracy and of the capacity of any socialist system to overcome its pitfalls. He went on to argue that Lange, Kalecki and Brus saw price-setting and the control of investment as critical components of the socialist model; the 'countervailing power towards bureaucracy' should be provided by 'workers' councils' (Kowalik, 1992b: p. 170). He pointed out that in the context of the Soviet approach to planning, Kalecki and other reformers regarded the socialist economy as having two fundamental elements: autonomous enterprises led by workers' councils; and the plan set forth by the central planning agency.[8] In sum, Kowalik dissented from the Balcerowicz plan both because it was based on distortions, both of the theoretical plausibility of real-world socialism as such, and of the possibility that workers' voice could find a place under socialism.

The Balcerowicz plan pushed aside the gradualist approach of the Round Table of February–April 1989, which had provided the basis for a peaceful transition from Communist Party rule by emphasising consultative deliberations and bargaining among stakeholders representing different economic sectors. The 'Shock Therapy' or 'Polish Big Bang' put in place later that year, and approved as a stabilisation program by the IMF in December 1989, took precisely the opposite approach – immediate, large-scale economic transformation via a series of non-negotiable top-down decisions. These changes included the introduction of a bankruptcy mechanism for state-owned firms, the end of special access to credit for state-owned companies, restrictions on wage increases, and so on. Bauman (1994: p. 19) refers to the replacement of the Round Table by the IMF program only obliquely, as the 'penalty paid by Poland for being in the lead'. Kowalik saw it as marking a critical divide in the transition period. He pointed out that the IMF programme delivered rates of unemployment higher than in other Eastern European countries; and it was based on the false premise that Poland required the same sort of primitive accumulation (via the reallocation of ownership rights and the amassing of a pool of savings that could seek out new investment opportunities) as might a developing country. This false premise provided a justification for radical across-the-board actions such as the attack on the 'welfare state' provisions that had been part of Poland's socialist system. These acts of social dismantling and the power to reallocate being given to new actors were consequences of seeing Poland as a developing – and not a transitioning – society.

In his 1997 *Dissent* article, Kowalik refers to this as a tragicomedy – the 'largest labor movement in Europe' bringing about one of the most inequitable societies in Europe (Kowalik, 1997: p. 26). This chapter clarifies his somewhat cryptic criticisms of Poland's commitment to primary capital accumulation in his 1996 paper. First, he was asserting his objection to the programmatic target of reducing labour share in national output. He rejected the view that modernisation and growth requires a reduction in the income share of workers and those dependent on the social safety net, in favour of making more income available to capital. Second, he was critical of the abandonment of consultation and joint decision-making. He went on to explain why, in his view, Solidarity squandered its popular mandate due to a conjuncture of factors. Chief among them was the inability of its leadership to see that the several important insights in the Balcerowicz program were incorporated into a neoliberal programme whose logic would undercut the working-class alliance that was the root of Solidarity's success. The economic strategy so suddenly adopted forced intellectuals to choose between economic growth and the need for inclusive and egalitarian growth.

3.6 Conclusion: democratic voice versus sustained prosperity in capitalism and socialism?

Some of Tadeusz Kowalik's most profound writings on capitalism and socialism focused on the question of 'crucial reform': whether it would be possible, as each system encountered limits on further expansion built into its structures of political and economic ownership and control, to extend each system's life through a fundamental re-engineering. In the case of capitalism, as Kalecki showed, the problem was that when full employment is reached, labour effort falls, labour militancy rises, and ultimately capitalists strike – they refuse to invest.[9] Further, when unemployment rises too high, accumulation also breaks down due to insufficient aggregate demand. Kalecki and Kowalik suggested that the lower-level binding constraint could be eased through either military expenditure or an augmented welfare-state safety net. In effect, capital would have to accept some socialisation of investment to avoid the problem of stagnation. The upper-level constraint was relaxed through a 'crucial reform' in which labour agreed to labour peace – cooperation with capital on the workshop floor – in exchange for wage stability. As these authors noted, this resolution proved unstable, but did provide a quarter-century of relative prosperity for much of the global North.

Kowalik turned to the problem of 'crucial reform' in socialism just as the real socialist economies were coming under insurmountable pressure from below. Some analysts – here we have highlighted the work of Kornai – argued that socialism's problems were fundamentally its flawed economic design: too much decision-making power was invested in corruptible elites, who were set in charge of competing firms that were not subject to market discipline. Kowalik disagreed, and asserted that the problems in socialism derived fundamentally from the excessive power of an unaccountable elite. The solutions were to democratise the economy and the polity. In particular, self-management and autonomous activity by productive firms would encourage higher productivity, while state and local government control could be retained over key industrial activities. The role of the state would shift from running a command economy to coordinating economic activity in the public interest. The enhancement of pathways by which popular groups and interests could make their needs and preferences known would ensure that governmental choices over economic output was sensitive to social needs. The success of this crucial reform depended on both the willingness of the political elites to surrender a part of their prerogatives, and the desire of the populations of the socialist nations to maintain the socialist form of economic governance.

In the event, continuous prosperity via either 'crucial reforms' that could guarantee stable accumulation and prosperity under either a capitalist or a socialist path proved to be blocked by contradictions involving democratic voice. A contradiction of democratic voice arises in both capitalist and socialist economies in different ways but with parallel consequences.

Consider just one example from among the capitalist nations: the case of the United States. The prominence on its 1960s–1970s political agenda of issues such as the negative income tax, a community-reinvestment requirement for banks, a right to shelter, extensive job-training, affirmative action for racial/ethnic minority businesses and so on, illustrates the threat posed by excessive democratic voice to capitalist profits. The capital–labour accord was undermined with the coming of the Neoliberal era in the 1980s. The shift toward deregulation and reduced welfare state protection in the leading global-North nations, together with the spread of production to offshore 'global factory' locations, eliminated the economic basis for capital's accommodation with a prosperous and pacified labour force. Labour militancy was mooted by the explosion of offshore production locations and an influx of migrant workers. Labour lost the capacity to defend its interests politically, as the discourse of labour rights gave way to that of consumer rights.

In the case of real socialism, the example of Poland has been examined briefly above. As Kowalik feared, workers were so anxious to overthrow the shackles of their subjugation to an overbearing political elite that they opened the doors to a radical anti-state, market-based approach.[10] The option of a socialist economy with substantial democratic voice and more room for autonomous economic activity was never posed; instead, the IMF 'shock therapy' program wiped away the possibility of gradualist change. An expanded democratic voice, as envisioned in Kowalik's 1986 working paper, would have threatened the privileges and position of the elite that had governed Poland during the Communist-bloc period. And in any case, normalised channels for forming and refining political alternatives democratically did not yet exist.

Following Kowalik's lead, we can speculate that either a capitalist or a socialist path can in principle generate stable, secure incomes along with some amount of consumer choice – but only via the empowerment of workers. However, such empowerment is destabilising for those with centralised control over resources – capitalists in the case of capitalism, and a bureaucratic elite in the case of socialism.

The 'crucial reforms' proposed by Kowalik for both capitalism and socialism require democratic empowerment of workers, an enlightened, long-term-oriented elite, and political and economic mechanisms for effectuating the necessary compromises. The fragility of these conditions is one reason why most real socialist systems have not been sustained and why real capitalist systems have collapsed into crisis and stagnation.

Kowalik's writings are clearly not solely of historical interest. The way forward for China is clearly compromised by that nation's inability to create mechanisms for validating the democratic voice in both the political and the economic realms. The situation Kowalik describes in the transitioning Polish economy – extreme inequality, lack of democratic accountability, and control by the rich, unresponsive and isolated government – closely resemble the situation in many nations of the world today. Kowalik's warnings about the inability of popular governments – even those based on national insurrections – to create reforms responding to the will of the people are an important starting point for those who hope that democratic mobilisation (via either the Occupy movement or more traditional forms of political action) can remake capitalism.

Notes

1. While most of his analysis of the sources of fluctuations in capitalist economies used formal models (for example, Kalecki, 1954), these two papers contained no mathematics.
2. Representative texts reflecting the ferment of the Eurocommunist movement – the possibilities for using popular mobilisation to inject a democratic voice into structures of economic control – are Colletti (1972) and Laclau and Mouffe (1977).
3. In Kalecki's 1956 essay on workers' councils, he writes, 'the essential structure of economic organization that is emerging after these reforms consists of enterprises directed by workers' councils which operate within the framework of central planning in the strict sense of the term' (Kalecki, 1999: p. 202).
4. Joseph Persky's (2000) essay on neoclassical economics would view Kornai's category mistake here as a recurring problem for those pre-committed (as Kornai has become) to the neoclassical framework:'Over the 20th century, repeated efforts have been made to expunge values and norms from neoclassical economics. But American neoclassical economics has never really capitulated. At root, neoclassicism has affirmed the necessity and usefulness of creating and defending a normative economics based on an idealisation of full competition. It did so in 1900 much as in 2000, not as an apology for the status quo, nor as a justification for laissez-faire, but rather as a prerequisite for constructive action by a progressive state.' (Persky, 2000: p. 107)

5. Toporowski (1999) argues that Kalecki's economics of socialism leads to the conclusion that 'errors of economic strategy and, in particular, weak planning of investment, rather than an absence of markets, [led] to the "Collapse of Communism" at the end of the 1980s' (p. 227).
6. Leszek Balcerowicz is an influential Polish economist closely affiliated with Solidarność. He served as both deputy prime minister and finance minister twice, including during the crucial September 1989–August 1991 period. In Balcerowicz (1992), he argues that Hayek's critique of socialist planning as impossible to implement was right; and centrally planned economies would invariably have shortages and a variety of problems arising from the centralisation of investment, including insufficient innovation and risk-taking. Efforts to maintain a mixed economy only serve to highlight the implausibility of the overall model; in his analysis, the freedom to establish private firms and the privatisation of state enterprises represent the inevitable endpoint of the centrally planned economy. He rationalises his plan in Balcerowicz (2000), arguing that '*extreme [...] inherited macroeconomic instability calls for the rapid implementation of a tough stabilization* program' (p. 233, italics in original).
7. Alec Nove (1992), in a contribution to the volume featuring Balcerowicz' essay, points out that the neoclassical model which Balcerowicz and others regarded as a superior tool for the guidance of real-world systems was itself based on implausible and unrealistic ideas about the determinants of investment, the abilities of agents in decentralised markets to achieve optima, and so on.
8. Many of these views were set forth in the pivotal year of 1956 – that is, just before a crackdown on such thinking led to the imposition (in Poland and elsewhere in the Eastern bloc) of a more sterilised, centrally controlled version of real-world socialism. In this sense, the democratic councils that sprang up as Solidarność-enforced concessions resembled a return to some of the core ideas of the democratic real-world socialism that had been swept aside 33 years earlier.
9. Dymski (2012) argues that accumulation can only proceed successfully inside a narrow zone, unless systemic parameters are changed.
10. In South Korea, the arrival of IMF intervention in the context of the 1997–1998 Asian financial crisis evinced similarly complex sentiments among Koreans, given their widespread resentment of the *chaebols* (multinationals). See Crotty and Dymski (1998).

4
Michał Kalecki's Capitalist Dynamics from Today's Perspective

D. Mario Nuti

4.1 Premise

In 1962, having just graduated in economics from the University of Rome 'La Sapienza' and hoping for a scholarship for Cambridge the following year, I decided to go to Warsaw, braving the coldest winter of the century, and learn more *in corpore vili* about the comparative economic systems which were to become my life's main research and teaching interest. At the time there was a thriving school of economics in Poland with, in addition to Kalecki, such eminent representatives as Oskar Lange, Kazimierz Łaski, Włodzimierz Brus, Ignacy Sachs, and many others. I learned Polish fast, and by September I was attending both Kalecki's and Lange's lectures and their courses, which were being given in English that year for students from developing countries, at SGPiS (the Higher School of Planning and Statistics, as it then was; it is now the Higher School of Commerce). I had a fellowship from the Polish Academy of Sciences and was associated with the PAN Department of Economic Sciences, on the 20th floor of the Russian-built Palace of Culture. It was there that I first met Tadeusz Kowalik, who used to attend our seminar although he was a member of the PAN History Department.

I learned a great deal, even though my youthful commitment to socialism was somewhat weakened, and I made new friends, among whom I definitely regard Tadeusz Kowalik as the closest and dearest. An independent scholar, a Swedish-style social democrat and a passionate egalitarian, he introduced me to the work of Lange and Kalecki and guided me through the intricacies of the Polish reform movement. A year later I went to King's College, Cambridge, but during that time and over the following 50 years I kept up my interest in Polish affairs and my connection with Tadeusz. I knew about his close collaboration with Solidarność and his lectures at the Flying University, and we exchanged papers and publications. We both were ardent critics of the Polish transition and above all the so-called Stabilisation Plan of Leszek Balcerowicz, which plunged Poland into an unnecessary transition recession under the guise of 'shock therapy'. In the periods 1994–1997 and 2002–2004, I acted as economic advisor to Deputy Premier Grzegorz Kołodko, a mutual friend of ours, in which capacity I visited Warsaw for about a week every month, so that Tadeusz and I could meet frequently and discuss current policies. Always a sober and unpretentious person, Tadeusz suggested, when he first heard of the initiative to edit a *festschrift* in his honour, that contributors – whom he expected to be just a few friends – might discuss some aspects of the economics of Lange and Kalecki, to whom he had devoted so much of his editorial work and his own research in the history of economic thought. In this vein I wish to contribute some thoughts on the vexed question of the relationship between Kalecki and Keynes, specifically on Kalecki's theory of the political cycle and its relevance today in view of the revival of what Joan Robinson used to call 'Pre-Keynesian Economics after Keynes' – that is, the return to fashion of fiscal austerity – and the so-called expansionary fiscal consolidation.

4.2 Kalecki and Keynes

In my Cambridge days (1963–1980) I heard Joan Robinson lavish repeated praise on Kalecki's anticipation of Keynes's *General Theory* (1936).

'It must be rather annoying for you', Robinson wrote to Kalecki in 1937, 'to see all this fuss being made over Keynes when so little notice was taken of your own contribution' (reproduced in Patinkin, 1982; she wrote similar acknowledgements in 1964, 1976 and elsewhere). She was not alone in making this claim on Kalecki's behalf: 'Kalecki's greatest achievement, among many, was undoubtedly his complete anticipation of Keynes' *General Theory*' (Klein, 1975, 1947; see also Lange, 1939). In fact, before the publication of Keynes's *General Theory*, Michał Kalecki had published in Polish (1933c, 1934; reprinted in English in Kalecki, 1971b) and in English (1935a), a demand-determined theory of national income and employment, centred on investment and with an expenditure multiplier, similar to that of Keynes. But his intellectual roots, methodology and arguments were original – and so were Keynes's;.there are many highly significant differences between the two (see Nuti, 2004).

First, money and the money interest rate, which figure prominently in Keynesian theory and in the very title of the *General Theory*, have no role in Kalecki, for whom only the long-term interest rate is relevant, within the limits set by the principle of increasing risk of credit-financed investment.

Second, Keynes had a view of the volatility of expectations and the dependence of investment on 'animal spirits' as well as 'the state of the news'. Kalecki's investors, instead, simply looked at the degree of capacity utilisation (a flexible accelerator or capital-stock adjustment) and projected the current profit rate into the future.

Third, Keynes had no particular views about income distribution, in spite of post-Keynesian developments in this area, while Kalecki had two distribution theories, one based on the relative propensities of capitalists and workers to consume – 'workers spend what they earn, capitalists earn what they spend' – akin to the post-Keynesian approach, and one based on the average degree of monopoly aggregated over all producers.

Fourth, Keynes's approach lent itself to combination with an accelerator to produce economic cycles – as did Roy Harrod's, followed by those of many others. Kalecki had an armoury of complete models of economic cycles.

Finally, both Kalecki and Keynes made outstanding contributions to other areas of economic thought. Keynes's ideas ranged from probability theory to fiscal policy to the design of the international monetary system, Kalecki's from the theory of growth of the capitalist economy to the theory and practice of socialist economic planning to original criteria for the selection of investment projects.

Both Kalecki and Keynes were great economists on their own account and merits; so, laying unnecessary stress on the relatively small overlapping of their demand-determined theory of employment and income – no matter how important –detracts from their greatness.

4.3 Kalecki's political cycle

Besides his mathematical models of the economic cycle, Kalecki (1943) produced a model based on the political economy of government fiscal policy and of capitalist behaviour.

In theory full employment could be achieved via additional government expenditure were it not for the government's and capitalists' need to reproduce labour unemployment in order to keep wage rates and labour discipline under control.

In a nutshell, 'A solid majority of economists is now of the opinion that, even in a capitalist system, full employment may be secured by a government spending programme, provided there is in existence adequate plant to employ all existing labour power, and provided adequate supplies of necessary foreign raw-materials may be obtained in exchange for exports' (Kalecki, 1943: p. 347). As long, of course, as such a government spending programme is 'financed by borrowing and not by taxation'. However,

> we may expect the opposition of the leaders of industry [to such a policy of full employment] on three planes: (i) opposition on principle to government spending based on a budget deficit; (ii) opposition to this spending being directed either towards public investment – which may foreshadow the intrusion of the state into the new spheres of economic activity – or towards subsidising mass consumption; (iii) opposition to maintaining full employment and not merely preventing deep and prolonged slumps. (Kalecki, 1943: p. 353)

Such objections subside in the slump, and are revived in the boom.

With lasting full employment workers would 'get out of hand', and the 'captains of industry' would be anxious to 'teach them a lesson'. Moreover, the price increase in the upswing is to the disadvantage of small and big rentiers and makes them 'boom-tired' and ready to ally with capitalists.

Their pressure would probably induce the government to return to the orthodox policy of cutting down the budget deficit. 'A slump would follow in which government spending policy would again come into its own.'

4.4 Today's world

Seventy years later, what has changed in economic theory, and in the state of the world? At least three fundamental things:

(1) labour markets have become globalised;
(2) the fiscal constraints on the sustainability of sovereign government debt have tightened;
(3) the economic profession's consensus about the possibility of achieving full employment has gradually faded – at least it did until 2008–2010.

Since Kalecki's time, especially since about 1970, there has been an increasing integration of international trade and movements of production factors, with a single temporary decrease of the average import–export share in world GDP in 2009 immediately reversed. The globalisation of world labour markets – through international migrations and delocalisation of output to lower-wage locations but primarily through international trade – has led, in the years 1985–2005 in advanced countries, to a deterioration of labour shares in national incomes by 10 percentage points, from 65 per cent to 55 per cent (IMF, 2007), without a parallel offsetting increase in emerging countries, where labour is still relatively abundant.

The global crisis has made unemployment a cyclical worldwide phenomenon; conversely, global calls for expansionary fiscal and monetary policies have been made (for example, in November 2008 at the G20 under IMF leadership) and implemented, though they were short lived and subjected to premature reversal. In other words, Kalecki's political cycle is still there, but it has grown globally synchronised and possibly weakened on average by both the general weakening of the power of organised labour and by persistent international divergences in the timing of the cycle.

The second feature that today differs markedly from Kalecki's time and framework is the record high level of sovereign debt. How can fiscal stimulus be feasible and sustainable in this situation?

Kalecki expected interest rate on public debt to be contained by monetary policy (as it was at the time of his writing, and would be today were it not for the so-called spread that distances the cost of credit for the southern members of the Eurozone from that of the more virtuous and credible Nordic members, like Germany). In any case Kalecki envisaged interest on public debt being financed out of a recurring capital tax, a solution technically unimpeachable though politically unpopular. Therefore the persistence of unemployment continues to be the result of political obstacles to alternative policies.

Finally, the economists' consensus on the effectiveness of expansionary fiscal policy, which Kalecki could confidently assert in 1943, was challenged soon after the war on a variety of grounds indicated in the next section, at least until the current global crisis, that began in 2008 and is not over yet, led to a re-consideration.

4.5 From deficit spending to expansionary contraction

First, it was argued that government expenditure would 'crowd out' private investment (see Blanchard, 2008 for a review of the argument).

The idea neglects the possibility of public investment 'crowding in' additional private expenditure due to the activation of its accelerator effect of higher primary demand. On the contrary, Dennis Robertson (in a talk given at Princeton in 1953) argued that at least some of the additional savings from the income generated by government spending would not represent a leakage but would be channelled into additional investment; he called this 'the Kalecki effect'.

Second, Ricardian equivalence, tentatively put forward by David Ricardo in the 1820s and rediscovered by Robert J. Barro in 1974, was invoked. When government expenditure, funded by borrowing, is raised, economic agents discount the future payments of higher taxes that they anticipate having to pay to service the higher debt. The effect is the same as it would be were expenditure funded directly by an immediate higher tax: lower private consumption offsets higher government expenditure.

Third, in the early seventies the theory of so-called rational expectations (a tendentious misnomer) was introduced by Lucas (1981) and others. They should have been called expectations *successful by definition*. The efficient utilisation of all information available by all economic agents makes markets efficient. Nobody is ever surprised. Multipliers could then be lower than unity.

The final blow to the full employment feasibility consensus invoked by Kalecki was given by the concept of an 'expansionary fiscal contraction' – indeed an *extreme* expansionary fiscal contraction. In the 1990s and 2000s a series of empirical studies purported to show that closing the budget deficit via higher taxes and/or lower expenditure could be, and by and large was, expansionary (see Giavazzi and Pagano, 1990, 1996; Alesina and Perotti, 1997; Alesina and Ardagna, 2010). Blanchard (1990), then a professor at MIT before joining the IMF as chief economist in 2008, explained how this was due to the promotion of private sector-led growth, for the reasons already mentioned above: Ricardian equivalence, increasing confidence, a favourable impact on expectations, declining borrowing costs and a weaker currency.

Giavazzi and Pagano (1990, 1996) showed that fiscal consolidations are sometimes correlated with expansions in private consumption within a year. They presented evidence based on case studies and regressions of private consumption on cyclically adjusted government revenue and spending for a panel of OECD economies.

Similarly, using case studies Alesina and Perotti (1997) found that fiscal consolidations are sometimes correlated with rapid output growth, particularly if implemented by cutting government spending rather than by increasing taxes. These findings were confirmed by subsequent research based on larger samples of countries and years, including a more recent paper of Alesina and Ardagna (2010).

But the culmination of the expansionary fiscal consolidation thesis, supported by the so-called austerians – 'advocates of fiscal austerity, of immediate sharp cuts in government spending' (Krugman's definition) – is a paper by Harvard economists Carmen Reinhart and Kenneth Rogoff, 'Growth in a Time of Debt' (2010). On the basis of a new dataset of 44 countries spanning about 200 years and incorporating 'over 3,700 annual observations covering a wide range of political systems, institutions, exchange rate arrangements, and historic circumstances', Reinhart and Rogoff find that 'the relationship between government debt and real GDP growth is weak for debt/GDP ratios below a threshold of 90 percent of GDP. Above 90 percent, median growth rates fall by one percent, and average growth falls considerably more.'

The notion that government debt exceeding 90 per cent of GDP has a significant negative effect on economic growth became a decisive supportive argument for austerity by national and international leaders, from the former US vice presidential candidate Congressman Paul Ryan, Chairman of the House Budget Committee, to the EC Commissioner Olli Rehn and other authoritative commentators. Thus Keynes's proposition that 'the boom, not the slump, is the right time for austerity' was falsified, austerity becoming a good policy for all seasons in highly indebted countries.

4.6 The tide is turning...

The proposition of expansionary fiscal consolidation was immediately subjected to many criticisms and was gradually discredited both on theoretical and on empirical grounds. Already in November 2008 the IMF Managing Director Dominique Strauss-Kahn took the initiative for a sizeable global fiscal stimulus on the order of 2 per cent of global GDP. In an interview with *IMF Survey Online* on 29 December 2008, Olivier Blanchard, then the IMF chief economist, and Carlo Cottarelli, chief of the IMF Fiscal Affairs Department, called for bank recapitalisation (time consuming) and monetary expansion (ineffective at low interest rates) and made the case for fiscal stimulus:

> In normal times, the Fund would indeed be recommending to many countries that they reduce their budget deficit and their public debt.

> But these are not normal times, and the balance of risks today is very different....
>
> If no fiscal stimulus is implemented, then demand may continue to fall. And with it, we may see some of the vicious cycles we have seen in the past: deflation and liquidity traps, expectations becoming more and more pessimistic and, as a result, a deeper and deeper recession. If, instead, a fiscal stimulus is implemented but proves unnecessary, the risk is that the economy recovers too fast. Surely, this risk is easier to control than the risk of an ever deepening recession.

The IMF raised its lending, increased its own resources and relaxed somewhat its conditionality, but its commitment was intermittent and short lived. The ECB, under the leadership of Jean-Claude Trichet, was soon advocating an early exit strategy from both monetary expansion and fiscal stimulus.

In October 2010, chapter 3 of the IMF *World Economic Outlook* examined 'the effects of fiscal consolidation – tax hikes and government spending cuts – on economic activity'. It found that fiscal consolidation typically reduces output and raises unemployment in the short term, especially if consolidation occurs simultaneously in many countries and if monetary policy is not in a position to offset them. Only in the longer term can interest rate cuts, a fall in the value of the currency and a rise in net exports usually 'soften' but not offset the contractionary impact.

Baker (2010) criticises Alesina and his various colleagues (1997, 2010) for their use of cyclically adjusted deficits, while policy-driven deficit adjustments behave in a Keynesian fashion, and the argument by Broadbent and Daly, on the ground that known cases of expansionary consolidation occurred for very narrow output gaps relative to the large ones that have occurred in the current crisis.

The September 2011 *IMF Fiscal Monitor* warned that 'too rapid consolidation during 2012 could exacerbate downside risks... Further tightening during a downturn could exacerbate rather than alleviate market tensions through its negative impact on growth'.

In 2012 Carlo Cottarelli stressed the 'schizophrenic' attitude of investors with regard to fiscal consolidation manoeuvres: their initial enthusiasm was followed by the fear of consequent recession, so that governments were 'damned if they do, damned if they don't'. The IMF *World Economic Outlook* (October 2012) contains a box by its chief economist, Olivier Blanchard, and Daniel Leigh arguing that fiscal multipliers have probably been underestimated by IMF forecasts and policy documents and by the OECD and the European Commission. Recent IMF research suggests that fiscal multipliers are in the range 0.9 to 1.7 rather than the customary assumption of around 0.5; in other words, the cost of fiscal consolidation has been grossly underestimated. In January 2013 Blanchard and Leigh presented a paper expanding their argument at the American Economic Association's annual conference. However, according to the authors 'more research is needed'.

But more research was already available to the IMF: Guajardo, Leigh and Pescatori (2011) investigated 'the short-term effects of fiscal consolidation on economic activity in OECD economies'.

> We examine the historical record, including Budget Speeches and IMF documents, to identify changes in fiscal policy motivated by a desire to reduce the budget deficit and not by responding to prospective economic conditions. Using this new dataset, our estimates suggest fiscal consolidation has contractionary effects on private domestic demand and GDP. By contrast, estimates based on conventional measures of the fiscal policy stance used in the literature support the expansionary fiscal contractions hypothesis but appear to be biased toward overstating expansionary effects.

And Batini, Callegari and Melina (2012)

- discredit the need for cutting public/social expenditure, for especially in a downturn expenditure multipliers can be up to ten times larger than tax multipliers;
- find absolute values for multipliers of the order of 2.5 instead of 0.9–1.7, as in the IMF *World Economic Outlook* (2012);
- find aggressive (rather than gradual) consolidation much more expensive in terms of GDP.

In May 2013 Jeffrey Frankel criticised Alesina's papers, with various co-authors, all of which claimed that fiscal consolidation is not contractionary in a recession. Frankel, reporting on a recent paper by Alesina's original co-author, Perotti (2012), that criticises the dating methodology used, points out that some of the fiscal consolidations used by Alesina were announced by governments but never implemented. Thus Frankel concludes that Alesina 'has not been receiving his fair share of abuse' (*Eurointelligence*, 2013). Alesina and Giavazzi then softened their original position very considerably; in May 2013 they actually recommended that the Italian government overstep the 3 per cent deficit threshold for two years – for 'that three per cent should not be a taboo' – offering the EC in exchange immediate tax reductions on labour incomes, and planned gradual and permanent expenditure cuts in the following three years. The European Commission would not close the excess deficit procedure for Italy at the end of May but should be willing to approve such a plan and verify its implementation. At the same time, credit to households and enterprises should resume through bank recapitalisation conditionally funded by the EMS.

The Reinhart–Rogoff notion of a critical 90 per cent threshold of the debt/GDP ratio was immediately criticised by Bivens and Irons (2010), who argued that causation run backwards, in that slower growth leads to higher debt-to-GDP ratios rather than the other way round. Moreover, 'there is no compelling reason to believe [...] that gross debt of about 90% will necessarily lead to slower economic growth [...]. In fact, the greatest threat to economic growth is policy inaction fueled by deficit fears'. The final blow to the Reinhart–Rogoff 90 per cent debt/GDP dogma came from Herndon, Ash and Pollin (2013), who replicated the 2010 analysis by Reinhart and Rogoff, using the original data; they found that coding errors, selective exclusion of available data and unconventional weighting of summary statistics had led Reinhart and Rogoff to serious errors. '[W]hen properly calculated, the average real GDP growth rate for countries carrying a public-debt-to-GDP ratio of over 90 percent is actually 2.2 percent, not 0.1 percent as published in Reinhart and Rogoff.' It turns out that 'average GDP growth at public debt/GDP ratios over 90 percent is not dramatically different than when debt/GDP ratios are lower'. Reinhart and Rogoff (2013) admitted some of their errors and omissions but argued that these do not alter their ultimate austerity-justifying conclusion: excessive debt depresses growth. But two subsequent studies have claimed that, on the contrary, slow growth appears to cause higher debt, as Bivens and Irons (2010) had already argued. Dube (2013) finds that growth tends to be slower in the five years before countries have high debt levels. In the five years after they have high debt levels, there is no noticeable difference in growth at all – certainly not at the 90 per cent debt-to-GDP level regarded by Reinhart and Rogoff as the threshold of non-sustainability. Kimball and Wang (2013) present similar findings. This point is accepted by Reinhart and Rogoff (2013): 'The frontier question for research is the issue of causality.'

4.7 ...but suicidal policies persist

Such an amazing, cumulative and final discrediting of the alleged expansionary (severe at that) fiscal contraction approach and the associated 90 per cent threshold to debt sustainability does not appear to have had much impact on actual policies, especially on German-led European policies, with EU and especially EMU countries tied to a 'suicide pact' (Joseph Stiglitz) of so-called growth and stability.

The latest EU fiscal compact, or TSCG (Treaty on Stability, Coordination and Governance), demanded that a balanced budget provision be inserted in member states' national constitutions, subject to a maximum structural deficit of 0.5 per cent of GDP. There are penalties and automatic adjustments in case of non-observance, subject to the verification and rulings of the European Court of Justice. Financial assistance programmes under the ESM – the European Stability Mechanism, which came into operation in March 2012 – were, from March 2013, conditional on prior TSGC ratification.

From 2014, countries exceeding the statutory debt/GDP ceiling of 60 per cent, required by both the Maastricht Treaty and the Stability and Growth Pact, are expected to reduce the excess debt by 1/20 of the current gap every year until the ceiling is reached. For a country like Italy, which is at over 130 per cent, this involves a budgetary surplus of over 3.5 per cent a year for 20 years.

Recently, the IMF criticised the handling of the Greek crisis over the last four years by the troika (EC, ECB, IMF) but concluded that all was for the best and that policies would not be any different today in the same circumstances. In July 2013 a conference of German economists advocated that a debt/GDP ratio of 90 per cent – Reinhart and Rogoff's fated but dubious threshold – should trigger automatic debt restructuring and bail-in.

In conclusion, the Keynesian–Kaleckian view of capitalist dynamics is alive and well. The IMF itself has been reviving it and providing theoretical and empirical backing for it by stressing the high cost of fiscal consolidation but at the same time continuing to officially recommend and impose such fiscal consolidation. While providing the strongest case for a fiscal stimulus, IMF research is being used even by more enlightened officials to recommend gradual fiscal consolidation instead of the fiscal stimulus that would be appropriate. Obstacles to full employment policies are still of a political nature today (resistance to a capital tax to service exceptionally high sovereign debt, in addition to the drive to maintain workers' discipline through unemployment). The time for a Kaleckian (and Keynesian) revival is now overdue, and until it takes place we are all condemned to suffer the impoverishment and the unemployment caused by the deepest man-made economic crisis in human history.

5
'Political Aspects of Persisting Unemployment': Kalecki and Beyond

Alessandro Vercelli

5.1 Introduction

Kalecki's 'Political Aspects of Full Employment' (Kalecki, 1943)[1] is a recognised masterpiece that is still widely quoted by economists of different orientation (a significant recent example may be found in Krugman, 2012: pp. 94–96 and 206). Its insights are still useful to clarify and understand many crucial issues lying on the border between macroeconomics, politics and macroeconomic policy. In this chapter we intend to reconsider his essay from the specular point of view of persisting structural (or involuntary) unemployment as experienced in the last three great crises that have upset developed countries in the last century: the Great Depression of the 1930s, the Great Stagflation of the 1970s and the Great Recession which started in 2007. Kalecki's insights on full employment economies were prompted by the Great Depression and the scientific, policy and political reactions to it, but succeeded in capturing a few crucial structural features of contemporary capitalism that may also shed light on what happened afterwards. In this chapter, we argue that in particular they help us to understand better not only the Great Depression as analysed by Kalecki himself, but also the Great Stagflation as has long been argued (for example by Robinson, 1976), and – as we are going to argue – the ongoing deep crisis often called Great Recession.

Kalecki's essay obtained the immediate appreciation of Keynes 'I have just read with much sympathy and interest your article on Political Aspects of Full Employment in Pl. Q. An exceedingly good article and very acute' (letter dated 20 December 1943, quoted in Osiatyński, 1990: p. 573). Notwithstanding the early endorsement by the most prestigious economist of his time, the success of Kalecki's short but extremely dense essay has not been immediate. The economic miracles of the 1950s and 1960s seemed at first out of tune with Kalecki's opinion that persistent full employment is in principle inconsistent with existing capitalism.[2] However, the increasing problems emerging since the late 1960s unfolded very much along the lines predicted by Kalecki (Section 5.2); the same is true with the evolution of business cycles (Section 5.3).

The subsequent Great Stagflation aroused a powerful reaction that went in the direction foreseen by him. The new mainstream macroeconomics (New Classical Macroeconomics as worked out and propounded by Lucas and his followers) prepared the terrain for a no less radical U-turn also in macroeconomic policy that diverged sharply from full employment macroeconomics. This originated a new cycle of growth, often called 'neoliberal' or 'neoconservative', that slowly took off in the 1980s but, after the 'roaring 90s', gradually declined, eventually crashing into the recent crisis (Section 5.4). Kalecki's essay goes a long way towards the explanation of the inner motivations of the mainstream reactions to the ongoing Great Recession that appear, at least on first sight, extremely irrational (Section 5.5). In the concluding remarks we claim that there is urgent need of a new U-turn in the policy regime reverting towards the forgotten principles of a full employment economy that have to be promptly resumed in an updated and developed form. If this does not happen in the near future the consequences might be catastrophic, as Kalecki's arguments help us to understand.

5.2 The Great Stagflation and the downfall of the full employment economy

The Bretton Woods peace conference that designed the institutions and dictated the rules of post-war economic activity seemed to be going in the direction of a 'full employment capitalism' although not without significant ambiguities. Its general underlying philosophy was based on the need to regulate markets to avoid new systemic failures such as those experienced in the 1930s. In order to stabilise the expectations and to check speculation on the international markets, the Bretton Woods monetary system was conceived in terms of fixed exchange rates of all currencies with the dollar, while the latter could be exchanged with gold at a fixed rate. The liberalisation of international exchanges was resumed after the protectionism and autarchy of the interwar years, but in a cautious way through recurring rounds of multilateral negotiations

(GATT). The new international institutions established at Bretton Woods to regulate the international markets (the International Monetary Fund and the World Bank) were designed to implement a policy strategy that we may interpret as broadly consistent with the Keynesian vision, though in an enfeebled way: the IMF was expected to pursue counter-cyclical policies by intervening in countries characterised by a lack of effective demand, to avoid contagion with other countries, while the World Bank was expected to support developing countries by financing investment in growth-promoting infrastructures. Notwithstanding the increasing inflationary tensions that started to emerge in the 1960s, the full employment philosophy continued to influence macroeconomic policy in developed countries until the breakdown in 1971 of the Bretton Woods monetary system based on the dollar standard.[3] This initiated a period of turmoil, exacerbated by two oil shocks, in 1973 and 1979, that brought the full employment perspective to an end. The main, and most disturbing, criticism was that the latter, as put forward by Keynes and his followers, had an intrinsic inflationary bias, jeopardising steady growth in the real economy.

This crucial problem had been clearly foreseen and lucidly analysed by Kalecki more than 20 years before in 1943. The reason for the inflationary bias of a full employment economy is not seen as a consequence of economic factors but of political and policy factors related to the distribution of income. Kalecki maintained that under reasonable conditions 'if the government intervention aims at achieving full employment but stops short of increasing effective demand over the full employment mark, there is no need to be afraid of inflation' (Kalecki, 1943: p. 348). The maintenance of full employment, however,

> would cause social and political changes that would give a new impetus to the opposition of the business leaders. Indeed, under a regime of permanent full employment, the 'sack' would cease to play its role as a disciplinary measure. The social position of the boss would be undermined, and the self-assurance and class-consciousness of the working class would grow. Strikes for wage increases and improvements in conditions of work would create political tensions. (Kalecki, 1943)

This is what started to happen, with growing intensity, in the 1960s. In many industrialised countries (such as the UK, the US, France and Italy) strikes and work stoppages of unprecedented intensity occurred in 1968–1969 in the hope of increasing real wages and improving work conditions. This triggered a highly intense political conflict involving not only industrial and public service workers and employees but also civil society (university students in particular) and political parties within and outside elected legislatures. This triggered a period of persistent stagflation (we call it the Great Stagflation to distinguish it from other shorter and milder episodes of stagflation in recent history).

The differential impact of class struggle in different countries produced increasing tensions on the currency exchange rates that eventually led to the breakdown of the monetary system based on the dollar standard when President Nixon in 1971 unilaterally declared the inconvertibility of dollar. The reversal to free fluctuations in the currency market was hailed by business leaders as the first step towards a renewed regime of laissez-faire. The two oil shocks in 1973 and 1979 further aggravated the stagflation, convincing an increasing number of economists, citizens and electors that the full employment economy was unsustainable and that industrialised countries had to revert to unfettered free markets. The debate in macroeconomics fully reflected the mounting opposition to full employment policies. The monetarists led by Milton Friedman progressively increased their influence in the 1960s undermining the influence of Keynesian Macroeconomics.

The final battle was fought on the analytical battleground of the Phillips curve. The inflationary bias of a full employment economy was not fully denied by the Keynesian macroeconomists, but they struggled to show that inflation could be kept under control within a fine-tuned full employment policy strategy. The main instrument used to this end since the late 1950s had been the Phillips curve (Phillips, 1958) an alleged long-term empirical regularity estimated by Phillips over a century of time series in the UK.[4] Its standard Keynesian interpretation was that a government could 'buy' more employment by accepting a limited and controllable increase in inflation. The Phillips curve was thus seen as a stable trade-off between employment and inflation, offering a reliable menu of policy choices. Unfortunately, the growing inflationary tensions emerging in the 1960s and 1970s were reflected by a progressive upward shift and an increasing slope of the short-run Phillips curves that seriously questioned the standard Keynesian interpretation of the Phillips curve.

The defence of the Keynesians in the 1960s was perceived as rather weak, being based on allegedly ad hoc explanations. The anti-Keynesian camp counterposed an explanation derived from one of the most revered principles of classical economics: the dichotomy between monetary and real variables. According to this principle, a long-term, negative-sloped, one-to-one relation between inflation (a monetary variable) and employment (a real variable) is a red herring, since the long-run Phillips curve has to be conceived as vertical in correspondence to the value of the 'natural' unemployment rate that measures the long-run equilibrium of the real system. In their view any attempt to reduce the unemployment rate below the natural rate would be self-defeating, since it would trigger accelerating inflationary processes fed by extrapolative expectations (Friedman, 1968). Inflation could thus be tamed only by increasing the unemployment rate well beyond its natural rate for a sufficiently long period.

5.3 Business cycles and countercyclical policies in a full employment economy

His insights into the sustainability of the full employment policy regime are perhaps the most original contribution of Kalecki's essay. However, the most quoted insights from this chapter are probably those referring to the so-called 'political business cycle' that are ground-breaking but hardly elaborated.[5] To understand the strength and limits of these insights we have to start, as Kalecki did, from an analysis of the industrial leaders' opposition to full employment achieved through government spending. First, 'budget deficits necessary to carry out government interventions [are] regarded as perilous. The social function of the doctrine of "sound finance" is to make the level of employment dependent on the state of confidence' (Kalecki, 1943: p. 350). Second, the business leaders dislike 'the direction of government spending (public investment and subsidizing consumption)'. Public investment is claimed to crowd out private investment, while the subsidising of mass consumption is believed to violate the sacred ethical principle of capitalism 'there is not such a thing as a free lunch', since the fundamentals of capitalist ethics require that 'you shall earn your bread in sweat – unless you have private means'. Subsidising mass consumption would amount to relaxing the dependency of workers on capital, a consequence that business leaders would never accept. Although Kalecki does not in this essay mention Marx, nor his language on this specific point, he does share his vision of the crucial role of an 'industrial reserve army' in the smooth functioning of the capitalist mode of production.

Updating and qualifying this basic insight, Kalecki shows that the interaction between the different policy orientations of big business and workers is likely to produce recurring 'political business cycles' reaching the full employment barrier at the peak of the boom, and never deviating too much from it even in the slump. This is because the workers are assumed to be always favourable to full employment policies while the business leaders 'tend to accept as a *pis aller* public investment financed by borrowing as a means of alleviating slumps' but are still 'consistently opposed to creating employment by subsidizing consumption and to *maintaining* full employment' (ibid: p. 354). This implies that when a slump starts, public investment will be undertaken to prevent large-scale unemployment. This considerably shortens the slump and accelerates the recovery. When full employment is reached, however, the business leaders oppose any measure meant to maintain it, finding the support of 'boom-tired' rentiers affected by the price increases brought about by the upswing. The powerful alliance formed between big business and rentier interests 'would most probably induce the government to return to the orthodox policy of cutting down the budget deficits. A slump would follow in which government spending policy would again come into its own' (ibid: p. 355). Kalecki conjectures that this sort of political cycle is 'symptomatic of future economic regime of capitalist democracies'. However, he claims that

> this pattern of a political business cycle is not entirely conjectural; something very similar happened in the USA in 1937–8. The breakdown of the boom in the second half of 1937 was actually due to the drastic reduction of the budget deficit. On the other hand, in the acute slump that followed the government promptly reverted to a spending policy. (ibid: p. 355)[6]

The conjecture by Kalecki proved to be substantially correct until the late 1970s. This is clearly confirmed by the so-called Phillips loops described along the long-term Phillips curve during the business cycles. These fluctuations reflect the stop-go policies pursued over this period by most governments of OECD countries.[7] We have to emphasise that many details of stop-go fluctuations are missing from Kalecki's account. In particular, in this essay he ignored the crucial role of central banks inclined to reduce the discount rate and increase liquidity during a slump but ready to increase the discount rate and reduce liquidity as soon as the economy shows signs of overheating during the upswing. In addition on this occasion he does not develop the crucial role played by the functional distribution of income in determining the timing and amplitude of these short-term fluctuations, although it is a crucial ingredient of his vision of the capitalist process as developed in other essays. As is well known, the literature on political business cycles has been subsequently developed in many directions, some fully independent of those suggested by Kalecki. His seminal insights, however, greatly contributed to the promotion of this significant research programme (an early critical review of the relevant literature may be found in Frey, 1978).

5.4 The neoliberal counter-revolution in the light of Kalecki's analysis

In this and the following section we have tentatively applied Kalecki's approach to the capitalist evolution beyond his death (in 1970), in the conviction that its fecundity may outreach his lifetime. The anti-Keynesian counter-revolution gathered momentum from the late 1960s, taking a direction fully consistent with that advocated by business leaders according to Kalecki's reconstruction. This is clearly visible in the U-turn of mainstream macroeconomics that in the 1970s forsook the full employment perspective and reverted to an extreme form of the classical paradigm (the New Classical paradigm advocated by Lucas and his collaborators and followers). In this view, full employment is considered as an arbitrary category, since its Keynesian definition implies absence of involuntary unemployment, while unemployment is in their opinion always voluntary by definition (Lucas, 1981). Full employment equilibrium is thus just assumed, without any distinction between short- and long-term. Within this conceptual framework, full employment policies cannot even be discussed: if one assumes that the aircraft is in flight, the take-off and landing procedures and associated risks cannot be even discussed as they are not an issue. According to the first version of this new paradigm, the monetary equilibrium business cycle (Lucas, 1975), the observed fluctuations of the real economy are the consequence of discretionary monetary policies that perturb the real markets. This may be avoided by adopting fixed policy rules: a predetermined rate of increase of the monetary base and persistent fiscal equilibrium. The economic failures observed in the past, including those experienced during the Great Depression, are interpreted as policy failures due to the discretional interventions of policy authorities disrupting the working of markets that would otherwise have been fully efficient. Countercyclical policies based on deficit spending are seen as counterproductive not only during the boom but also during the slump. In this view, the only meaningful policies would be the structural policies meant to transfer the decision-making power from the state to the market through deregulation, privatisation and the progressive dismantling of the welfare state.

This point of view gives full 'scientific' support to the point of view of business leaders as reconstructed by Kalecki, but in a much more radical version since deficit spending is excluded even in the slumps. According to Kalecki, writing in 1943, the reason why the business leaders – contrary to their previous harsh opposition – had eventually accepted that 'something must be done in the slump' was due to three factors (i) the experience of very full employment during the war, (ii) development of the economic doctrine of full employment, (iii) 'partly as a result of these two factors, the slogan "Unemployment never again" is [...] deeply rooted in the consciousness of the masses' (Kalecki, 1943: p. 353). By the 1970s these three factors had disappeared since (i) the recent experience of stagflation had convinced many observers that full employment policies were flawed, (ii) the systematic criticism of Keynesian economics had undermined the prestige of full employment economics, (iii) even the masses struggling with the dire consequences of stagflation were eventually ready to look for a better alternative.

The new policy regime seemed to be able to solve the alleged unsustainability of the full employment regime, but eventually it proved to be unsustainable in a much deeper and more irremediable way. To describe and understand the historical parable of the neoliberal regime, we have to distinguish four phases of its evolution: recession and recovery (1979–1989), the roaring 90s (1990–1999), the 'big zero' years (2000–2007), and the Great Recession (2008-?). Each of these periods has been characterised by significant structural changes made possible and shaped by the neoliberal policy regime taking account of its evolution and national variants. The first period is characterised by a strictly monetarist policy inspired by Friedman's monetarism and Lucas's equilibrium monetary business cycle. This view was implemented in the US by Volcker, President of the Federal Reserve from 1979 to 1986, soon followed by the other central banks of the OECD countries. The ensuing severe recession (1980–1983) succeeded in curbing inflation and restoring monetary stability within a few years. In addition, the significant increase in unemployment weakened the power of trade unions to such an extent that the neoconservative governments emerging from the crisis, led in the UK by Mrs Thatcher from 1979, and in the US the Reagan administration from early 1981, were able to introduce radical reforms in the labour market and in the industrial relations rules. These reforms aimed to make the labour market and industrial relations much more flexible than before, allegedly to strengthen competitive markets by transferring from the workers to the employers the power of decision on the supply of labour. After a few years, the supporters of the new policy regime emphasised that the enhanced flexibility of labour markets and industrial relations had succeeded in shifting the short-term Phillips curve downwards and reducing its steepness; they claimed that these structural changes had succeeded in eliminating the inflationary bias perturbing the full employment policy regime. This also reduced the volatility of the real macroeconomic variables, later called the 'Great Moderation' and popularised by Bernanke (2004). Unfortunately this alleged great success of the bitter (mainly for workers) pills prescribed by the neoliberal policies came with dire collateral effects that made the new policy regime much more unsustainable than the full employment one.

The first side effect was the inversion in the OECD countries of the falling trend of income inequality that had started at the beginning of the century. This was due to the stagnating purchasing power of the lower and middle classes' per capita income, while the income of the top two per cent of the population rocketed to unprecedented levels. This determined a tendency of aggregate demand to stagnate, undermining the sustainability of decent growth rates. The average growth rate in the period 1979–2007 did not equal that of the full employment period 1951–1971, notwithstanding a series of countermeasures taken by private citizens and public institutions to sustain it (see, for example, Maddison, 2007). Households increased their indebtedness to maintain their lifestyle, with the active support of banks and public authorities. Also the governments allowed a progressive increase in the sovereign debt to sustain growth through public spending. According to data from the IMF, the debt/GDP ratio of the G7 countries followed a capital U pattern after WWII: it progressively diminished from 1950 (120 per cent) to the late 1970s (about 60 per cent) to then increase progressively to a value of over 100 per cent in the early 2010s (see IMF statistics). The increase of sovereign debt is thus a structural feature of the neoliberal policy regime and was only aggravated by, but did not originate in, the Great Recession.

The second side effect was the structural impact of a change in monetary policy that started in the US when Volcker was succeeded by Greenspan (1987–2006). The new chairman took advantage of the emerging Great Moderation to relax the monetarist rules in the financial system. Under his leadership, soon followed by most other OECD central banks, the FED reacted to any potentially persistent fall in the trend of share prices by flooding the markets with liquidity. This policy, called the 'Greenspan put', succeeded in maintaining a growing trend in the stock index from the late 1980s until the early 2006. This policy made a significant contribution to sustaining the declining rates of growth because long-selling speculation greatly increased the profits of financial institutions while the continuous revaluation of shares sustained the viability of balance sheets and increased the income of all shareholders through a persistent wealth effect. In addition this policy reduced the depth and length of slumps, further strengthening the Great Moderation regime in the real economy.

Also in this case, however, the positive short-run returns from this policy were accompanied by negative side effects that progressively cumulated a disruptive potential. First of all, the increased price stability and the reduced volatility in the real economy was accompanied by increasing inflation and augmented volatility in the financial system. In addition, the expectations of financial institutions and rentiers rapidly adapted to the new monetary regime, reducing the perception of risk in financial trading and investment as if it were covered by an implicit insurance. This encouraged an unprecedented increase in the leverage of financial institutions and in the indebtedness of households that in turn progressively increased the financial fragility of economic units and nurtured a growing number of financial bubbles, followed by financial crises of growing depth and scope. The South-East Asian crisis of 1997–1998 had a wide impact but was still centred in the periphery of the financial system. The 'dot.com crisis' was the first global financial crisis centred in the core of the financial system; however the 'Greenspan put' policy still proved successful in averting the crisis well before it was expected – and this further increased faith in the invisible hand operating in the financial markets guided by the visible hand of Greenspan. The forewarnings of the catastrophic financial crisis were not understood, and the way out of the crisis was sought in the direction of 'business as usual'. The only significant change was that investment turned from the immaterial goods of the 'new economy' to the brick-and-mortar goods of the real estate sector. Therefore in around 2001 the housing bubble started in the US, the UK, Spain and many other countries, paving the way to the first global contraction of the 21st century.

5.5 The reactions to the Great Recession

The policy reactions to the ongoing crisis have been criticised as highly irrational and extremely counterproductive by many top commentators and analysts (including the opinions expressed by two Nobel laureates: Stiglitz, 2010, and Krugman, 2012). Two main waves in the financial earthquake that started in 2007 can be distinguished; the subprime crisis and its immediate aftermath (the Lehman bankruptcy and the subsequent bailout of many big financial institutions), and the Eurozone sovereign debt crisis. The political aspects of the reaction to the first wave is understandable; the bailout, without any significant conditions, of big financial institutions that were virtually broke in 2008 was in sharp contrast to the market fundamentalism that had inspired economic policy in the preceding decades, but clearly reflected the power acquired by finance not only in the economy but also in the political process. But the reaction to the sovereign debt crisis is much more difficult to understand. The austerity policy hit not only wage and salary earners (with the scandalous exception of the top managers of financial institutions, including those just bailed out) but also the profits of businesses, including financial businesses. The motivations of business leaders and financiers may still be clarified by resorting to Kalecki's insights. The main declared purpose of his essay was exactly the explanation of the apparently irrational policy pursued by business leaders and by governments influenced by them: 'The entrepreneurs in the slump are longing for a boom; why do they not gladly accept the synthetic boom which the government is able to offer them? It is this difficult and fascinating question with which we intend to deal in this article' (Kalecki, 1943: p. 349).

I answered this question by distinguishing the economic interests of a social class from its political interests, showing that in case of conflict it is the latter that prevails. Kalecki did not provide a general explanation of this observation, but we may speculate that this is because in the long term economic interests depend crucially on political interests. In any case, a thorough analysis of this kind should distinguish a plurality of social classes sufficiently articulate to reveal the underlying political processes. The essential analysis put forward by Kalecki limits itself to the basic distinction between big business and workers, occasionally introducing rentiers as a third actor. In his view of capitalism, the economic and political interests of capital are mainly represented by big business ,while the economic and political interests of small business do not necessarily coincide with those of big business but are believed to be much less influential (in any case, that issue is not analysed in the paper). Within big business there is no distinction between big manufacturing entrepreneurs and finance; this is a significant shortcoming of Kalecki's analysis, probably due to the moment at which he wrote his contribution.[8] After the financial crisis of the 1930s the financial capital had been downsized and tamed by strict controls and constraints enforced by law (a case in point is the 1933 Glass–Steagall

Act that introduced a clear distinction between investment banking and commercial banking). In any case, an extension of Kalecki's analysis to the post-1970 period requires this crucial distinction to be made. The process of financialisation that characterised the 30 years from 1980 has produced a growing tension between the interests of finance and those of the real economy, a tension that cannot be ignored. This distinction, however, needs to be understood in functional, but not corporate or personal, terms. In the financial sector, the interests of speculation in trading and investment banking have progressively overwhelmed the interests of support to the real economy; however, the same financial institutions are often in charge of both. Analogously, even households have increasingly absorbed the financial perspective of pension and investment funds as the percentage of household wealth held in the form of financial assets has steadily increased in the last decades.

The reaction to the second wave of the ongoing turmoil seems at first sight more difficult to understand. The austerity policy inaugurated in the early 2010s negatively affected workers, reducing the earnings and purchasing power of all citizens and even affecting business leaders, by significantly reducing the aggregate demand for their products and finance, by reducing the demand for its services. The representatives of big business both in finance and in manufacturing fully supported these measures, notwithstanding the negative impact on their balance sheets. Big financial institutions obtained a huge flow of funds from public authorities to avoid bankruptcy. However a more expansionary policy would have also benefited big businesses, both financial and non-financial. What may explain their full support to austerity policies and their sharp opposition to a more expansionary policy? The explanation given by Kalecki in 1943 still seems to be the right one; the political interest is stronger than the economic interest. First of all the focus of mainstream indignation was redirected almost overnight from the avidity of Wall Street to the corruption of the State and profligacy of people, especially in the PIIGS countries. This abrupt change of focus was implemented through a systematic campaign through friendly economists and sympathetic mass media, and crony policy officials sought to postpone, and maybe to avoid or at least to water down, the radical reforms of finance and corporate governance that in the 2008 and 2009 had obtained great popular support. This sudden shift in public opinion after the subprime crisis and its apparent early support by many economists, policy officials, and high-level practitioners terrified big businessmen, mainly in finance, and their supporters and beneficiaries, convincing them that in the absence of a prompt, vigorous and relentless counter-offensive they would lose much of their power and privilege. The sovereign debt issue, particularly in the Eurozone, created an excellent diversion and alibi; in addition, the structural reforms introduced through the austerity policies shifted the balance of power well their way. The weakening of workers and trade unions, the significant reduction of their rights and the reduction of unit labour costs are objectives cherished by business leaders, in the anticipation that when the recovery is eventually triggered, this new balance of power, recalling that of the Ancien Régime, will translate into the renewal of huge profits for them.

5.6 Concluding remarks

Adam Smith is seen as the founding father of an economics conceived of as an independent discipline since its conceptualisation of a perfect-competition market as a gravitational system defines the emblematic object of economic analysis as independent of political decision making ruled by an autonomous, invisible hand. Smith, however, would not have accepted this interpretation: he was fully aware of the intrinsic limits of real markets that require regulation by public authorities. In addition, in his view the State has to provide public goods that the market is unable to produce efficiently in the right quantity and quality. Finally, he never underplayed the importance of an approach to economic problems broad enough to understand the interaction between the economic, social and institutional issues. For those fundamental reasons, Smith maintained that 'political economy', not yet viewed as a discrete 'economics', could not sever the connection between economic and political decisions.

Kalecki's contribution is in line with the tradition of political economy and, under the influence of Marx, suggests a basic structural explanation of the political influence on the economic process in terms of the conflicting interests of the social classes. Although his explanation is very simple and requires further specification, articulation and updating, the depth of his basic intuition is confirmed by the basic soundness of his predictions throughout the remainder of his lifetime (almost 30 years!). Its applicability to the Great Stagflation has been already argued in the past, and we have confirmed it. We have shown in this chapter that his conceptual framework has continued to be useful in the interpretation of what happened after his death provided that we update it to take account of the structural transformations that have occurred in this period; the main change that needs to be incorporated into his analysis is the emergence of finance as crucial economic and political power, to be clearly distinguished in functional terms from non-financial business.

Notes

1. Kalecki's article was first published in *Political Quarterly* in 1943 and 'corresponds roughly to a lecture given to the Marshall Society in Cambridge in the spring 1942' (Kalecki, 1943: p. 347, note 1). This article has been often reprinted, sometimes in a shortened version drafted by Kalecki himself. We refer here to the original long version as reprinted in Osiatyński (1990).
2. Kalecki did not exclude the possibility of a 'Full employment capitalism', that is a capitalism radically reformed by developing 'new social and political institutions which will reflect the increased power of the working class'. However, he was rather sceptical about the viability of its concrete implementation: 'If capitalism can adjust itself to full employment, a fundamental reform will have been incorporated in it. If not, it will show itself an outmoded system which must be scrapped' (Kalecki, 1943: p. 356).
3. As is well known, the first government that struggled to realise the new policy strategy was that in the UK, led by Ms Thatcher from 1979. Reagan was the first to pursue the new track in the USA, from early 1981. Most other countries soon followed.
4. His first version, as put forward by Keynes in the *General Theory* and by Kalecki himself, was untenable; this amounted to assuming that the Phillips curve had the form of a backwards capital L, becoming vertical at the point of full employment. As a matter of fact we find many qualifications in Keynes and Kalecki. Keynes, for example, admitted that inflationary tensions materialise long before reaching the full employment barrier because of bottlenecks in specific sectors and the increased power of the trade unions.
5. This contribution by Kalecki is also mentioned in popular economics textbooks (see for example, Samuelson, *Economics*, 10th and subsequent editions
6. Fisher had already given a similar interpretation.
7. Joan Robinson maintained that Kalecki's conjecture 'was fairly accurate prediction of what we have experienced, both in the US and in Britain, in the last 30 years of alternating *go* and *stop*' She also rightly maintains, however, that Kalecki's diagnosis 'underestimated the importance of financial policy and exchange rates, putting his main emphasis on the role of government spending' (Robinson, 1976).
8. Keynes, however seems to make exactly this criticism in the private letter to Kalecki dated 20 December 1943. After his commendation of Kalecki's paper quoted above, he says 'If I have been writing it myself, I might have added as an important influence [ ] old fashioned sound finance which [resists (?) *illegible*] against any public expenditures and a high deficit [...]' (in Osiatyński, 1990: p. 573).

6
The Dynamics of Competition

Ewa Karwowski

6.1 Introduction

This chapter links Michał Kalecki's and Josef Steindl's analysis of dynamics of competition (Kalecki, 1932, 1933b, 1935, 1939; Steindl, 1945a, 1952) to the concept of overcapitalisation and the theory of capital market inflation (Toporowski, 1993, 2000). In this way it extends the Kalecki–Steindl argument that the maldistribution of profits, meaning the concentration of profits in industries with market power, be it cartels or oligopolies, introduces economic instability into the financial realm, where that maldistribution leads to financial fragility.

Economic instability is generated by oligopolistic profits since they have the potential to exacerbate the business cycle while depressing long-term growth through low investment activity due to the excess capacity of oligopolies. Oligopolistic profits can induce financial fragility if held as excess capital on firms' balance sheets, that is as large volumes of liquid (financial) assets. Consequently, oligopolistic profits contribute to capital market inflation because they induce increased demand for liquid financial assets such as corporate equity.

The chapter is organised as follows. In Section 6.1, the arguments supporting cartelisation will be presented. Section 6.2 will discuss the Kalecki–Steindl analysis, showing that concentration of profits in cartels and oligopolies destabilises the economy as a whole. Furthermore, financial fragility might be induced because oligopolistic profits are a potential source of excess capital, that is, large volumes of liquid asset holdings not utilised in productive operations. This contributes to capital market inflation as argued in Section 6.3. Finally in Section 6.4, relevant data for the South African economy, which shows strong evidence of capital concentration and existence of oligopolistic profits, will be examined to support the hypothesis that oligopolistic profits are a source of excess capital.

6.2 The case for cartelisation

The idea that cartelisation counteracts the anarchy of market competition, rendering capitalism more rational and therefore more stable, was particularly popular in Germany around the turn of the 19th/20th centuries (Bernstein, 1899; Grunzel, 1902; Liefmann, 1903). There is an economic and a social dimension to the case for cartelisation.

6.2.1 The case for cartelisation: the economic dimension

At the heart of the economic argument was the belief that cartelisation can stabilise investment because it reduces the entrepreneur's risk of capital loss in investment activity (or *Kapitalrisiko,* Grunzel, 1902). The claim was that increased efficiency and economic stability brought about by cartelisation would lower *Kapitalrisiko* by ensuring continuous production, averting or at least moderating temporary crises, stabilising demand, and optimising capacity utilisation among other beneficial impacts on economic activity.[1]

Over the course of the business cycle, unconstrained market forces were believed to destabilise the production process, since there is no coordination among capitalists in investment and production. As a consequence, economic booms would inevitably end in overproduction because capitalists do not know the limits of market demand and, even if they did, would not be willing to respect them, scrambling for larger market share (Grunzel, 1902).

Therefore, a major function of cartels was to reduce downward pressure on prices during periods of business cycle downswings. In this way, the less competitive (mostly smaller) firms would be salvaged while the profit margins for the more competitive (typically large-scale) producers would be preserved. The eradication of cut-throat competition was believed to moderate economic crises, stabilising the business cycle. The chamber of commerce in Essen, for example, shared this view on cartelisation, declaring that the activity of the coal cartel in Rhineland and Westphalia during the German economic crisis of 1901 had alleviated the business cycle downswing (Grunzel, 1902).

Joining a cartel secured the industrialist a relatively stable cash flow. Investing became less risky (or *Kapitalrisiko* decreased) since he could either rely on internal finance for investment if his profit margins were large enough or have a stable income stream to service his debt if he had had to use external funds such as bank borrowing.

6.2.2 The case for cartelisation: the social dimension

Cartels could arguably also alleviate the social consequences of industrialisation or even contribute to the socialist transformation by either giving capitalism a more social face or contributing to its demise. Socialist thinkers such as Eduard Bernstein (1899) believed that cartelisation could bring about the socio-economic preconditions for socialist transformation because nationalisation of production would be easier once industries were centrally controlled by sectoral cartels.

Less radical social reformers (or *Kathedersozialisten*) such as Lujo Brentano suggested cartelisation as a means to alleviate the miserable social conditions of the German working class (Krzywicki, 1957). If cartels agreed to set up and contribute towards industry-wide funds to provide social benefits for workers, the negative impact of mechanisation on employment could be mitigated. Similarly, reformers saw a role for cartels in establishing health and safety regulations, improving working conditions, and shortening the working day (Grunzel, 1902).

While the above-mentioned proponents of cartels were content with a partial cartelisation of the economy, Rudolf Hilferding (1910) pointed out that only a general cartel of the economy as a whole could mitigate business cycle swings. The coexistence of cartelised alongside non-cartelised industries would simply shift the brunt of business cycle fluctuations to non-cartelised branches while stabilising prices and profit margins for cartel members. Hilferding argued that this could in fact worsen economic cycles, because industrialists are dependent on cheapening input prices, which would remain high due to cartel action, during the early phases of economic recovery when their financial position is fragile. Whereas Hilferding seemed to view general cartelisation as desirable but politically not attainable, others, like the Polish scholar Ludwik Krzywicki, were suspicious of the socio-economic stability that general cartelisation might create in society.

Krzywicki cautioned against industrial feudalism (Krzywicki, 1957). Leaving the institution of private property (and therefore the concentration of the means of production in the hands of capitalists) untouched while ensuring employment and stable wages to the workers would cement social classes, elevating the capitalists into the position of landed gentry, with workers in the role of socially and economically dependent landless farmers. This is likely to result in a stable but stagnant society where a financial elite receives large rents which are tolerated by society in exchange for economic stability and social protection. But such a setup would only alleviate some of the symptoms of fundamental inequality in class society, while not solving its underlying causes. Crucially, Krzywicki viewed industrial feudalism as a potential danger to a socialist transformation, offering an alternative and stable, albeit highly unequal, social system (Kalecki and Kowalik, 1971).

During the 1930s, it was hoped that the stabilising influence of cartels or trusts would alleviate the economic and social consequences of the Great Depression in the US. The National Recovery Administration (NRA) allowed for the creation of so-called codes of fair competition, which in certain industries, such as sugar manufacturing, set wages and prices, and introduced production quotas and entry barriers (Bridgeman et al., 2009; OECD, 2011). Nevertheless, price stability and limitations to output in cartelised industries to bring about the economic recovery were awaited in vain .

6.3 Opposing oligopolistic profits

In his analysis of competition dynamics, Michał Kalecki addressed US policies favouring cartelisation (Kalecki, 1933b) as well as claims that cartels moderated business cycles in Europe (Kalecki, 1932). After a brief comment on the suitability of Kaleckian methodology to analyse competition dynamics, this section will show the close link between cartels and oligopolies, both generating oligopolistic profits. The Kalecki–Steindl analysis argues that oligopolistic profits destabilise the business cycle in the short run and depress economic growth in the long run. While the analysis focuses on the economic dimension the impact of competition dynamics on employment has profound social implications.

6.3.1 Methodology

Kalecki's (and Kaleckian) methodology is particularly suitable for the analysis of competition dynamics because it treats microeconomic and macroeconomic aspects as interwoven elements of the economic system. Mainstream theory such as New Keynesian approaches and the New Macroeconomic Consensus, in contrast, claim microeconomic foundations for their macroeconomic models (Woodford, 2003). Typically, they merely project microeconomic concepts onto the macroeconomy, using for example the representative agent, who behaves in the same profit- (or utility-) maximising way, regardless of whether it represents a household, firm, bank, or even the State. Here perfect competition is ensured through a large number of agents present in the same product market, resulting in the absence of supernormal profits – meaning no revenue beyond cost coverage (Varian, 1992).

In the Kaleckian framework, the issue of competition is more complex since it encompasses not only product competition but also competition between different types of capital, that is, for example, between small and large producers with fundamentally different access to technology, finance and the market itself. Crucially, in the Kaleckian framework, patterns of competition – typically considered to be a microeconomic issue – determine income distribution on the macroeconomic level through pricing power.

Kalecki's early versions of cycle analysis did not explicitly reject perfect competition, but he had definitely abandoned perfect competition by 1938 when he adopted Abba Lerner's 'degree of monopoly' concept (Osiatyński, 1990). The 1939 business cycle theory (Kalecki, 1939) therefore deals with economic fluctuations in the presence of oligopoly profits. Nevertheless, Kalecki had prior to 1938 been considering dynamics of competition mainly through the issue of cartelisation (Kalecki, 1932, 1933b, 1935).

6.3.2 Connecting cartels and oligopolies

Cartels and oligopolies are both types of economic organisation aiming at securing and potentially increasing their pricing power in order to protect and/or raise profit margins. In the absence of cartelisation, pricing power crucially depends on the excess capacity of oligopolies being used to deter new entrants. A certain degree of concentration is necessary for successful cartelisation, since oligopolistic excess capacity can be expected to enforce the cartel's price agreements (Kalecki, 1939).

Firms operating in oligopolistic industries have a tendency to maintain or even increase their profit margins over time. Oligopolistic profit maximisation does not depend on full capacity utilisation and unit cost minimisation. Therefore, during an economic downswing oligopolistic industries tend to adapt output more than prices in order to protect profit margins. During business cycle upswings, in contrast, they respond to increased demand through raising prices to a greater extent than increasing production (Toporowski, 2005a). Hence, they behave similarly to cartel members in the course of the business cycle.

Since cartels and oligopolies can be treated as closely related economic phenomena, corporate profits derived from cartelisation and from oligopolistic market power will be both subsumed under the term 'oligopolistic profits' below.

6.3.3 Opposing oligopolistic profits: the economic dimension

While the proponents of cartels believed that the key to economic and social stability was to reduce *Kapitalrisiko* through cartelisation, Kalecki pointed out that the riskiness of a firm's investment position in fact depends on the relationship of company debt to own assets: the gearing ratio. This is Kalecki's principle of increasing risk (Kalecki, 1937; Steindl, 1945b). In this context, cartelisation or the emergence of oligopolies might in fact reduce the debt of cartel members or oligopolistic firms by providing them with relatively stable profit margins and cash flow.

The corporation receiving oligopolistic profits is able to reduce its risk stemming from the gearing ratio in several ways. First, pricing power enables oligopolistic firms and cartels to protect their profit margins, ensuring stable cash flow. These internal funds can be used to finance investment instead of borrowing, or to repay lenders, reducing the company's total debt. Further, the typically large production capacity these corporations possess means that the volume of own assets is large, resulting in a relatively small gearing ratio. Finally, oligopolies and the larger cartel members, at least, have excess capacity, leading to a low propensity to invest. Therefore, they are unlikely to borrow in order to expand capacity, which once again prevents the gearing ratio (and *Kapitalrisiko*) from rising.

However, a low riskiness of investment for entrepreneurs is not sufficient to eradicate fluctuations in corporate investment, which would be necessary to stabilise the business cycle. During economic upswings demand increases, cartels adjust their output quotas, albeit less than the overall rise in demand, to allow for a stronger price increase than under perfect competition. Since quotas are typically assigned on the basis of production capacity, cartel members are likely to engage in an investment race to expand their capacity in order to secure a higher quota. Since cartel members then enter economic downswings with excessively increased production capacity, their investment activity will be low during the recession despite relatively stable profit margins. In actual fact, this behaviour resulted in more volatile investment expenditure relative to a free competition situation (Kalecki, 1932).

A different facet of the belief in the economic organising powers of cartelisation deals with the lack of coordination among investment decisions. The idea that crises emerge because of overproduction stems from Austrian theories of the business cycle focusing on malinvestment, that is badly allocated investment, due to the abundance and cheapness of entrepreneurial credit (see Ellis, 1934). In the Kaleckian framework, crises are the result of underinvestment rather than overinvestment, because investment activity is crucially determined by capitalist profits, which equal in aggregate the sum of their consumption and investment expenditure, as shown in Kalecki's profit equation (Toporowski, 2003). If investment slows down profit decreases, further dampening investment and setting off a spiral of contracting economic activity.

6.3.4 Opposing oligopolistic profits: the social dimension

Equally, cartelisation or the presence of oligopolies cannot contribute to higher or stabilised employment, since falling demand due to economic downswings is mainly addressed through volume adjustments in cartelised industries rather than through changes in both volume *and* price. As a consequence, unemployment rises more severely during economic slowdowns and crises under cartelisation or oligopolistic competition than it does under free competition. Conversely, during economic upswings, cartels and oligopolies adapt output volumes less to increased demand, in order to raise price and profit margins. During economic booms unemployment is comparatively higher with the presence of oligopolistic profits than without.

These effects are further exacerbated because the concentration of oligopolistic profits in certain sectors is likely to dampen labour demand in sectors that do not enjoy pricing power, operating under competitive conditions. On the one hand, lack of productive investment due to excess capacity decreases demand for capital goods produced outside cartels and oligopolies. On the other hand, lower employment levels across the economy negatively affect demand for the consumption goods typically produced by competitive sectors.

In the course of the business cycle, the condition of workers is depressed in the presence of oligopolistic profits, since unemployment increases more severely during an economic crisis, while hiring is less pronounced in an economic boom. Interestingly, the case of general cartelisation as advocated by Rudolf Hilferding (1910) comes close to oligopolistic industries dominating the economy as a whole in the long run. The concentration of profits, as described in Kalecki's *Trend and Business Cycle* (1968) and Steindl's *Maturity and Stagnation of American Capitalism* (1952), can lead to a low growth and low employment situation with dire welfare and social consequences.

6.4 Opposing overcapitalisation

As Josef Steindl (1952) pointed out, the concentration of oligopolistic profits, that is the maldistribution of profits, is likely to be reinforced by capital markets. Since oligopolies tend to have a higher profit rate than competitive industries, they are likely to absorb most of the cash obtained by share issues. In this manner, their gearing ratio will decrease, reducing the riskiness of their financial positions while they become overcapitalised; that is, oligopolies tend to hold large volumes of liquid assets unused in actual productive operations. This section will discuss how liquidity management of listed firms can induce financial fragility, which is further exacerbated through oligopolistic profits.

6.4.1 Listed firms' liquidity

In the Kalecki–Steindl analysis, gearing mainly refers to the share of total liabilities in total own assets. In modern financial parlance, gearing or financial leverage can be expressed in a range of different measures such as the debt-to-equity ratio, the equity ratio (meaning total equity as share of total assets), or the debt ratio (the relationship between total debt and total assets). Because listed non-financial companies make considerable use of capital markets in their balance sheet operations, it seems that a financial gearing ratio becomes indicative of the riskiness of their financial position. This financial gearing ratio, that is the relation of total liabilities to liquid assets such as cash, cash equivalents, and financial assets, determines both a company's ability to service its debt at short notice, and the degree of liquidity of its assets.

Liquidity of assets is particularly important for listed non-financial corporations due to the inherent volatility of capital markets. The increased presence of financial investors with large pools of liquid funds such as pension and investment funds since the 1980s has led to a process of capital market inflation (Toporowski, 2000). Prices for financial instruments and particularly corporate equity seem to have ceased being a reflection of expected future corporate profits[2] as suggested by Hilferding (1910) and Keynes's, and Veblen's financial theory in general. It is also doubtful that they are a combination of the return on risk-free financial paper such as government bonds plus some individual premium for the equity's riskiness measured by its volatility vis-à-vis market returns as formalised in capital asset pricing models (Tobin, 1958; Sharpe, 1965; Black and Scholes, 1973).

Instead, equity prices in particular depend on how investor demand can be absorbed in the primary and secondary capital markets. If rising demand faces an equivalent increase in newly issued equity or a withdrawal of the same amount of invested funds from the secondary markets, prices will remain unchanged. However, if there is additional demand which cannot be absorbed via new issuance or financial paper offered in the secondary markets, prices will rise. Since investors typically expect past price gains to continue into the future, rising prices can trigger a dynamic of capital market inflation. No substitution effect occurs within investors' portfolios, as would be suggested by textbook microeconomic analysis from more expensive financial paper towards relatively cheaper paper. Instead, increasing prices are interpreted as a signal to invest. This continues until investors are unable or unwilling to channel further funds into the market, for example because their income or credit access does not allow for it any more. At this point the upward price dynamic stalls, potentially triggering a price deflation if investors decided to cash in on their positions.

Facing capital market inflation, the liquidity preference of listed non-financial firms is likely to grow. During economic downswings, large volumes of liquid assets enable listed companies to buy back their own equity in order to stabilise share prices. Furthermore, calls for dividend payments, which are often more pressing during recessions as share-holders cannot sell equity profitably, leaving dividends as the only viable source of income, can be met despite decreasing cash flow from productive operations. During economic booms, liquid assets can be invested into corporate equity in order to make asset price gains from capital market inflation. Through the latter action, non-financial firms contribute to equity price inflation, increasing capital market volatility while becoming rentiers.

6.4.2 Fostering financial fragility

The consequence of low financial gearing is the emergence of overcapi-talisation (Steindl, 1945a; Toporowski, 1993). 'That is, that companies with high profits tend to have a higher amount of "good will" or other fictitious items in their assets' (Steindl, 1945a: p. 42). Goodwill is ficti-tious, because it does not reflect any tangible or quantifiable value but rather, as is often somewhat cryptically argued, derives from the reputa-tion, the brand and other corporate characteristics. Steindl clearly had the inflation of listed companies' equity in mind because goodwill is an accounting item on firms' balance sheets, which can conveniently be adjusted to ensure the equality of corporate assets with the sum of their liabilities and equity. Therefore, strong gains in share prices of a company in the absence of increased productive capacity, or substantial gains in cashflow or production output, could be put down as rising goodwill. Hence, capital market inflation can lead to such increases in the value of fictitious items on corporate balance sheets including goodwill.

An alternative measure for the inflation of corporate balance sheets, meaning the expansion of assets and liabilities without simultaneous growth in production or its capacity, is excess capital (Toporowski, 2008). The concept refers to 'the excess of a company's liabilities over its productive capital, i.e., the plant, equipment, materials, and stocks of unsold products and semi-fabricates that a firm holds' (Toporowski, 2008: p. 1). Hence, excess capital measures how much of the firm's acquired liabilities are not used for productive activity, and is instead invested into financial assets or simply held as cash and cash equivalents. Liquid assets typically generate no or marginal cash flow, which makes it costly to hold them, so according to conventional economic theory, and even in a Kaleckian business cycle framework, liquid assets should be used to pay off liabilities or finance productive investment internally in order to minimise cost.

Typically, it is suggested that listed companies obtain excess capital through their easy access to financial markets and favourable borrowing conditions (Toporowski, 2000). Both dynamics reinforce themselves. As mentioned before, investment in corporate paper by non-financial firms can contribute to capital market inflation making it even more lucrative to issue equity for further acquisition of shares. Equally, holding liquid assets such as financial paper and cash enables firms to borrow at very favourable conditions, since large volumes of liquid assets constitute high-quality collateral. Their loans create bank deposits (Withers, 1912). Since it is conceivable that banks target a specific ratio of corporate to household credit held on their balance sheets, household credit growth might be facilitated. This can inflate housing markets, as seen during the early 2000s in South Africa (Karwowski, 2012). Crucially, in both instances corporate balance sheet management contributes to financial fragility in the economy as a whole.

6.4.3 Overcapitalisation and oligopolistic profits

Apart from external sources of overcapitalisation, namely capital markets and external borrowing, there are also origins of excess capital which are internal to the corporation. Oligopolistic profits can be one of them. Oligopolies enjoy high profit rates while they possess excess capacity by definition. As consequence, their propensity to invest will be low, while their profits will continue to accrue. The logical question arises as to where oligopolistic profits will be channelled. The acquisition of foreign companies and emergence of multinational concerns is a probable outcome. The expansion of South African banks into other Southern African countries is an example in place. Also, oligopolistic companies sometimes branch out into other domestic industries, as exemplified in East Asian conglomerates.

While these seem to be possible long-term strategies, the short and medium-term alternative is to accumulate excess capital in order to strengthen the corporate balance sheet. In this sense, excess capacity, which is a characteristic of oligopolistic firms, results in excess capital. Here, accumulated oligopolistic profits may have advantages over external finance as source of excess capital. Fundamentally, accumulating excess capital internally avoids raising total liabilities, which results in a faster fall of financial gearing and conversely, a quicker rise of the liquidity ratio that is the ratio of liquid assets to total liabilities.

Financial gearing and liquidity ratio are defined as shown below:

Financial gearing: $$g_f = \frac{L_t}{A_t} \qquad (6.1)$$

Liquidity ratio: $$l = \frac{A_l}{L_t} \qquad (6.2)$$

where L_t are total liabilities and A_l refer to liquid assets. Hence, financial gearing is simply the inverse of the liquidity ratio, meaning that listed companies will attempt to reduce their financial gearing while increasing the liquidity ratio in order to strengthen their individual balance sheets.

When increasing liquid assets by the same amount (Δq) using external sources instead of internal ones such as oligopolistic profits, listed firms will see a slower fall (rise) in their financial gearing (liquidity ratio) because external financing adds to total liabilities while oligopolistic profits accrue to the company as an asset without creating a liability:

Changes in financial gearing due to external finance and due to oligopolistic profits:

$$\frac{L_t+\Delta q}{A_l+\Delta q} > \frac{L_t}{A_t+\Delta q} \qquad (6.3)$$

Changes in liquidity ratio due to external finance and due to oligopolistic profits:

$$\frac{A_l+\Delta q}{L_t+\Delta q} < \frac{A_l+\Delta q}{L_t} \qquad (6.4)$$

One result of these considerations is that overcapitalisation as measured by the liquidity ratio will increase faster if generated internally. Furthermore, since oligopolies tend to preserve their profit margins during economic slumps, overcapitalisation might be more persistent in oligopolies than in competitive listed firms that are more dependent on favourable capital market and credit conditions to generate excess capital. Hence, fluctuations of overcapitalisation in the course of the business cycle are likely to be less severe in oligopolistic corporations.

Finally, these considerations show that even assuming an extreme position where external financing through capital and credit markets would be severely curtailed, such as under a full-reserve-banking regime (Benes and Kumhof, 2012) oligopolistic profits could nevertheless induce overcapitalisation. In such a situation, overcapitalised non-financial firms with large volumes of liquid assets could become intermediaries, fostering financial fragility in the economy as a whole.

In the long run, heightened levels of financial fragility in the economy may increase the precautionary liquidity preference of all non-financial firms across the economy, regardless of their competition patterns, depressing investment in favour of cash and liquid asset holdings.

6.5 Some empirical evidence

In the following, South African data will be presented to support the hypothesis that oligopoly profits might be a source of overcapitalisation. The South African case is relevant since in manufacturing there is evidence of capital concentration resulting in exceptionally high markups, that is net income over input cost (Fedderke and Szalontai, 2005; Aghion et al., 2006). Furthermore, it demonstrates that overcapitalisation and resultant financial fragility is a phenomenon not only present in advanced economies but also affecting emerging markets.

To analyse the presence of oligopolistic profits in South African manufacturing and their impact on firms' financial positions, a sample of 17 relevant companies has been created. These companies are non-financial firms, which are listed on the Johannesburg Stock Exchange (JSE) and can be classified as involved in manufacturing. All corporations engaged in mining, which often includes steel manufacturers, have been excluded, since their large profit margins depend on resource prices rather than primarily on oligopolistic pricing power. Equally, firms purely involved in agricultural production of basic foods such as sugar have been excluded, since their activity is part of primary production rather than manufacturing.

The 17 firms have been chosen out of the top 120 JSE-listed companies according to market capitalisation of their stock, in order to include the most important South African manufacturers. The sample of firms, their position in terms of JSE market capitalisation, and type of manufacturing production are described in Table 6.1.

Using balance sheet data provided by McGregor BFA, profit margins in the form of net income to revenue ratios have been calculated for the years 2000 to 2012. The average profit margins are also provided in Table 6.1. According to Quantec data for the years 2000 to 2009, the average profit margin in South African manufacturing was 8.8 per cent with a standard deviation of 1.47 percentage points over that period (Quantec, 2010).

Table 6.1 provides p-values for the hypothesis that average profit margins for the companies in the sample are significantly different from the sector average of 8.8 per cent.[3] Aspen, Pretoria Portland Cement (PPC) and Caxton and CTP Group all have significantly higher profit margins. The case of Adcock Ingram is somewhat difficult, since data are only available for 2008 to 2012; abstracting from the latest observation, the profit margin is in fact significantly higher. Since data for 2012 might not be consolidated yet, the company will be grouped with the firms with high profit margins.

Mondi, Sappi, Nampak, Pioneer Foods, Allied Electronics, AECI, Rainbow Chicken and Astral Food all have profit margins significantly below the average for the manufacturing sector.

Following Steindl's understanding of competitive behaviour (1952), firms with high profit margins are likely to be enjoying oligopolistic profits while companies that face below-average profit margins are probably operating in a competitive environment. The rationale behind this definition of oligopolistic competition is the insight that the sheer number of companies present in an industry does not characterise competition behaviour. Therefore, concentration indices are not an tool adequate to identify oligopolistic companies. Instead, sales effort – that is companies' active competition for market share through product innovation or advertising – determines what type of competition is predominant.

Generally, if firms are subject to competitive conditions they will only be able to reap high profit margins temporarily before competitors catch up. This is consistent with Schumpeterian ideas. Hence, if a firm experiences structurally high profit margins it is likely to possess oligopolistic

Table 6.1 South African listed manufacturing and service industry firms

Rank of capitalisation as of September 2010	Company	Industry	Average profit margin, 2000–2012 (%)	p-values
21	Aspen pharmacare	Pharmaceutical manufacturer	20.7	0.00
24	Tiger Brands	Food and household goods manufacturer	9.4	0.63
26	Mondi	Packaging and paper manufacturer	3.5	0.01
28	Steinhoff International	Furniture and household goods retailer/ manufacturer	8.4	0.60
40	Sappi	Paper and paper products manufacturer	1.2	0.00
43	Pretoria Portland Cement	Cement manufacturer	21.9	0.00
49	Distell	Alcoholic beverage manufacturer	8.3	0.62
53	Nampak	Packaging manufacturer	5.4	0.00
54	Reunert	Electronics manufacturer	9.2	0.68
57	Adcock Ingram	Pharmaceutical manufacturer and healthcare services provider	14.5	0.20
63	Pioneer Foods	Food manufacturer	3.6	0.00
67	AVI	Food and beauty products manufacturer and fashion and beauty retailer	8.5	0.70
69	Allied Electronics	Multimedia service provider and electronics manufacturer	5.9	0.00
71	AECI	Chemicals manufacturer	4.9	0.00
85	Caxton and CTP Group	Publishing and printing	13.4	0.00
103	Rainbow Chicken	Food manufacturer	6.3	0.01
106	Astral Foods	Food manufacturer	6.0	0.00

Source: McGregor BFA and author's calculations.

power, protecting these margins through its oligopolistic position in the market.

There is evidence that the four firms in the sample identified as oligopolistic (Aspen, PPC, Caxton and Adcock Ingram) are overcapitalised. Figure 6.1 depicts their liquidity ratios for the period 2000 to 2012, which on average were all above 20 per cent as share of total liabilities.

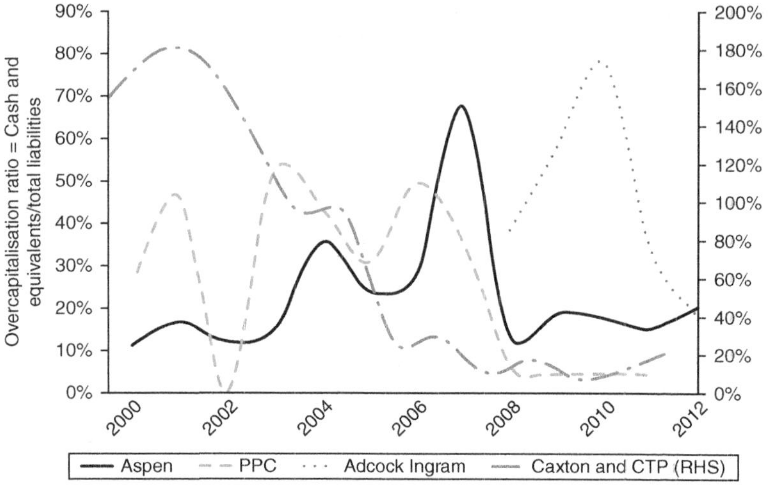

Figure 6.1 Liquidity ratios for oligopolistic firms
Source: McGregor BFA and author's calculations.

Adcock Ingram's ratio of cash and cash equivalents to total liabilities for the period was even well above 40 per cent, while for Caxton the same ratio exceeded 70 per cent.

The 20 per cent threshold appears to be useful for identifying overcapitalised companies. Amongst large listed companies in advanced economies, 10 per cent of cash and cash equivalents as share of total assets appears to be the norm (see Kim et al., 1998; Baum et al., 2004; Khurana et al., 2006; Bates et al., 2009). Hence, doubling this ratio could be regarded as a conservative measure to identify firms that carry cash and cash equivalents on their balance sheet well above the average. Research conducted for Malaysian listed non-financial companies also supports a liquidity ratio of 20 per cent as threshold for overcapitalisation (Karwowski, 2009).

The lack of a clear secular upward trend in liquidity ratios for the oligopolistic company group can be explained with losses incurred during crises and economic downswings. South Africa was hit by a currency crisis in late 2001, which is particularly visible in a sharp reduction of cash holdings as share of total liabilities for PPC and Caxton. The latest global financial crisis, fully present in South Africa by the end of 2008, appears to have reduced liquidity ratios for all of these companies with a delayed response by Adcock Ingram. Despite the recent reduction

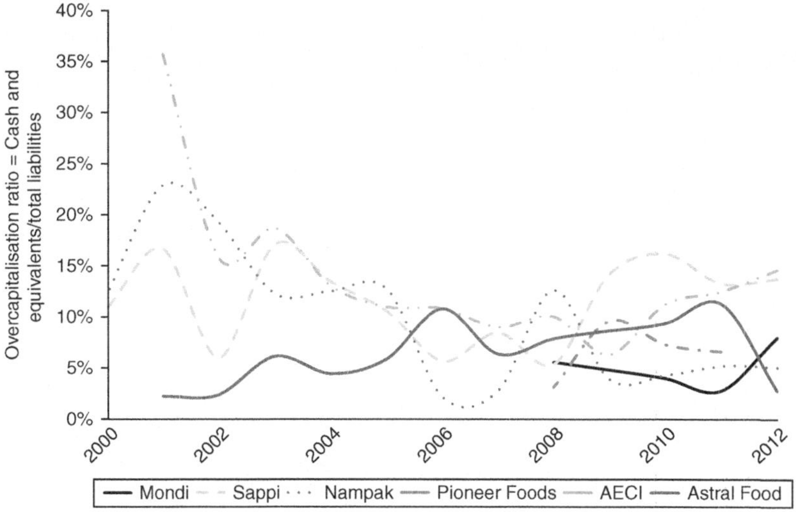

Figure 6.2 Liquidity ratios for competitive firms
Source: McGregor BFA and author's calculations.

in liquidity ratios, levels of cash and cash equivalents to total liabilities remain noticeably high. Only PPC has not managed to restore a liquidity ratio of around 20 per cent since the onset of the global financial crisis. This impression is further strengthened considering liquidity ratios for the competitive firms as shown in Figure 6.2.

Liquidity ratios for Mondi, Sappi, Nampak, Pioneer Foods, AECI and Astral Food have been between 5 and 14 per cent for the period 2000 to 2012. With the exception of AECI and Nampak there have not been any strong variations in these ratios, indicating that levels of cash holdings are relatively low and liquid assets are less actively and less aggressively managed in competitive firms in comparison to oligopolistic companies.

However, all of these companies are large and listed corporations with favourable access to capital markets and bank credit. As consequence, all could accumulate excess capital using external finance. Oligopolistic profits represent only one possible source of overcapitalisation. This might explain why Rainbow Chicken and to lesser extent Allied Technologies have relatively high liquidity ratios – as shown in Figure 6.3 – despite their comparatively low profit margins.

Generally, the visibly higher liquidity ratios of Aspen, PPC, Caxton and Adcock Ingram – on average 20 per cent and more – support the

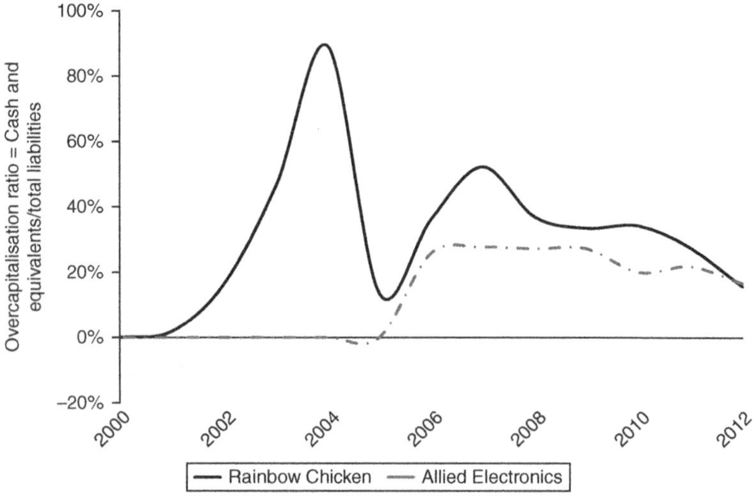

Figure 6.3 Liquidity ratios for competitive firms
Source: McGregor BFA and author's calculations.

hypothesis that oligopolistic profits can be used to accumulate excess capital. Interestingly, the hypothesis that oligopolistic profits as source of overcapitalisation might lead to a more stable liquidity ratio as suggested in Section 6.4. does not seem to be reflected in data for South African listed non-financial firms. Stabilising cash flow using liquid assets leads to volatility in corporate balance sheets, implying a potential source of financial fragility.

Other sources of excess capital – such as capital market funds – are also conceivable. Nevertheless, it is striking that only a small number of firms in the competitive companies group – namely Rainbow Chicken and possibly Allied Electronics – is visible overcapitalised.

6.6 Conclusion

While the proponents of cartelisation believed that reducing *Kapitalrisiko* would be sufficient to induce stable investment activity, the Kalecki–Steindl analysis exposed this claim as a misconception. In fact, the accumulation of oligopolistic profits by cartels and oligopolies exacerbate the business cycle in the short run while introducing economic instability in the form of high unemployment and stagnant growth in the long run. In a contemporary economic setting with developed financial markets, present in advanced but also in some emerging economies, the attempt to reduce financial risk for the individual company introduces financial fragility in the form of capital market inflation (Toporowski, 2000) fuelled by corporate excess capital. In this context, oligopolistic profits can constitute an internal source of excess capital.

Notes

1. 'Ein Moment größerer Wirtschaftlichkeit liegt schließlich darin, dass das Kapitalrisiko der kartellierten Industrien vermindert wird. Diese Verminderung wird hervorgerufen durch die Stetigkeit der Produktion, durch die Verhütung oder Vermilderung der zeitweise auftretenden Krisen, durch die Gleichmäßigkeit des Absatzes, durch die zweckmäßige Ausnutzung der Betriebseinrichtungen u.s.w.' [Increased efficiency of cartels consists of the fact that the entrepreneur's risk of capital loss in investment activity is reduced for the cartelised industries. This reduction is a result of the continuity of production, the prevention or moderation of temporary crises, the regularity of sales, the appropriate utilisation of capacity and so on] (Grunzel, 1902: p. 121).
2. The analysis of so-called fundamentals to determine share prices strongly resembles Hilferding's idea that the firm's ability to generate profit in the future shapes equity price. Nowadays, the fundamentals considered are cash flow, return on assets, return on equity, and the gearing ratios amongst others. Governance indicators and historical company performance are also often analysed.
3. This is based on a two-sided t-test under the assumptions that variances of the two samples, that is the sample underlying industry data and the sample underlying company data, are different from each other. p-values of 0.01 and smaller imply support for the hypothesis that the company's profit margin differs significantly from that of the industry average.

7
Net Private Savings in Relation to the Government's Financial Balance

Kazimierz Łaski and Leon Podkaminer

7.1 The basic identities

Looking at a national economy from both the income and expenditure sides, we get the following identity:

$$YD + T + M = CP + IP + G + X \tag{7.1}$$

where YD denotes the disposable income of the private sector, T is the disposable income of the government (all taxes net of all monetary transfers to the private sector) and M is the income of the rest of the world (RoW) from imports of the national economy in question (the left-hand side of (7.1)). On the right-hand side of (7.1) we have private sector expenditures on consumption (CP) and that sector's gross investment (IP), government expenditure on goods and services (G), and RoW expenditure on the national economy's exports (X). By simple rearrangement, we get

$$[(YD - CP) - IP)] = (G - T) + (X - M) \tag{7.1}$$

This is equivalent to:

$$(SP - IP) = (G - T) + (X - M)$$

or, finally:

$$NPS = D + E \tag{7.2}$$

Private savings (SP = YD – CP) comprise household savings and profits retained by firms. In (7.2) we denote by NPS = (SP – IP) the *net* private savings, by D = (G – T) the budget deficit, and by E = (X – M) the RoW deficit (or the current account of the country concerned).

Ex post, formula (7.2) always holds because it is an identity. However, even as an identity it points up interesting relationships between sectors, especially when statistical data covering longer periods are available. For the world as a whole, we obviously have NPS = D; this is an identity which links the balances of the private and government sectors aggregated globally. Budget surpluses (D < 0) and even balanced budgets D = 0) do occur, albeit rarely; thus, for monetary economies worldwide, budget deficits (D > 0) seem to be the rule rather than an exception. This applies not only to times of war and disasters, but – at least for the industrial countries disposing of longer statistical records – also to periods of peace as well (for example, Łaski, 2008). Hence, given that for the world as a whole E = 0 by definition and D > 0 (as shown by long-term statistical records) we have, according to (7.2), NPS > 0. The private sector of the entire global economy displays a sustained tendency to save more than it invests. The same observation can be made with respect to the European Union (EU), which is a group of countries with negligible E. Almost all EU countries have consistently run budget deficits (very much in violation of the Maastricht Treaty). Thus, for the EU as a whole we also have D > 0. It follows that the NPS for the EU as a whole is also positive. Last but not least, we observe that for NPS = 0 – which can be understood as a minimum requirement to the effect that the private sector should not become indebted in the long run – all countries with a current account deficit (E < 0) must record budget deficits D > 0. All these observations are to be understood as referring to a trend and average values for longer periods – and not as a rule for each country and every year. We also observe that those countries which happen to report budget surpluses (D < 0), very often (although not always) record high E. This must be the case if E > NPS > 0 (for example, the case of Norway since becoming a major oil exporting country).

Within the private sector we have two subsectors: private households and firms. It is normally assumed that for most of the time firms invest more than they save (in the form of profits retained), hence incurring a flow of debt whose volume increases over time. This debt makes it possible to increase the firms' productive capacities beyond the levels funded from their own savings (that is profits retained). It is also assumed that private households are net savers whose financial assets increase over time. The assumption NPS > 0 is thus normally interpreted as a situation in which private households save more than the debts that firms are ready to incur.

The fact that as a rule (or mostly so) NPS is positive can be interpreted as reflecting the *desired* level of private savings (SP) being higher than actual private investment. Positive (D + E) helps to narrow that gap. Alternatively, it can be said that the positive NPS must be reflected in the sum (D + E) being positive as well. However, NPS equal to (D + E) is an identity; as such, it does not say anything about the direction of causality. In any event, positive NPS must be *counterbalanced* by the sum of the Government and foreign deficits. The private sector's desire to run a financial surplus (NPS > 0) cannot be realised without the willingness of government and foreign sectors (taken together) to run a deficit. Similarly, the government and foreign sectors (once again taken together) cannot run financial surpluses (D + E < 0) without the private sector's net dis-saving (NPS falling below 0) – for example, without private sector savings falling short of private sector investment.

At present, the trend throughout much of the industrialised world is for the private sector to increase net savings (ΔNPS > 0). Deleveraging should strengthen private sector balance sheets. That trend, however, actually clashes with the present overall orientation of fiscal policies. Those policies prescribe fiscal austerity – reducing budgetary deficits. Should austerity prevail, the result would be ΔD < 0. Should the private sector deleverage, ΔNPS > 0 would be the outcome. Clearly, the identity ΔNPS = ΔD would be violated. However, by their very nature, the identities hold under any circumstances. In reality, the identity ΔNPS = ΔD *will* hold no matter what policy is pursued and irrespective of private sector preferences. What kind of outcome will emerge out of the two conflicting tendencies or which of them will ultimately prevail is very much an open issue, but in any case, that conflict is likely to incur some 'collateral damage' in the form of weaker growth and higher unemployment.

7.2 Why do net private savings tend to be positive?

One consequence of (7.2) is that in a 'textbook economy' (consisting solely of a private sector and devoid of government and the 'outside world'), NPS would have to be zero. Indeed, in such an economy D = E = 0, hence NPS = 0. In such a textbook economy, investment is equal to savings (both are private) so that SP – IP = 0. It must be understood that in such an economy, the private sector as a whole would be unable to accumulate *net* (outside) financial wealth, simply because there would be no party beyond the private sector to supply the financial debt that would constitute the private sector's financial wealth. Surely, economies that rule out accumulation of private sector net financial wealth are conceivable; in all probability, the early 'natural' economies would have fitted that description. However, it is hard to imagine (unless one adheres to 'mainstream ideas') a modern monetary economy without private sector accumulation of net (outside) financial wealth. In such an economy, the private sector would accumulate net financial wealth, if not in the form of government bonds, then at least in the form of cash/money amassed and issued by the government's own central bank. To gain access to the money so hoarded, the private sector must have willingly supplied the government with goods and services that it had produced on its own. (Thereby the government would have had to acquire such goods and services without paying for them fully with the proceeds of proper taxation levied on the private sector.) The private sector's net (outside) wealth would have to be matched by the debt issued by the government (plus, eventually, the debt issued by foreign parties that the private sector had acquired, Wray, 1998: ch. 4).

Why does the private sector tend to accumulate outside debt (in particular, that of its own government)? The simplest answer is that the private sector greatly values such debt. For the private sector, public debt *must be* wealth – no matter what the proponents of 'Ricardian equivalence' claim. Otherwise, the private sector would not waste 'good money' on acquiring it.

What kinds of benefits follow from the ownership of public debt? The opportunity to earn interest income on that debt may certainly be one motive. That motive alone, however, does not seem to be decisive. In many countries, the rate of interest on public debt is purely symbolic; Japan with its soaring public debt has no difficulty in floating its massively expanding public deficits at interest rates of less than 1 per cent, and interest rates on Switzerland's public debt gravitate towards zero. Essentially, public debt is in such great demand in the private sector for liquidity reasons (as, of course, stressed by Keynes), or as the trusted store of value, or as the necessary capital reserves that facilitate firms' access to capital markets (and thus private investment, as in Kalecki). In Łaski and Podkaminer (2012) our hypothesis was that private sector demand for public debt is even likely to strengthen around a positive secular trend, accompanied by private sector savings in general rising more rapidly than private investment. Changes observed in the structure of private sector income (with rising inequality in disposable incomes and the emergence of a super-rich class whose members derive their incomes from trade/speculation in various assets and financial instruments rather than from capital investment in productive capacities) contribute to the gap between private sector savings and investment. The emergence of the super-rich is, of course, intimately linked to the ever-progressing financialisation/privatisation of services traditionally provided by the public sector (inter alia, health, education and pensions). Financialisation/privatisation also induces a higher propensity to save for precautionary reasons – without the requisite rise in the propensity to invest productively. The flip side of financialisation of the services formerly provided by the public sector is the rise in private funds, such as pension funds (Toporowski, 2000). These funds may tend to acquire – especially in turbulent times – growing chunks of public debt. Ageing in a time of ever-increasing financialisation of the pension system may add strength to the private propensity to save. Moreover, technological change may be another factor; the productivity of fixed assets is likely to improve secularly owing to advances in technology – the investment of smaller amounts of real assets is capable of producing more output. This trend may be temporarily interrupted by major inventions (such as the electrical system, which called for high initial investment in the construction of power stations, transmission grids, and so on). In the long term, as the supply of goods produced by the private business sector can perhaps be expected to outstrip demand for the same, the desire to save could systematically outstrip the desire to invest.

7.3 Destructive fiscal consolidation

The EU policy stance has always stressed the need to limit public-sector deficits. Actually, the Stability and Growth Pact 'lays down the obligation for Member States to adhere to the medium-term objective for their budgetary positions of close to balance or in surplus'.[1] The recent Fiscal Pact agreed upon by the EU leaders is designed to strengthen 'fiscal discipline' across the euro area (and beyond). Moreover, the Fiscal Pact imposes the obligation to reduce public debt/GDP ratios. In so doing, it actually imposes on most euro-area countries the obligation to run – on a long-term basis – the budgetary surpluses. Taxation of the private sector (net of transfers to the same) should be persistently higher than income earned by the private sector on sales on goods and services to the government. The private sector in most euro-area countries will 'bleed' for many years to come – for the sake of 'healthy public finances', the latter being deemed indispensable to the long-term robustness of the private sector itself. (An analogy with mediaeval 'medical science' and the practice of bloodletting inevitably comes to mind.) The economic and social costs of this austerity hysteria will no doubt be immense. The question worth asking is whether it will be possible at all – and under what conditions – to run a Eurozone-wide policy which in fact requires that the net private savings of the member states are persistently negative. In view of (7.2), a negative D (that is a budgetary surplus) implies that the NPS would also have to be negative. Of course, the current account E for some Eurozone countries may, on occasion, be positive and high enough to render D + E still positive. A small country (such as Luxembourg) can combine large budgetary surpluses with current account surpluses over extended periods of time without this having a perceptible impact on its trading partners. A large country (such as Germany) is, however, unlikely to persist indefinitely with high budgetary surpluses combined with massive current account surpluses, the reason being that German current account surpluses are the current account deficits of its partners, such as Italy. The latter country's NPS would then have to be unambiguously negative – on account of both E and D being negative. Thus, any attempts to run budgetary surpluses in one (or more) Eurozone countries can only be successful (via expansion of current account surpluses), if those attempts fail in some other euro-area countries.[2] Incidentally, under the present circumstances it is futile to expect that the EU as whole could become a major net exporter to the rest of the world.

Given the limitations of the scenario in which budgetary surpluses are persistently combined with current account surpluses, it is useful to return to the analysis of a simple form of (7.2):

$$NPS = D$$

Supposing D is negative (as required by the Fiscal Pact), NPS would have to be negative as well. Or (remembering that NPS = SP – IP) private sector savings would have to be consistently lower than private sector investment. The private sector's financial wealth would then have to drop: for example, via the government redeeming its debt to the private sector (with the proceeds then serving to finance private investment). It is at least debatable whether the private sector would be eager to engage in investment under such conditions. The falling financial wealth and contracting domestic consumer demand might more likely induce falling investment and rising savings, thereby initiating spiralling recessionary adjustment. Of course, recessionary adjustment could ultimately steer NPS into negative territory (consistent with the budgetary surpluses).

That outcome, however, would feature low income and high unemployment levels. At a very low level of private savings, the requisite negative net private savings could eventually be achieved; however, even if economically imaginable, such an outcome would be unacceptable, both politically and socially. We doubt whether this is the outcome that the EU leaders actually desire. On the other hand, we deeply deplore the fact that the economic advisors to the EU heads of state have apparently failed to grasp the actual consequences of the policies that they so doggedly advocate.

Notes

1. See Council Regulation No. 1055/2005 amending the Growth and Stability Pact. *Official Journal of the European Union*, 7 July 2005, L. 174/1.
2. We abstract here from another difficulty. A combination of current account surpluses with t budgetary surpluses implies a shift in a country's private sector net financial wealth. To an increasing degree that wealth would consist of foreign (private or public) debt. At the same time, the share/size of debt issued by that country's government would decline. It is doubtful whether the German private sector would actually be eager to substitute *bunds* for private/public Greek (or even Italian) debt.

8
Confidence, Increasing Risks, Income Distribution and Crisis in a Post-Kaleckian Stock-Flow Consistent Model

Edwin Le Heron

I have found out what economics is; it is the science of confusing stocks with flows.

Michał Kalecki as cited by Joan Robinson (1982: pp. 295–296)

8.1 Introduction

Today, PK usually stands for the post-Keynesian school. But it can also stand for the post-Kaleckian or post-Kaldorian schools; Michał Kalecki certainly seems to be the more important reference, because he is said to have discovered Keynes's principle of effective demand on his own in 1933, and he strongly influenced Cambridge economists, Nicholas Kaldor in particular. With Rosa Luxemburg and Gunnar Myrdal, Kalecki was one of the first to show the importance of demand in growth theory. In this chapter, we have blended some ideas from Kalecki, Kaldor and Keynes – but in honour of Tadeusz Kowalik, we shall focus on the Kaleckian aspects. From Kalecki, we have taken the mark-up pricing theory, with fixed technical coefficient, capacity utilisation, and two classes of households: workers and capitalists.

We have used a dynamic growth model introducing lags and time, with the long run being conceived of as a chain of short terms. With the corporate retained profits, we have introduced the principle of increasing risk (Kalecki, 1937) with borrower's and lender's risk. The long-term interest rate is linked to the level of debt of firms. The risk and the interest rate increase with lower self-financing and the size of investment. The relevance of income distribution is introduced in the consumption function, perfectly summarised by Kaldor Kalecki's approach with the sentence (Kaldor 1956: p. 96): 'capitalists earn what they spend, and workers spend what they earn'.

Our challenge is to understand how the 2007 financial crisis in the US became a real global economic crisis after 2008, especially in Europe and particularly in France, and what kinds of income policies are best. Many transmission channels can be considered, and have certainly had an influence. Kalecki and Keynes's thoughts give us answers, but these answers raise a very difficult question. With the principle of effective demand, Keynes stressed the importance of psychological variables in determining economic growth, especially because of radical uncertainty, and expectations are often self-fulfilling. But how can we model this brilliant insight?

This chapter aims at showing that one of the main channels through which the financial crisis in the US became a real global economic crisis is the 'confidence channel', that is, that the financial crisis affected firms' and banks' expectations and confidence, thus leading to the events that they were fearing. This 'confidence channel' is reinforced by the principle of increasing risk. I propose to model expectations and the state of confidence of private agents using the indexes calculated by national statistical services from monthly polls; these illustrate the state of confidence in an economy in real time. This data is genuinely forward looking.

First, I shall build a post-Kaleckian stock-flow consistent (SFC) model (Godley and Lavoie, 2001, 2007; Dos Santos and Zezza, 2004; Le Heron, 2011) to study the link between a local financial crisis and a global real crisis, to make clear the nature of the 'confidence channel' in a demand-led model. I shall introduce the question of the state of confidence in the private sectors and other features of Kalecki's models (Toporowski, 2005b). Second, I shall simulate the model to study the effects of the current financial crisis involving increasing risks and a crisis in confidence; the aim is to analyse the channel of transmission of changes in the state of confidence in the private sectors to the real world. I shall explore the confidence channel with a model based on French indexes of the state of confidence (firms and banks) from 2005 to 2012. Third, I shall analyse two kinds of income policy to inform the search for an exit strategy to the crisis.

8.2 A post-Kaleckian stock-flow consistent growth model

I shall develop in more detail the features influenced by Kalecki and the most specific matter of the model.[1] The economy is comprised of six sectors: government, firms, worker households, capitalist households, private banks and central bank. SFC modelling is based on two tables: the transactions matrix (flows, Appendix 8.3) and the balance sheet matrix (stocks, Appendix 8.4). The complete dynamic model (Appendix 8.2) contains 58 equations.

All production must be financed. However, current production is financed by the working capital of entrepreneurs (retained earnings) and by contracted revolving funds granted by banks at the current rate of interest; these two factors constitute a shock absorber to possible monetary rationing by banks. I am essentially limiting my study to the effects that a fall in the state of confidence of banks, firms and households might have on new financing for investment and growth of production. Let us proceed to examine the gross supply (φ) and the net supply (ΔL) of finance by banks – that is to say, the new flow of money, as opposed to the existing stock of money (D). Also, there is a stock of money demand equal to transaction, precaution, finance and speculative motives, whereas the desired gross finance demand (φ^d) represents the new flow of financing required by firms for the desired investment (I^d) and for the redemption of the debt (amortisation = $amort_L$) minus the undistributed profits (P^u). Thus the internal funds of firms (IF) represent the undistributed profits (P^u) minus the redemption of the debt ($amort_L$). Assuming a closed economy, demand for money can be satisfied by banks, either by the stock markets or by credit. At the end of the period, net financing demand (ΔLD) can be constrained by net money supply from banks (ΔL). ΔD determines monetary creation in the period, issued from loans (L) to firms and Treasury bonds (B) of the Government.

The national income (Y) adds the household consumption (C), investment of the firms (I) and the public expenditure (G). The rate of growth of the national income is gr_y.

8.3 Investment of firms

The investment function is the most important one in a growth model. The stock of capital (K) increases with the flow of net investment (I) that is financed by the total of the corporate retained profits of firms and by external funds from commercial banks (gross finance = φ). Firms prefer self-financing (Kalecki, 1937; Eichner, 1976), because the borrower's risk begins with external funds. The self-financing of firms corresponds to the net retained profits, that is the retained earnings (P^u) minus the redemption of the debts of firms ($amort_L$). Firms borrow money from banks to finance investments (loan at variable rate) (L).

$$I \equiv \varphi + IF \qquad (8.1)$$

$$IF = P^u - amort_L \qquad (8.2)$$

$$amort_L = a_l \cdot L_{-1} \qquad (8.3)$$

In this model, I differentiate between the effective investment (I) and the desired investment of firms (I_D). The banks finance the latter totally or in part according their lender's risk (LR) (see Equations 8.19, 8.20, 8.21 and 8.26). Rationing in investment financing can exist ($\varphi < \varphi^d$ or $I < I_D$). The desired rate of accumulation (gr_{kD}) is a function of an exogenous state of confidence (γ_0), of the capacity utilisation rate (u) and of the increasing risk of the borrower (BR), which is measured by the rate of cash flow (r_{cf}) and by the financial condition index (FCI). The rate of cash flow is the ratio of retained profits to capital, and the financial condition index captures the sensitivity of investment to the level of indebtedness and to the long-term interest rate. The borrower's risk captures Kalecki's principle of increasing risk. The risk and the long-term interest rate increase with lower self-financing and the size of investment.

$$I_D = gr_{kD} \cdot K\!-\!1 \qquad (8.4)$$

$$\varphi^d = I^d - IF \qquad (8.5)$$

$$gr_{kD} = \gamma_0 + (\gamma_1 \cdot r_{cf-1}) + (\gamma_2 \cdot u_{-1}) - (\gamma_3 \cdot FCI_{\,-1}) \qquad (8.6)$$

with γ_i: constant

Where the rate of capacity utilisation is defined as the ratio of output to full capacity output (Y_{fc}):

$$r_{cf} = P^u/K_{-1} \qquad (8.7)$$

$$u = Y/Y_{fc} \qquad (8.8)$$

The capital to full capacity ratio (σ) is defined as a constant:

$$Y_{fc} = K_{-1} \cdot \sigma \qquad (8.9)$$

with σ: constant

$$FCI = \mu_1 \cdot i_l \cdot L/K \qquad (8.10)$$

with μ_i: constants.

I measure the output gap in ratio, with Y_{fc} the output of full capacity and not of the capacity that corresponds to the potential output. Distributed profits (P^d) are a fraction of profits realised in the previous period:

$$P^d = (1 - s_f) \cdot P_{f-1} \tag{8.11}$$

with s_f: constant.

8.3 Two classes of households: workers and capitalists

Income distribution is relevant. I assume that households (denoted H) determine their consumption expenditure (*C*) on the basis of their expected disposable income ($Y_H{}^a = Y_W{}^a + Y_K{}^a$) and their wealth of the previous period that consists entirely of bank deposits. Following the Kaleckian tradition and the Kaldorian equation (1956), there are two classes of households: workers (W) and capitalists (K). Working households essentially earn wages and consume a large part of their income (Y_w) while the financial income of capitalist households (Y_k), consisting of distributed profit (P^d) and interest, is largely devoted to saving ($\alpha_1 > \alpha_2$ and $\alpha_3 > \alpha_4$). Consumption decisions depend on the social class of the households and determine the amount that they will save out of their disposable income. The financial behaviour of workers is simplified; they only hold banking deposit accounts that earn interest. The capitalists, however, hold equities and banking deposits. The consumption decision and the level of taxes (T_W and T_K) determine the amount (ΔD) that households will save out of their disposable income (essentially the capitalist households). A small part of the household wealth (D) is consumed.

$$C = C_W + C_K \tag{8.12}$$

$$C_W = (\alpha_1 \cdot Y_W{}^a) + (\alpha_3 \cdot D_{W-1}) \tag{8.13}$$

with α_i: constant

$$C_K = (\alpha_2 \cdot Y_K{}^a) + (\alpha_4 \cdot D_{K-1}) \tag{8.14}$$

with α_i: constant

$$Y_W{}^a = Y_{W-1} + \theta_h \cdot (Y_{W-1} - Y_W{}^a{}_{-1}) \tag{8.15}$$

with θ_h: constant

$$Y_K^a = Y_{K-1} + \theta_h \cdot (Y_{K-1} - Y_{K\ -1}^a) \qquad (8.16)$$

with θ_h: constant

$$Y_W = W + (i_{d-1} \cdot D_{W-1}) - T_W \qquad (8.17)$$

$$Y_K = P^d + (i_{d-1} \cdot D_{K-1}) - T_K \qquad (8.18)$$

8.4 Financing by private banks

Banks do not make loans to households, but firms' financing is fundamental in a monetary economy of production. Firms begin by being self-financed, then turn to external finance (ΔLD). Banks only finance projects they consider profitable, but confidence in their judgement is variable and can justify various strategies. Banks examine firms' productive and financial expectations and also their financial structure. This investigation is carried out according to their confidence in the state of long-term expectations of yields on capital assets, influencing what Keynes referred to as 'animal spirits'. The state of confidence of banks is notably taken into account by an exogenous variable (γ_4). After studying expected production and the demand for financing that incorporates the firm's borrowing risk, bankers can refuse to finance. The state of confidence of banks summarises these factors.

Banks experience a lender's risk (*LR*) when underwriting finance and creating money. Lender's risk is the sum of three fundamental risks: risk of default, risk of liquidity and market risk. In Equations (8.19, 8.20, 8.21 and 8.26), the risks of default and of liquidity are taken into account by the gap of the leverage ratio with a conventional leverage ratio. Monetary policy involves a money market risk when fluctuations in the money interest rates occur.

When the lender's risk is maximum ($LR = 1$), commercial banks refuse to finance the net investment of firms: $\Delta L = 0$. Desired investment (I_D) faces a serious finance rationing. The flow of net investment is only financed by self-funding, that is the retained earnings (P^u), minus the amortisation of the debt ($amort_L$). Thus the stock of money supply can be reduced by the redemption of the debt. If the lender's risk is null ($LR = 0$), desired investment is fully financed: $\Delta L = \Delta LD$ or $\varphi = \varphi^d$. It corresponds to the endogenous money (horizontalism) of Kaldor (1982).

$$\varphi = \varphi d \cdot (1 - LR) \qquad (8.19)$$

with $0 \leq LR \leq 1$

$$\Delta L = \varphi - amort_L \qquad (8.20)$$

In the model, the lender's risk (*LR*) is measured by the difference between the current and the conventional leverage ratios (amount of indebtedness considered normal) and by the spread on the interest rates, that is the difference between the long-term and short-term interest rates ($i_l - i_{cb}$). The higher the current indebtedness of firms (*L/K*) over the accepted indebtedness, the greater the lender's risk. The accepted indebtedness is conventional, but this conventional indebtedness can increase during a boom and decrease during a crisis: γ_5 is linked to growth and to the state of confidence (measured by the Index of Business Climate (*BCI*) in this model) and is thus endogenous.

$$LR = -\gamma_4 + a_1 \cdot (lev_{-1} - \gamma_5 \cdot lev_c) + (b_1 \cdot spread) \qquad (8.21)$$

with γ_4, a_1, b_1 et lev_c: constant

$$lev = L/K \qquad (8.22)$$

$$\gamma_5 = a_2 \cdot BCI \qquad (8.23)$$

with a_2: constant

$$spread = i_l - i_{cb} \qquad (8.24)$$

Monetary authorities endogenously determine the key rate on the money market (i_{cb}) following a Taylor rule (1993). While central banks fix the short-term rates, the private banks' liquidity preference determines banking rates (short-, medium- and long-term interest); it is the long-term interest rates (i_l) that are significant for growth and financing (loan), and the link between short-term and long-term interest rates is complex. Macroeconomic banking interest rates (i_l) are the production costs of money plus a risk premium. The first element corresponds to: functioning costs (wages, investment, immobilisation); payment costs for monetary liabilities (subject to the firms' competition for households savings) and the cost of high-powered money determined by the central bank; and to a rate of margin (χ) corresponding to standard profits of banks. The production costs of money are equal to (i_{cb}) plus a relatively constant mark-up (χ).

Risk premiums are not constant, because they are the results of the banks' liquidity preference, which covers lender's risk (*lr*). There is an increasing risk (Kalecki, 1937) as a consequence of the size of investment and of the level of self-financing. With an increase in prosperity, the volume of investment and the leverage ratio both rise, involving an increasing long-term interest rate. In the model, I use a lender's risk similar to the one above (Equation 8.21), that is, a mix of state of confidence and of leverage ratio plus the expectation of inflation (Π^a). But with the different coefficients (γ_5) and (a_3), (l_r) can be negative and reduce the mark-up. Therefore the long-term interest rate becomes in part endogenous, and the spread between (i_{cb}) and (i_l) is not constant. To explain the short-term interest rate (i_d), i_{cb} and χ are sufficient. Meanwhile, (l_r) is the primary variable in order to explain the long-term interest rate (i_l). Banks apply a spread (χ_2) between the key rate and the rate on deposits in order to realise profit.

$$i_l = i_{cb} + lr + \chi_1 \tag{8.25}$$

with χ_1: constant $\chi_1 > \chi_2$

$$lr = -\gamma_6 + a_3 \cdot (lev_{-1} - \gamma_5 \cdot lev_c) + \Pi^a \tag{8.26}$$

with γ_6, a_3, lev_c constant and c = convention on the 'normal' debt ratio

$$i_d = i_{cb} - \chi_2 \tag{8.27}$$

The initial structure of interest rates is as follows: $i_l = i_b > i_{cb} > i_d$

Economic activity also depends on the 'animal spirits' of banks. A scarcity of finance can only be the consequence of a deliberate choice. 'Desired scarcity' of financing is the sign of banks' liquidity preference. From an optimal structure of their balance sheet, I measure the profits of commercial banks (P_b) obtained by monetary financing:

$$P_b \equiv i_{b-1} \cdot B_{-1} + i_{l-1} \cdot L_{-1} - T_B - i_{d-1} \cdot D_{-1} - i_{cb-1} \cdot REF_{-1} \tag{8.28}$$

8.5 Fiscal policy of the government

The government collects taxes from workers on wages and from capitalists, firms and commercial banks on profits. The government finances any deficit by issuing bonds, so that the supply of treasury bonds (*B*) in the economy is identical to the stock of government debt. In other words, it is given by the pre-existing stock of debt plus its current deficit (*DG*). The current deficit of the government includes the redemption of the national debt. I assume that private banks give limitless credit to government at the long-term rate of interest (i_l).

To analyse the consequences of a supply shock, I assume a stabilising effect of the fiscal policy. Public expenditure (*G*) always grows at the same rate (gr_y) as the national income (*Y*) with a lag of one year, whereas tax revenue is proportional to income, and hence varies in line with public expenditure. With State debt, the global impact is linked to the key interest rate and thus to the monetary policy; this resembles a form of co-ordination between the monetary and the fiscal policies. The final effect of the fiscal policy is measured by the government deficit (*DG*). Our economy has a self-stabilising tendency due to the fiscal policy.

$$G = G_{-1}.\ (1 + gr_{y\,-1}) \quad (8.29)$$

$$DG = G + (i_{b-1} \cdot B_{-1}) - T - P_{cb} - amort_B \quad (8.30)$$

$$T = T_H + T_F + T_B \quad (8.31)$$

$$T_H = T_W + T_K \quad (8.32)$$

$$T_W = \tau_1 \cdot Y_{W-1} \quad (8.33)$$

with τ_1: constant

$$T_K = \tau_2 \cdot Y_{K-1} \quad (8.34)$$

with τ_2: constant

$$T_F = \tau_3 \cdot P_{f-1} \quad (8.35)$$

with τ_3: constant

$$T_B = \tau_4 \cdot P_{b-1} \quad (8.36)$$

with τ_4: constant.

8.6 Monetary policy of the central bank

Following the theory of endogenous money (Kaldor, 1982), I assume that the central bank is fully accommodating. Clearly, central banks in Europe (ECB, BoE) are not post-Keynesian. Then, I use a Taylor rule as a central bank reaction function for the modelling of central bank interest policy. First, the central bank fixes the key rate of interest (i_{cb}) using a Taylor rule, that is the central bankers react to output gap and inflation gap; and second, it provides whatever advances (*REF*) are demanded by banks at that rate. Taylor propounded his first instrument rule in 1993, modelling the dual mandate of the Federal Reserve Bank. It was founded on the output gap and on the inflation gap. From the Taylor rule, I can summarise monetary policy in three ways: strategy, flexibility and intensity. Strategy represents the mandate and therefore the long-term policy. Flexibility measures the deviation in the short term of the policy from the strategy. Intensity is the weight put on output gap and inflation gap respectively. With the Taylor principle, coefficients must be higher than one to prevent expectations of inflation from producing inflation.

I assume that central bank uses a flexible Taylor rule. The key interest rate (i_{cb}) is a negative function of the output gap and a positive function of the inflation gap. The output gap is the difference between the full capacity output[2] (Y_{fc}) and the current output (Y). The output gap ratio is output over the output gap, and the inflation gap is the difference between current inflation and the target of inflation (Π^*). As in the standard Taylor rule, I add a neutral interest rate, exogenously fixed at 2 per cent as Keynes in the *General Theory*. The inflation target is also 2 per cent. At the steady state, the key interest rate is equal to 3 per cent. The key interest rate should be 4 per cent for the real key interest rate, which equals the neutral interest rate ($i_{cb} - \Pi^* = i^* = 2$ per cent) and for the three gaps (output, inflation and interest rate) which are equal to zero. But the output gap is always positive, involving a lower key interest rate (3 per cent).

The monetary rule of the central bank is:

$$i_{cb} = i^* + \Pi - \alpha_4 \cdot OG_R + \alpha_6 (\Pi - \Pi^*) \tag{8.37}$$

8.7 Inflation

I am assuming that income distribution is constant in the short term.[3] This approach corresponds to the Kaleckian view where the long run is conceived as a 'slowly changing component of a chain of short period situations' (Kalecki, 1971b: p. 165).

$$W = Y/(1 + \rho) \tag{8.38}$$

with ρ: constant.

We adopt the Kaleckian mark-up pricing principle to explain prices; this asserts that prices are determined by unit costs, however measured, to which entrepreneurs add a mark-up. Entrepreneurs set prices after the determination of nominal wages; so entrepreneurs have a profit target and themselves set real wages and income distribution. This explains why income distribution is constant, even with inflation. According to Kalecki, the mark-up depends on the degree of monopoly, and this measures the balance of power between entrepreneurs and workers relating to nominal wages in the labour market. So the theory of price inflation is not explained by a change in income distribution, but by the requirements of the nominal wages of workers. This balance of power is measured by the output gap.

If GDP growth is strong and reduces the output gap, workers may demand higher nominal wages. If they are successful, the entrepreneurs will transmit the extra costs to their prices without delay to maintain their profit rates (the mark-up being constant). The result is an acceleration of inflation. But with an economic crisis and rising unemployment, wages rise more slowly than inflation. Inflation is slowed as long as entrepreneurs prefer to maintain the same income distribution and lower prices, trying to sell their total production; a deflationary trend may even develop.

So inflation and deflation stem from the productive sector. Except with significant supply and demand shocks, workers demand an increase in their wages that corresponds to the level of inflation in the steady state. Their inflation expectations are anchored on the inflation target of the central bank: the inflation target of the monetary policy becomes self-fulfilling. So there is a 'corridor of stability' where inflation expectations are anchored on the target (inflation targeting). Leijonhufvud (1981: p. 112) coined the word 'corridor', meaning the idea that for small disturbances the inflation rate is stable while for large disturbances it is unstable; the economy has stability inside the corridor, while it will lose stability outside.) Such a 'corridor of stability' can provide another way of looking at Keynes's insight that the economy is not violently unstable. When inflation is low and close to its target, I consider that the expectations of inflation are anchored on the target; in this case, inflation does not react to the variations of output gap (OG_R). Inflation depends only on the anticipated inflation (Π^a) that is anchored on the target: $\Pi^a = \Pi^*$. This leads to a horizontal curve. But if the variations in output are too significant (for instance, close to full capacity output) or if an exogenous supply shock occurs (for instance, a shock in productivity or in the oil price), inflation is the reaction. Inflation reappears over OG_{Rmini}, and disinflation under OG_{Rmaxi}.

Inflation can also occur from exogenous supply shocks, that is a cost-push (*CoP*), as productivity gains or a sharp rise in the price of oil. So we introduce this cost-push element.

To write the equation of inflation, I use the output gap:

$$\Pi = \Pi^a + d_1 \cdot (OG_{Rmini} - OG_R) + d_2 \cdot (OG_{Rmaxi} - OG_R) + CoP \quad (8.39)$$

$$\Pi^a = \Pi_{-1} + \theta_h \cdot (\Pi_{-1} - \Pi^a_{-1}) \quad (8.40)$$

To simplify, inflation is only used to determine the reaction of the central bank (monetary policy), and thus the changes in the short-term interest rates. All the values (flows and stocks) are nominal values and there are no fixed prices in the model. But it would be possible to introduce price explicitly into the set of equations to separate the changes in volume and prices in nominal flows or to introduce real wealth effects.

8.8 Experiments on confidence, income distribution, financial risks and crisis: the case of France

The purpose of this chapter is to understand how the US financial crisis has became a real global economic crisis, especially in Europe. Many transmission channels can be considered. For some European countries, the explanation may be found fairly easily: in Great Britain and Iceland, banks and financial activities were an important part of the GDP, and were highly globalised with distressed assets that contaminated banks around the world; in Spain and Ireland, speculative bubbles in the housing market developed apace, and in Spain the building sector was over 26 per cent of the GDP; the Irish business cycle was linked to the US business cycle; the British pound has depreciated greatly since 2007; Greece had already been experiencing structural problems, especially of governance, that could only be amplified by the financial crisis.

However, a large part of continental Europe had no specific reason for suffering its deepest depression since WWII. In much of Europe, there was no bubble in the housing markets; banks were moderately engaged in the speculative markets and their profitability remained strong. Households were unlikely to suffer a negative wealth effect, since their incomes or pensions were not linked to stock markets. Household debt was low when compared to the situation in the United States. European entrepreneurs are certainly living in a globalised world, but the US market is not an important outlet for European trade. Moreover, the US crisis involved a great moderation in prices of raw materials, and particularly a strong and rapid drop in the price of oil. It was good news for production, and Europe could expect lower inflation and lower interest rates. The euro has allowed 17 European countries to maintain stability of exchange rates with their key economic partners; Germany, for example, exports to many emerging countries, which have not experienced a major crisis and where high rates of growth are starting to rebound quickly. Finally no restrictive fiscal policy was conducted during the period 2005–2012. Instead, after the outbreak of the crisis, budget expenditures were substituted for the weakness of private initiative, with the danger of a sovereign debt crisis in Europe, but only after August 2011. Today, the search for a balanced budget in Europe increases the importance of the confidence of entrepreneurs and bankers, since the European government economic policies are no longer countercyclical.

My thesis is that the most important channel of transmission of the US financial crisis is confidence, and business confidence in particular, as this is what determines effective demand. Of course, I do not say it is the only factor. But I am particularly interested in psychological variables such as the state of confidence, because these variables play a key role in the post-Keynesian framework. With radical uncertainty, agents' expectations can become self-fulfilling prophecies. As Keynes said, in economics when people go out with umbrellas, it rains. Group expectations are the strongest predictor of future events, and the most important expectations are those of entrepreneurs. In the *General Theory*, Keynes stressed the importance of psychological variables in determining economic growth, particularly because of radical uncertainty.

The state of confidence of private agents affects the economy through two psychological laws which lie at the heart of the model:

- For entrepreneurs: the marginal efficiency of capital (expectations of the profits) that determines the 'effective demand' and therefore the current production, income and demand of external finance.
- For commercial banks: the liquidity preference that determines 'effective finance'. Indeed, as previously (Le Heron, 2007), we generalise the liquidity preference, understood as an increasing risk, to commercial banks.

A loss of confidence, which corresponds to a generalised liquidity preference, that is to say the fear of long-term commitment, leads rapidly to an economic crisis. Entrepreneurs want to stop investing, banks reduce lending and then households limit consuming. With the collapse of effective demand, household incomes decline, resulting *de facto* in a decrease of consumption.

As Keynes defined it so well in the *General Theory* (ch. 12, 1936: pp. 147–148):

> The considerations upon which expectations of prospective yields are based are partly existing facts which we can assume to be known

> more or less for certain, and partly future events which can only be forecasted with more or less confidence. [...] We may sum up the state of psychological expectation, which covers the latter as being the *state of long-term expectations*; [...]. The state of long-term expectation, upon which our decisions are based, does not solely depend, therefore, on the most probable forecast we can make. It also depends on the confidence with which we make this forecast – on how we rate the likelihood of our best forecast turning out quite wrong. [...]
>
> The *state of confidence*, as they term it, is a matter to which practical men always pay the closest and most anxious attention. But economists have not analysed it carefully and have been content, as a rule, to discuss it in general terms. In particular it has not been made clear that its relevance to economic problems comes in through its important influence on the schedule of the marginal efficiency of capital.

The entrepreneurs' vision of the future, and also the confidence that entrepreneurs have in this vision, largely determine the present and therefore what our future will really be. Thus Keynes demonstrated the simultaneous importance, in part contradictory, of animal spirits (spontaneous risk taking) and conventions (confidence in the stability of present). The crisis is reflected in lower animal spirits and the questioning of conventions.

Our reasoning applies to many European countries; nevertheless, I shall keep the specific French example as support for my modelling. The rate of growth in France dropped dramatically, to –4.5 per cent in the first quarter of 2009, and the unemployment rate rose from 7.6 per cent in May 2008 to 10 per cent in 2010–2012.

This model is a mathematical model of a closed modern economy, but it is not fully calibrated on the French economy. Therefore these experiments are only an attempt to simulate the state of confidence with some established confidence index figures in order to ascertain if we can define the stylised facts of the current period. Our thesis is that an important channel of transmission of the US financial crisis to the French growth crisis is confidence. But of course, it is not the only one.

8.9 Crisis in the state of confidence

I make simulations by imposing changes in the state of confidence corresponding to the period 2005–2012. To take into account the end of the speculative boom and the current crisis, I have taken the six-year period from January 2005 (INDEX = 100) to April 2012.[4] I have used the different monthly indicators elaborated by the French National Institute of Statistics and Economic Studies (INSEE); these indexes are calculated from monthly polls on a representative population. I have used the seasonally adjusted series. The calculated index of confidence drives our model and impacts the GDP and the real economy. I have not tried to explain these changes in the state of confidence; I have assumed that these changes impact the real economy and I have no feedback loop from the real economy (the GDP for instance) to the state of confidence of the private sectors. Then the state of confidence of the private sectors moves exogenously with the calculated expectations of the private agents; the model is thus 'forward looking'. Radical uncertainty is taken into account, since only the state of confidence of economic agents explains the variations from the model's steady state. However, to simplify the experiments and presentation of results and reduce the uncertainties in calculation, monthly inflation will be introduced as an exogenous variable by the true values and not by our inflation Equation (8.37), even if it provides a very good approximation. At steady state, inflation is 2 per cent; that is the situation of the early 2000s and the key interest rate is 3 per cent.

I assume that the financial crisis essentially involved a drop in the state of confidence of the economic agents, which then depressed the real economy. The aim is to deal with the channels of transmission of these psychological variables; I intend to show that psychological reactions (lower confidence) were sufficient to explain the spread of the financial crisis to the real sector. I follow the development of changes in the state of confidence of firms, and of commercial banks.

Following Kalecki and Keynes, the state of confidence of entrepreneurs affects the economy through investment and the effective demand, but the state of confidence of households (workers) cannot have a strong impact on economic growth as they merely spend what they earn. Indeed, as previously (Le Heron, 2007), we include the lender's risks and then, depending on their state of confidence, commercial banks can ration the finance requested by firms.

Although our economy is closed, the taking into account of the international dimension of the crisis in polls conducted among private agents justifies our integration of the global dimension of the real world.

8.10 The state of confidence of firms

In a post-Kaleckian framework, firms' expectations are the most important, because they explain 'effective demand'. For firms, I use an indicator of the state of confidence of firms (*SCF*) that summarises more than 18 issues: turning point indicator, recent changes in output, personal production expectations, inventory levels of finished goods, demand and total order books, demand and total export books, personal price expectations, general production expectations, and so on. I am taking into account expectations relating to international demand. The changes in the state of confidence of firms ($\gamma 0$) impact the desired rate of accumulation. It is a good proxy for the marginal efficiency of capital and the effective demand. Pessimistic expectations of firms depress effective demand and involve a supply shock and then a demand shock.

$$gr_{kD} = \gamma_0 + (\gamma_1 \cdot r_{cf-1}) + (\gamma_2 \cdot u_{-1}) - (\gamma_3 \cdot FCI_{-1}) \quad (8.6)$$

$$\gamma_0 = a_5 \cdot SCF \quad (8.6bis)$$

8.11 The central bank monetary policy and the state of confidence of commercial banks

The key interest rate of the central bank (*i*cb) reacts to the changes in inflation rate through a Taylor rule (Equation 8.37). According to Schumpeter, the bankers are considered entrepreneurs in money. For banks, there is not a specific index on the state of confidence of this sector, so I have used the French business climate index (*BCI*) that summarises the business tendency surveys of the different economic sectors in the way the banks usually did. This indicator of the French business climate influences the conventional level of the leverage ratio and the lender's risk. The index changes the coefficients (γ_4), (γ_5) and (γ_6) in Equations of lender's risk (8.21 and 8.26). Moreover, it changes the level of the conventional leverage ratio (quantity of firms indebtedness considered as normal (*levc*)).

$$LR = -\gamma'_4 + a_1 . (lev_{-1} - \gamma_5 \cdot lev_c) + b_1 \cdot spread \quad (8.21bis)$$

$$lr = -\gamma'_6 + a_3 \cdot (lev_{-1} - \gamma_5 \cdot lev_c) + \Pi^a \quad (8.26bis)$$

$$\gamma'_4 = \gamma_4 \cdot a_4 \cdot BCI \text{ and } \gamma'_6 = \gamma_6 \cdot a_6 \cdot BCI \quad (8.21ter)$$

$$\gamma_5 = a_2 \cdot BCI \quad (8.23)$$

I have put these processes together for an analysis of the state of confidence of the private sectors (banks and firms) with changes in inflation rate. In the trials, the respective importance of the different economic sectors (banks and firms) on the economic situation is not relevant; the objective is only to find the stylised facts. The changes in the state of confidence of banks and firms and in the key interest rate involve supply shocks, and then impact the household income, involving a shock of demand.

8.12 Experiments with inflation and the state of confidence of the French private sector

The drop in the state of confidence of firms at the beginning of 2008 mainly explains the decline of the growth rate of the economy, because it depressed effective demand, that is the desired growth rate of accumulation of capital. The crisis deepened after August 2008, and the rate of utilisation of productive capacity fell. However, it is the state of confidence of firms (effective demand) that is the driving sector in the economy; the economy is demand-led.

If we compare the observed rate of French real growth (growth rate compared to the same quarter of the previous year, seasonally adjusted, Trim-year GYSA, OECD) and our simulation with the state of confidence of firms, we note a strong convergence (Figure 8.1). Thus, introducing only the recorded confidence of French firms, the model reproduces the reality of the French production crisis and notably the shape in W: first, a sharp drop in 2008–2009, then a good recovery due to the fiscal deficit in 2010–2011, and then a new drop during the

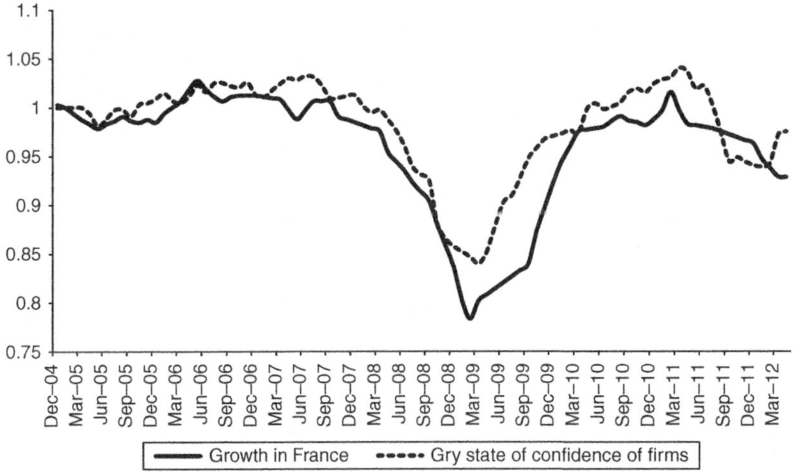

Figure 8.1 State of confidence of firms in France: effects on economic growth

second half of 2011. With the current public debt crisis and the new Stability and Growth Pact in Europe and its 'Golden Rule', economic recession continued in 2012. Of course, in real life, the crisis certainly influences the state of confidence and *vice versa*: they are clearly self-fulfilling prophecies.

Now we can add to inflation and the state of confidence of commercial banks. Inflation is introduced by the true monthly figures recorded, and the central bank responds by changing its key interest rate. With the deep crisis, monetary policy tries to avoid deflation, and then the flexible Taylor rule focuses on unemployment. The key interest rate drops rapidly to stop the fall in prices and asset prices. The influence of the output gap on the key interest rate is the same, but is lower than that of inflation. Commercial banks have also a responsibility, because financing conditions deteriorate. The consequence is a weak finance rationing of the investment of firms by private banks: $\varphi < \varphi d$ during the end of the boom. But during the crisis, the firms greatly reduce their demands for financing and consequently, there is no credit crunch, even if there is a significant fall in the profit of banks.

A credit crunch is not a satisfactory way to understand the transmission channel of this financial crisis to the real world. With the policy mix, the increased government deficit allows an increase in the cash flow of firms, and their self-financing increases. Government indebtedness substitutes that of firms, and the negative impact of the crisis in the banking sector on the government deficit is evident. A fall of the state of confidence in the private sector and the crisis suggest that the government should appear optimistic and support the effective demand with a huge fiscal deficit. In 2008, this was the case in France, with a deficit reaching 8.5 per cent of GDP. With these three variables (inflation, state of confidence of firms, state of confidence of banks), we obtain a good approximation of the crisis in France (Figure 8.2). So it is clear that the channel of confidence is an important explanation of the recent crisis.

In contrast to IS-LM, New Keynesians or the usual PK-SFC models, the interest rate curve is not exogenous. The spread between the short-term and long-term interest rates is not constant. First, the model shows the same evolution as the stylised facts of the last crisis: a rise of this spread, corresponding to higher lender's risk, when the key rate was decreasing at the central bank. Second, the central bank lowered its key interest rate faster than inflation, specifically to boost the prices of capital assets.

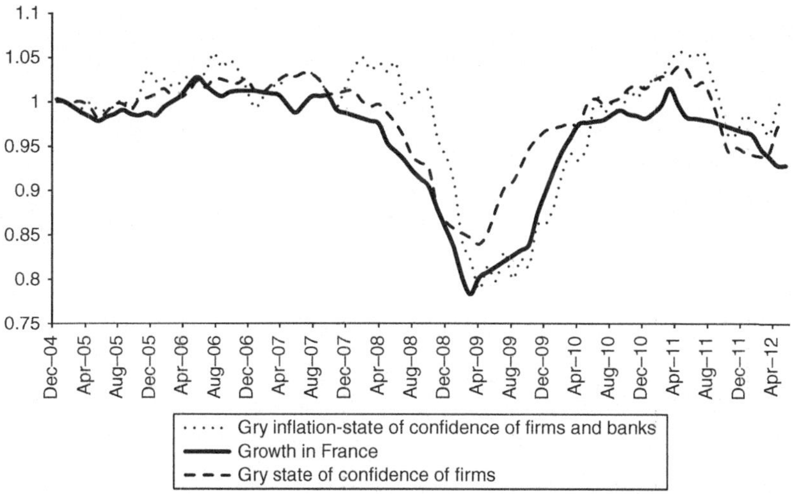

Figure 8.2 Inflation and state of confidence of firms and banks in France: effects on economic growth

We find that the real long-term interest rate decreased more slowly than other rates, which reduces the effect of expansionary monetary policy.

8.13 Income distribution: what policy to overcome the crisis?

We can use our post-Kaleckian model to examine two kinds of income policy currently proposed in Europe. First, we can make a better income distribution, lowering the tax rate on workers and increasing the tax rate on capitalists. However, we stabilise the tax rate of households as a whole, at 28 per cent of GDP; this income policy on households is at no cost for the State budget. The initial rate on workers and on capitalists was 50 per cent of their income, that is 22.5 per cent of GDP for the workers and 5.5 per cent for the capitalists. The tax rate on workers is reduced to 40 per cent, representing a decrease of about 3.5 per cent of GDP. Second, as has been requested in Greece, we can impose lower wages, representing a decrease of 2.5 per cent of GDP.

Of course, if we find that these income policies cannot prevent the crisis, more even income distribution allows better growth and reduces the fiscal deficit. On the other hand, lowering wages, by depressing the

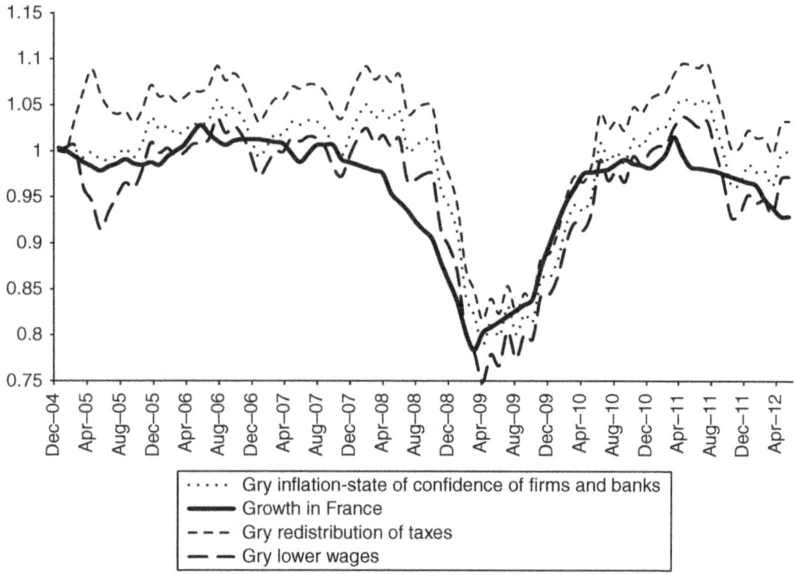

Figure 8.3 Two income policies: effects on economic growth

effective demand, exacerbates both the crisis and the fiscal deficit; wage cuts will never form the solution to a public debt crisis (Figure 8.3). So Angela Merkel is clearly not Kaleckian.

8.14 Conclusion

To better understand the latest financial crisis and its generalisation to the real world, I have tried to take into account the behaviour of private banks, the financial risks of firms and banks, and the psychological variables along with the state of confidence of private sectors. In order to achieve this, Kalecki, Kaldor and Keynes give an adequate framework. I can argue that confidence is a fundamental transmission channel of a financial crisis to the real world in a global society. First, I have tried to show that expectations play a key role in the transmission of the financial sector crisis to the real sector and could well be self-fulfilling. Firms' expectations are the keystone to understand the present. Second, a better income distribution is today's solution to restore economic growth without worsening public debt; choosing to reduce wages would reproduce the worst mistakes of the 1929 crisis.

Appendix 8.1 Glossary of variables

Y	National income
Y_{fc}	Output of full capacity
gr_y	Growth rate in the national income
Π	Inflation
Π^a	Expected inflation
Π^*	Inflation target
N	Employment
N_{fe}	Full employment
OG	Output gap
OG_R	Ratio of output gap
Un	Unemployment
r_{un}	Rate of unemployment
CoP	Cost push

Central Bank

P_{cb}	Central bank profits
REF	Reserve requirements (CB refunds)
H	High-powered money
i_{cb}	Central bank key interest rate
i^*	Neutral interest rate

Commercial Banks

L	Loans
P_b	Banks' profits
V_b	Net wealth of banks
i_d	Interest rate on deposits
i_l	Interest rate on loans
i_b	Interest rate on treasury bonds
FCI	Financial Condition Index
LR	Lender's risk
lr	Lender's risk for long-term interest rate
γ_4, γ_5	State of confidence of banks
lev	Leverage ratio
amort	Debt redemption

Firms

I	Net investment
I_D	Investment demand
W	Wages
K	Stock of capital
V_f	Net wealth of firms

u	Capacity utilisation rate
gr_k	Growth rate in the stock of capital
gr_{kD}	Desired growth rate in the stock of capital
ΔL	Net finance
φ	Gross finance
φ^d	Desired gross investment
IF	Internal Funds
$amort_L$	Amortisation of loans
P_f	Firms profits
P^d	Distributed profits
P^u	Undistributed profits
r_{cf}	Borrower's risk (ratio of cash flow)
γ_0	State of confidence of firms
Government	
G	Government expenditure
DG	Government deficit
g_{dg}	Constant ratio of government deficit
P_{cb}	Central bank profits
T	Taxes
T_H	Taxes on households
T_W	Taxes on workers
T_K	Taxes on capitalists
T_F	Taxes on firms
T_B	Taxes on banks
B	Treasury bonds
$amort_B$	Amortisation of bonds
Households	
C	Consumption of households
C_W	Consumption of workers
C_K	Consumption of capitalists
D	Bank deposits
D_W	Bank deposits of workers
D_K	Bank deposits of capitalists
${Y_W}^a$	Expected disposable income of workers
${Y_K}^a$	Exp. disposable income of capitalists
Y_H	Disposable income of households
Y_W	Disposable income of workers
Y_K	Disposable income of capitalists

Appendix 8.2 The complete model

(8.1)	$Y = C + I + G$	National income
(8.2)	$gr_y = \Delta Y / Y_{-1}$	Growth rate of national income
(8.3)	$OG_R = Y_{fc} - Y / Y_{fc}$	Output gap ratio
(8.4)	$Y_{fc} = K_{-1} \cdot \sigma$	Output of full capacity with σ: constant
(8.5)	$K = K_{-1} + I$	Stock of capital
(8.6-i)	$I \equiv \varphi + IF$	Net investment
(8.7)	$IF = P^u - amort_L$	Self financing
(8.8)	$amort_L = a_l \cdot L_{-1}$	Internal Funds
(8.9)	$I_D = gr_{kD} \cdot K-1$	Demand of investment
(8.10)	$\varphi^d = I^d - IF$	Desired gross investment
(8.11)	$gr_{kD} = \gamma_0 + \gamma_1 . r_{cf-1} + \gamma_2 . u_{-1} - \gamma_3 \cdot FCI_{-1}$	Desired growth in the stock of capital with γ_i: constant
(8.12)	$r_{cf} = P^u / K_{-1}$	Ratio of cash flow
(8.13)	$u = Y / Y_{fc}$	Capacity utilisation rate
(8.14)	$FCI = \mu_1 \cdot i_l \cdot L/K$	Financial Condition Index with μ_1: constant
(8.15)	$W = Y / (1 + \rho)$	Wages with ρ: constant
(8.16-ii)	$P_f \equiv Y - W - T_F - i_{l-1} \cdot L_{-1}$	Firms profits
(8.17)	$P^d = (1 - s_f) . P_{-1}$	Distributed profits with s_f: constant
(8.18-x)	$P^u \equiv P_f - P^d$	Non Distributed profits
(8.19)	$C = C_W + C_K$	Consumption of households
(8.20)	$C_W = (\alpha_1 . Y_W^a) + (\alpha_3 . D_{W-1})$	Consumption of workers with α_i: constant
(8.21)	$C_K = (\alpha_2 . Y_K^a) + (\alpha_4 . D_{K-1})$	Consumption of capitalists
(8.22)	$Y_w^a = Y_{W-1} + \theta_h . (Y_{W-1} - Y_W{}^a{}_{-1})$	Expected disposable income of workers with θ_h: constant
(8.23)	$Y_k^a = Y_{K-1} + \theta_h . (Y_{K-1} - Y_K{}^a{}_{-1})$	Exp. disposable income of capitalists with θ_h : constant
(8.24)	$Y_H = Y_W + Y_K$	Disposable income of households
(8.25)	$Y_W = W + i_{d-1} \cdot D_{W-1} - T_W$	Disposable income of workers
(8.26)	$Y_K = P^d + i_{d-1} \cdot D_{K-1} - T_K$	Disposable income of capitalists
(8.27-iii)	$D_W \equiv D_{W-1} + Y_W - C_W$	Bank deposits of workers
(8.28-iv)	$D_K \equiv D_{K-1} + Y_K - C_K$	Bank deposits of capitalists
(29)	$D = D_W + D_K$	Bank deposits
(8.30-xi)	$T \equiv T_H + T_F + T_B$	Taxes
(8.31)	$T_H = T_W = T_K$	Taxes on households
(8.32)	$T_W = \tau_1 \cdot W_{-1}$	Taxes on workers with τ_i: constant
(8.33)	$T_K = \tau_2 \cdot P^d{}_{-1}$	Taxes on capitalists

Continued

Appendix 8.2 *Continued*

(8.34)	$T_F = \tau_3 \cdot P^u_{-1}$	Taxes on firms
(8.35)	$T_B = \tau_4 \cdot P_{B-1}$	Taxes on commercial banks
(8.36)	$\Delta B = DG$	Treasury bonds
(8.37)	$i_b = i_l$	Interest rate on treasury bonds
(38)	$G = G_{-1} \cdot (1 + gr_{y\,-1})$	Government expenditure
(8.39-v)	$DG \equiv G + i_{b-1} \cdot B_{-1} - T - P_{cb} - amort_B$	Government deficit
(8.40)	$amort_B = a_b \cdot B_{-1}$	Amortisation of Government debt
(8.41)	$\varphi = \varphi^d \,.\, (1 - LR)$	Gross finance
(8.42)	$\Delta L = \varphi - amort_L$	Net finance
(8.43)	$LR = -\gamma_4 + a_1 .\, (lev_{-1} - \gamma_5 \cdot lev_c) + b_1 \cdot spread$	Lender's risk with $\gamma_{4,}$ a_1, b_1, and lev_c : constant
(8.44)	$lev = L / K$	Leverage ratio
(8.45)	$\gamma 5 = a_2 \,.\, BCI$	Changes in conventional leverage
(8.46)	$spread = i_l - i_{cb}$	Spread in interest rates
(8.47)	$i_l = i_{cb} + lr + \chi_1$	Interest rate on loans with χ_1: constant
(8.48)	$lr = \gamma_6 + a_3 \cdot (lev_{-1} - \gamma_5 \cdot lev_c + \Pi^a)$	Lender's risk for long-term interest rate with γ_6, a_3 and lev_c constant = convention on leverage ratio
(8.49)	$i_d = i_{cb} - \chi_3$	Interest rate on deposits
(8.50-vi)	$P_b \equiv i_{b-1} \,.\, B_{-1} + i_{l-1} \cdot L_{-1} - T_B - i_{d-1} \,.\, D_{-1} - i_{cb-1} \cdot REF_{-1}$	Banks profits
(8.51)	$H = \eta \,.\, D$	High powered money (bank reserves)
(8.52-vii)	$P_{cb} \equiv i_{cb-1} \cdot REF_{-1}$	Central bank profits
(8.53)	$i_{cb} = i^* + \Pi^a - \alpha_4 \,.OG + \alpha_5 \,(\Pi - \Pi^*)$	Central bank key interest rate
(8.54-viii)	$REF \equiv REF_{-1} + \Delta H + \Delta B + \Delta L - P_b - \Delta D - amort$	Reserve requirements (CB refunds)
(8.55-xii)	$amort \equiv amort_B + amort_L$	Amortisation of debt
(8.56)	$\Pi = \Pi^a + d_1 \,.(\, OGRmini + OGR) + d_2 \,.\, (OGRmaxi + OGR) + CoP$	Inflation
(8.57)	$\Pi^a = \Pi_{-1} + \theta_h \,.\, (\Pi_{-1} - \Pi a_{-1})$	Expected inflation
(8.58-ix)	$REF = H$	Missing equation[5]

Appendix 8.3 Transactions matrix

Sector / Operation	Govt	Firms		Households		Private banks		Central Bank		Σ
		Current	Capital	Workers	Capitalists	Current	Capital	Current	Capital	
Consumption		$+C$		$-C_W$	$-C_K$					0
Government expenditures	$-G$	$+G$								0
Net investment		$-I$	$-I$							0
Wages		$-W$		$+W$						0
Taxes	$+T$	$-T_F$		$-T_W$	$-T_K$	$-T_B$				0
Interest on Treasury Bonds	$-i_{b-1}.B_{-1}$					$+i_{b-1}.B_{-1}$				0
Interest on loans		$-i_{l-1}.L_{-1}$				$+i_{l-1}.L_{-1}$				0
Interest on bank deposits				$+i_{d-1}.D_{W-1}$	$+i_{d-1}.D_{K-1}$	$-i_{d-1}.D_{-1}$				0
Interest on CB advances						$-i_{cb-1}.REF_{-1}$		$+i_{cb-1}.REF_{-1}$		0
Profits of firms		$-P$	$+P^u$		$+P^d$					0
Profits of banks						$-P_b$	$+P_b$			0
Profits of CB	$+P_{cb}$							$-P_{cb}$		0
Δ HPM							$-\Delta H$		$+\Delta H$	0
Δ T Bonds	$+\Delta B$						$-\Delta B$			0
Δ Loans			$+\Delta L$				$-\Delta L$			0
Amortisation	$-amort_B$		$-amort_L$				$+amort$			0
Δ Bank deposits				$-\Delta D_W$	$-\Delta D_K$		$+\Delta D$			0
Δ CB advances							$+\Delta REF$		$-\Delta REF$	0
Σ	0	0	0	0	0	0	0	0	0	0

Appendix 8.4 Balance sheet matrix

Sector Assets	**Government**	**Firms**	**Households**	**Private banks**	**Central Bank**	**Σ**
Capital		+ K				+ K
HPM High powered money				+ H	− H	0
Treasury Bonds	− B			+ B		0
Loans		− L		+ L		0
Bank deposits			+ D	− D		0
CB advances				− REF	+ REF	0
Net wealth	− B	+ V_f	+ D	+ V_b	0	+ K

Notes

1. More explanations can be found in Le Heron and Mouakil (2008) and Le Heron (2009) for a post-Keynesian model, and in Le Heron (2008 and 2011) for a Keynesian stock-flow consistent model, even if this model is a new one.
2. I totally reject the New Keynesian potential output founded on a NAIRU.
3. This has been the case in France for the last 15 years. The ratio W/Y and P/Y are the same even in 1970 and 2009. Changes in income distribution exist, but inside W/Y and P/Y
4. We have used the E-views 5.5 software. December 2004 is in fact the stationary state of the model.
5. We have defined the 34 variables of the transactions matrix introducing 24 new variables, and we now have the same number of equations (58) and unknowns. Furthermore, we have managed to use the M + N − 1 = 12 accounting identities (Latin numbering) issued from the transcription of the transactions matrix.

9

Kalecki's Macroeconomic Analysis and the 'Great Recession'

Malcolm Sawyer

9.1 Introduction

Kalecki wrote extensively on macroeconomic policies during the 1940s, which were years not only of war but also of high levels of employment; there was a sharp contrast with the preceding decade with its years of depression, often seen as following the Wall Street crash of 1929 and bank collapses in the early 1930s. Kalecki also looked ahead to the post-war world, where he saw the potential return of depression and unemployment. The recovery from the Great Depression had not been completed in the late 1930s, and for many countries (including the UK and the US) full employment was only secured with the onset of war. The 'Great Recession' has been running now for some five years, and, at the time of writing, unemployment in the euro area, for example, remains at over 11 per cent and output remains below the level of 2007. The prospects are for continuing high levels of unemployment and slow growth.

In this chapter we draw on Kalecki's writings in the mid-1940s written against a back-drop of an inter-war period plagued by high unemployment when any market-driven forces of recovery were clearly weak. One key part of Kalecki's approach related to the balance between savings and investment. For example, he argued that 'the problem of employment was already before the war more difficult in the USA than in the UK because the percentage of income saved at the same degree of employment of the available labour force was substantially higher, and because this percentage was not normally offset by corresponding higher ratio of private investment plus export surplus to the aggregate income' (Osiatyński, 1990: p. 586). The Great Recession has seen investment fall sharply, which has been one of the factors driving the recession. But even before the Great Recession there was a tendency for savings intentions to exceed investment intentions. In the aftermath of the Great Recession it would seem likely that investment will recover but in general is not likely to exceed the sort of levels (relative to GDP) observed prior to the financial crisis.

In his writings on macroeconomic policy and employment of the mid-1940s, Kalecki made significant contributions, of which we highlight the following.

First, in Kalecki (1943) he argued that full employment was technically possible through budget deficits and aggregate demand policies, but that there would be large social and political obstacles to full employment. Kalecki saw *laissez-faire* capitalism as inconsistent with sustained full employment. In rather typical laconic style, he concluded by saying that '"full employment capitalism" will, of course, have to develop new social and political institutions which will reflect the increased power of the working class. If capitalism can adjust itself to full employment, a fundamental reform will have been incorporated in it' (Osiatyński, 1990: p. 356).

Second, in Kalecki (1944a), he examined the budget deficit, investment stimulation and income redistribution as ways of raising and sustaining high levels of demand consistent with full employment. These are all ways of stimulating demand, though Kalecki saw limits to the possible stimulation of investment essentially because a tendency for the capital–output ratio to rise would entail some combination of falling capacity utilisation and reduced rate of profit. 'It must be realised that a permanent budget deficit is not the only way in which lasting full employment can be secured. The same end can be achieved by redistribution from higher- to lower-income grades which tends to increase consumption out of a given national income (because the propensity to save of the rich – especially if one takes into account undistributed profits – is higher than that of the poor' (Kalecki, 1997: p. 243)

Third, in Kalecki (1944b), he argued for the need for permanent budget deficits in the face of intentions to save exceeding intentions to invest. He criticised those who accepted that budget deficits would rise during economic downswings but who did not accept the arguments for the need for permanent budget deficits. As he argued

> there will emerge out of a consistent anti-cyclical policy a certain more or less stable level of private investment which by itself, i.e. without considerable assistance by loan expenditure of the public authorities, may fall short of the level required to 'fill the gap' of

> savings out of a full employment income. The White Paper does not propose to use public loan expenditure to push employment up to the level where unemployment, other than frictional, is abolished. (Osiatyński, 1997: p. 243)

Fourth, in Kalecki (1945) he argued that securing full employment in the post-war era would require budget deficits in effect to offset the tendencies for intentions to save to exceed those of investment.

> The solution of the problem of employment after the transition will require a much more unorthodox policy in public finance in the USA than in the UK. The latter will certainly experience serious difficulties in the sphere of foreign trade [...] However, the financial problems involved in securing a national expenditure adequate to maintain full employment is likely to be of a much smaller order than in the USA. (Osiatyński, 1990: pp. 400–401)

In the outturn, there were much higher levels of employment than in the inter-war period through a combination of higher rates of investment and budget deficits, where expenditure on armaments played a significant role especially in the USA (Osiatyński, 1991: part 4).

9.2 Imbalances between savings and investment and budget deficits

In Kalecki's analysis, investment is a relatively volatile component of aggregate demand driving cyclical fluctuations, and the general rate of investment depends on a range of factors such as technological opportunities and degree of monopoly. Savings are largely undertaken out of profits, and Kalecki often used the working assumption of low or zero savings out of wages. Although savings and investment decisions are often made by firms, and profits are a source of savings and influence upon investment, savings intentions are not matched by investment intentions. When workers undertake savings (often in the form of pension funds), the possible mismatch between savings and investment is intensified in that if savings and investment are to be in balance, the firms' demands for external funds have to match the savings undertaken by workers and rentiers – a line of argument which was emphasised by Kalecki's colleague, Josef Steindl.[1]

There are two well-known conclusions to be drawn from Kalecki's general approach. First, there are no mechanisms which would aid the equality between savings behaviour and investment decisions to readily arise (as envisaged in much of the pre-Keynesian macroeconomics where the rate of interest was often seen as being set to achieve that outcome). Savings and investment are brought into equality through changes in the level of economic activity. But when there is a general tendency for savings intentions to exceed investment intentions, then there is a strong need for budget deficits, in effect, to absorb the difference between savings and investment. Second, the general tendency and pressures to invest will differ across time and across countries: the range of technological opportunities, the pressures or otherwise of competition, the terms on which loans and finance are available and so on.

With, broadly speaking, the capital–output ratio constant, the rate of investment (relative to GDP) is closely related to the growth rate of the economy. The experience of most industrialised countries in the past 40 years may suggest a growth rate of the order of 2 to 3 per cent per annum. Taking that range (without accepting that it is some 'natural' rate of growth, and acknowledging that pace of demand can have impact on the growth rate) with a capital–output ratio of 4 would indicate net investment to GDP of around 8 to 12 per cent, and then gross investment of the order of 16 to 20 per cent. A key question then becomes: how would a rate of gross investment of that order of magnitude compare with the ratio of intended savings to income? If there are marked differences, there is little that interest rate changes and the like can do to reconcile them. But if they cannot be brought into some equality then either there needs to be substantial budget deficits (in the case that savings rate exceeds investment ratio) or there will be deflation and unemployment.

A feature of the past two to three decades has been a general tendency in the direction of income inequality and a shift from wages to profits tending to increase the rate of savings. Some summary figures for the major European economies and the euro area are given in Table 9.1., averaged over the years 2001–2007 as indicative of the average rates of investment and savings (relative to GDP) covering a cycle prior to the onset of the financial crisis. The significance we draw from those figures is the general tendency for savings to exceed investment.

In Table 9.2, the corresponding figures for budget deficit and current account position are given, and, of course, conform to the national income accounts identity of S – I = BD + CA where S is private savings, I private investment, BD budget deficit and CA capital account position (equal to negative of current account position).

Table 9.1 Savings and investment relative to GDP, 2002–2007

	Private savings/GDP	Private investment/GDP
Germany	23.6	16.8
France	19.0	16.6
Italy	20.7	18.5
UK	15.3	15.3
euro area	20.8	17.7

Note: All figures are in percentages.*Sources:* Calculated from Eurostat, OECD Economic Outlook.

Table 9.2 Budget deficit and current account relative to GDP

	Budget deficit/GDP	Current account position/GDP
Germany	2.7	4.1
France	2.9	–0.6
Italy	3.2	–0.9
UK	2.4	–2.5
euro area	2.0	1.2

Note: All figures are in percentages.*Sources:* Calculated from Eurostat, OECD Economic Outlook.

Kalecki argued that there would be a need for permanent budget deficits, and not just deficits during some parts of the cycle offset by surpluses elsewhere. He pointed out that the conditions in which a deficit is required are those in which the funding of the deficit does not present difficulties, simply because there is an excess of private savings over private investment (which can only be realised if there is a budget deficit). The 'Treasury view', which has come back with a vengeance in the form of the euro area Fiscal Compact as discussed below, was associated with the idea of the government seeking to balance the budget on an annual basis. It was realised that, in a downswing of economic activity, tax receipts would fall, opening up a budget deficit, and that attempts to correct that budget deficit through expenditure cuts and tax rate rises would make matters worse. There was therefore an appreciation of the role of 'automatic stabilisers', and the role of 'big government' in providing a cushion against fluctuations in private economic activity. The White Paper on Employment Policy cemented that view; it argued that 'to the extent that the policies proposed in this Paper affect the balancing of the Budget in a particular year, they certainly do not contemplate any departure from the principle that the Budget must be balanced over a longer period', and there was also concern in reducing 'that part of the public debt which is a dead-weight war debt' (Ministry of Reconstruction, 1944: p. 25). Kalecki (1944a) argued that the White Paper on Employment Policy had 'not presented a programme for lasting full employment which must be based either on a long-run budget deficit policy or on the redistribution of income' (ibid: p. 135). The rationale for this view was straightforward: either a budget deficit was needed to mop up with the difference between full employment savings and investment, or full employment savings had to be reduced through a redistribution of income (from rich to poor). Kalecki regarded the third logical possibility, stimulating investment, as limited: 'private investment must be pushed up to the level sufficient to expand the productive capacity of capital equipment *pari passu* with the increase in population and productivity of labour' (Kalecki, 1944b: p. 57) but no further, because of a rising capital–output ratio and falling rate of profit. (In this Kalecki was incorrect since, for a higher investment to output ratio, the capital–output ratio initially rises but then levels out.) He also argued that

> the proper role of private investment is to provide tools for the production of consumption goods, and not to provide enough work to employ all available labour [...]. Both public and private investment should be carried out only to the extent to which they are considered useful. If the effective demand thus generated fails to provide full employment, the gap should be filled by increasing consumption and not by piling up unwanted public or private capital equipment. (Kalecki, 1944b: pp. 52–53)

The perspectives coming from the writings of Kalecki make the implementation of the Fiscal Compact by the euro area countries problematic to say the least (suicidal may be a more appropriate term). The Treaty on Stability, Coordination and Governance in the Economic and Monetary Union (European Union, 2012, hereafter referred to as the Treaty) of which the Fiscal Compact is the central part, and the associated so-called 'six pack' of policy measures, seek to enshrine balanced budget requirements on all member countries. These involve the imposition of a 'structural budget deficit' rule such that that notion of budget deficit does not exceed 0.5 per cent of GDP, with a stricter policy imposed on countries with a debt ratio exceeding 60 per cent of GDP to run surpluses to bring down the debt ratio. The deficit requirement is to be written into a country's national constitution or equivalent.

The writing of requirements on the achievement of a structural balanced budget into the national constitution embeds economic policy into the constitution, whereas ideas on appropriate economic policy are not unchanging over time. It seems a folly to incorporate ideas that some, but no means all, think are appropriate policies into a document which is difficult to change, especially when those ideas are mistaken. It can also be seen as an attempt to tie the hands of the electorate and future governments on economic policies. Further, the implementation of a balanced structural budget requirement will be made difficult by disputes over the measurement of the structural budget position.

The key point which comes from the writings of Kalecki is that there is little reason to think that full employment and a balanced budget are mutually compatible. In the context of the Fiscal Compact, this has shifted to whether a zero output gap (actual output equal to potential output) and balanced budget are compatible. The Kaleckian response would have to be that since there is little reason to think that savings intentions and investment intentions would be equal at full employment or at a zero output gap, there is little reason to think that a structural balanced budget is possible. The argument needs to be modified insofar as a country's net exports and corresponding lending abroad can absorb the excess private savings over investment. But that is clearly not a universal option since global net exports must sum to zero. The Fiscal Compact seeks to impose a 'structural balanced budget' which may often be impossible to achieve (and recall that the Fiscal Compact is to be imposed on all members of the EMU).

The post-war period unemployment situation turned out to be much better than the pre-war situation, and better than would have been anticipated from the writings of Kalecki. Although lower rates of unemployment were generally achieved in the industrialised world, it was rare for full employment to be achieved. Along with budget deficits and forms of 'military Keynesianism', the rate of investment was substantially higher, along with faster rates of growth. These were mutually reinforcing, and meant that a higher rate of investment did not lead to the rising capital–output ratio and falling rate of profit which Kalecki had seen as a major limit on the use of investment as a stimulus for demand. A major question now is whether investment rates (relative to GDP) will be higher in the future than they have been during the recession – and, more significantly, higher than in the pre-crisis decade. If the investment rate is indeed higher, then the budget deficit requirements diminish and a 'structural balanced budget' may become feasible. But – recognising the hazards of forecasting in a world of path dependency and fundamental uncertainty – it would seem much more likely that the investment rate will be lower in the future. The processes of financialisation have tended to lower investment rates.[2] Of particular importance is the requirement that a higher sustainable investment rate would have to be matched by a higher rate of economic growth, which runs into issues of environmental sustainability.

9.3 A Kaleckian model

Some of Kalecki's central ideas on income distribution and macroeconomics can be readily summarised: the distribution of income between wages and profits can be viewed in terms of the degree of monopoly which in its simplest form refers to market power and the ability of firms to mark up price over costs, the volume of profits being closely related to the amount of investment (in the simple form where there are no savings out of wages in a closed economy, profits equal to investment/propensity to save out of profits). Two further aspects of Kalecki's approach are worth noting, though they play a much less prominent role. First, in Kalecki (1971a), he sought to broaden the idea on the degree of monopoly with the power of trade unions, in effect placing limits on the degree of monopoly. Second, labour payments were divided into wages (of manual workers) which were marked up in pricing, and salaries (of non-manual workers) which were not marked up and in effect were paid out of the surplus and a deduction from profits. Since Kalecki wrote on this in the 1930s, the balance between manual and non-manual workers has, of course, changed dramatically and the division as represented by Kalecki no longer relevant. However, the distinction amongst employees between those who manage and make key decisions and those who are managed remains highly pertinent. Employment income cannot then be treated as homogenous, but rather the income of top managers be treated as more akin to an extraction from profits, and the propensity to spend out of employment income of top managers would differ (being much lower) than the propensity to spend out of other employment income.

The Kaleckian models (which involve some differences from Kalecki but can be used to highlight some salient features) stemming from Bhadhuri and Marglin (1990) are along the following lines:

We start with a savings function of the form:

$$\frac{S}{K} = \frac{sP}{K} = s\frac{P}{Y}\frac{Y}{Y^c}\frac{Y^c}{K} = \frac{smu}{v} \tag{9.1}$$

This is a classical savings function whereby there are savings (S) out of profits (P), but with no savings out of wages. The inclusion of savings out of wages, provided that the propensity to save out of wages is less than the propensity to save out of profits, would make no essential difference to the analysis (though it would if the relative ownership of the capital stock by capitalists and workers were relevant). The actual output is Y; then Yc is capacity output (in the sense of the physical limit), K a measure of the capital stock, v the capital–capacity output ratio, and $u = Y/Yc$ is capacity utilisation.

Investment, I, is modelled as dependent on the rate of capacity utilisation u, the profit margin being expressed as profits/output and denoted by m, and a variable μ a range of factors which influence investment, such as the state of 'animal spirits', the impact of technological opportunities and so on, and which vary over time; as a shorthand below μ is referred to as 'animal spirits'. Savings and investment are normalised by the capital stock K which provides a ready entry into growth rate (of capital stock). The rate of profit (P/K) is given by mu/v, and hence could be viewed as influencing investment through m and u (Bhadhuri and Marglin, 1990). A linear form of the investment function is used for convenience:

$$\frac{I}{K} = \alpha u + \beta m + \mu \tag{9.2}$$

As a prelude to the discussion below, we denote by u^* a socially desired rate of capacity utilisation. It is anticipated from a Kaleckian perspective that in terms of the notation above in general (but not always) $u < u^*$, and the employment rate is less than what would be considered full employment.

In a Kaleckian framework, the inadequacy of aggregate demand to secure high levels of capacity utilisation can be readily interpreted such that at the desired level of capacity utilisation the intention to save would exceed the intention to invest, that is:

$$\frac{smu^*}{v} > \alpha u^* + \beta m + \mu \tag{9.3}$$

This equation encapsulates some key features of a Kaleckian approach, in that there is a tendency towards an excess of savings over investment, and where there is a lack of market forces which would reconcile savings and investment at a high level of economic activity (whether that is represented by full employment, target capacity utilisation and so on) it is changes in the level of economic activity which serve to bring actual savings and investment into line with each other.

The fiscal policy stance and foreign trade are now introduced into the savings and investment behaviour. Fiscal policy is represented here by the inclusion of the term d, the fiscal deficit relative to the capital stock, and net exports relative to the capital stock by the term x. The condition injections = leakages then becomes:

$$\frac{smu}{v} = \alpha u + \beta m + \mu + d + x \quad (9.4)$$

This can be also read as domestic private savings equal to domestic investment, budget deficit and capital account deficit (equal to net exports). Time subscripts are introduced to indicate that variables such as profit margin and 'animal spirits' vary over time. From equation (9.4), the rate of capacity utilisation is given by:

$$u(t) = \frac{(\beta m+\mu+d+x)v}{sm-\alpha v} \quad (9.5)$$

The rate of growth is set by the rate of investment, and the differences between savings and investment are absorbed by the budget deficit. It can be readily seen from equation (9.4) that the budget deficit is funded from the difference between savings and investment, and that the budget deficit 'crowds in' with its positive effect on capacity utilisation.

The growth of the capital stock (equal to I/K) is given by:

$$g_K(t) = \frac{\alpha(d+x)v + sm(\beta m+\mu)}{sm-\alpha v} \quad (9.6)$$

In this framework it can be readily seen from equation (9.5) that a budget deficit has a positive effect on capacity utilisation. From equation (9.6), it can also be seen that the budget deficit would impact positively on the (one period) rate of growth of the capital stock. The one period rate of growth of output would be based on the growth of the capital stock and change in capacity utilisation. There would be limits, coming from the growth of the labour force and of labour productivity on the rate of growth of output and of the capital stock, which are sustainable. This is not to accept some simple 'natural rate of growth' story, since the growth of supply potential would itself be dependent on the growth of demand (Sawyer, 2011). But it is to recognise that there is some upper limit on sustainable investment and growth of the capital stock.

In effect, the budget deficit is set to enable investment expenditures to come through without being held back by savings behaviour. The appropriate scale of budget deficit can be readily calculated from these equations, where appropriate means the budget deficit required to secure the target level of economic activity, and capacity utilisation u^*. Thus from equation (9.5) the appropriate budget to secure u^* is:

$$d = \frac{smu^*}{v} - \mu - \beta m + \alpha u^* \tag{9.7}$$

This is easy to write down algebraically, but it would be extremely difficult in practice to make precise calculations of what is required. But it does represent a general principle, namely that the budget deficit should be targeted to achieve macroeconomic objectives, here represented as a desired rate of capacity utilisation. As such it stands in contrast with the prevalent view that budgets have to be balanced. The appropriate budget deficit would depend on a wide range of factors, which are here seen to be the profit margin (and hence the distribution of income between wages and profits), 'animal spirits', which drive investment (and more generally the tendencies and pressures on investment) and the savings propensity. The calculation of that budget deficit at any point in time is clearly not a straightforward exercise, for even in this simple model (in which, for example, foreign trade has been ignored) knowledge of key parameters is required, yet those parameters vary over time.

A fuller analysis of the role of fiscal policy would need to enquire into the composition of taxation and of public expenditure. The structure and level of tax rates would have effects on the savings and investment functions. The latter would need to distinguish components of public expenditure (notably public investment, but also education expenditure) which impact on the growth rate of the capital stock both directly and indirectly through their impact on private investment decisions. The relevant capital stock for growth purposes would be extended to include (at least part of) public capital (for example, infrastructure). The growth of the productive potential of an economy would depend on both private and public investment – and public investment, through its demand- and capacity-building effects, can be an effective stimulant of private investment.

The budget deficit which is relevant for the scale of fiscal stimulus is the total budget deficit (that is primary deficit plus interest payments). A continuing budget deficit (relative to capital stock) of d would then lead to the government debt (relative to the capital stock) stabilising at d/g when d has been measured in real terms (that is with allowance for the depreciation of the national debt as a consequence of inflation). In the absence of appropriate fiscal policy, the Kaleckian approach would imply that the economy would languish with a low level of capacity utilisation (and general implication of substantial unemployment) and low growth rate (which is demand-determined). A budget deficit of d raises the growth rate by $\alpha d/(sm - \alpha v)$ (as compared with a balanced budget).

A key element in a Kaleckian approach is the distribution of income and its impact on the level of aggregate demand. As indicated in the introduction, Kalecki envisaged that shifts in the distribution of income in the direction of less inequality and higher wage share would stimulate the level of demand. This perspective places a different view on the roles of 'structural reforms' in the promotion of high levels of employment – simply, where de-regulation, more 'flexible labour markets', lowering of minimum wages are advocated, the effects on demand are likely to be negative, having an adverse impact on employment. In the model presented here, it is only the share of wages and profits which appear, and a fuller analysis would clearly require full consideration of the structure of taxes and earnings inequalities. It is well known that over the past three decades there have been substantial shifts in the direction of inequality and of higher profit shares. These shifts could have been anticipated to have raised tendencies to save, and hence to have raised the need for budget deficits. Indeed, as we have argued elsewhere (Sawyer, 2011), the progressive way to reduce budget deficits would be to reduce inequality, which would have the effect of reducing the need for a budget deficit to sustain demand.

9.4 Concluding comments

In this chapter we have drawn on the work of Kalecki to argue that budget deficits and reduction of inequality are two major ways to secure a level of demand appropriate for full employment. At the present juncture it would have to be recognised that a shortage of productive capacity following the Great Recession would be a significant constraint on the achievement of full employment. Kalecki's analysis is often portrayed with firms operating with excess capacity alongside labour being unemployed. There seems the implicit suggestion that there would be sufficient productive capacity to generate full employment if only there was sufficient effective demand. But Kalecki argued that the right balance between capital equipment and available labour, with sufficient capital equipment needs to employ all the available labour and to leave some capacity in reserve, would be needed to enable full employment without inflationary pressures. 'If the maximum capacity of equipment is inadequate to absorb the available labour, as will be the case in backward countries, the immediate achievement of full employment is clearly hopeless. If the reserve capacities are non-existent or insufficient, the attempt to secure full employment in the short run may easily lead to inflationary tendencies in large sections of the economy, because the structure of equipment does not necessarily match the structure of demand' (Osiatyński, 1990: pp. 361–362). The argument put here is that the extent to which countries are 'backward' (using the terminology of this quote) is more extensive than envisaged by Kalecki, and that shortage of capital equipment is a more widespread phenomenon.

Kalecki (1943) was a clear expression that although the economic conditions in terms of level of demand which were required for full employment were established and that the tools (budget deficits) which could be used to achieve that were also established, there were close to insurmountable political and social obstacles. The 'fundamental reforms' which Kalecki saw as necessary are more remote than ever. On an analysis from the work of Kalecki, the present directions of policy travel of fiscal consolidation and lack of any measures to seriously confront inequality will seriously jeopardise a return to low unemployment.

Notes

1. For example, Steindl (1979, 1982), and for a recent essay on Steindl's work see Shapiro (2012).
2. Hein (2012) argues that 'from a macroeconomic point of view financialization has affected long-run economic developments through the following three channels. With regard to distribution, financialization has been conducive to a rising gross profit share [...] and to increasing inequality of wages and top management salaries. [...It has] had partially negative effects on firms' real

investment in capital stock and hence on long-run growth of the economy to the extent that productivity growth is capital embodied. [...] it also generated increasing debt-income ratios of private households and thus increasing financial fragility' (pp. 2–3).

10
'The Accumulation of Capital' of Rosa Luxemburg, and Systemic and Structural Reasons for the Present Crisis

Janusz J. Tomidajewicz

10.1 Introduction

The global financial and economic crisis that arose in September 2008[1] has again raised questions of the sources and causes of crises in capitalistic economies. The explanation of the reasons and causes of the present financial and economic crisis that we find in so-called mainstream economics focuses mainly on the organisational, technical and subjective sources of the crisis.

Thus, it has been pointed out that the crisis on the real estate market in the United States is related to demand, with the occurrence of significant demand for mortgage credits, which is supported by the policy of the state or refers to subprime (Rosati, 2010: p. 114) credits.

However, from the supply point of view, the rising of the credit bubble on the market of the real estate credits is related to the increase in the liquidity of American banks and, accompanying it, the misjudgment of credit risk (over-optimism), as well as the influence of the securitisation on the evaluation and transfer of the credit risk (ibid: p. 120; Helwig, 2008).

Generally speaking, in such an approach to the problem explanations for reasons for the crisis can be presented by some simplification, such as exaggerated greed, or sometimes irresponsibility, or even simple mistakes made in assessments by managers of financial institutions, as well as weaknesses in the regulation of financial markets, which did not manage to restrain irresponsible operations by financial institutions. [2]

In this picture, the further spread of the crisis and its transmission to the real sphere, as well as the functioning of the global economy, result from such features in the modern economy as: the development of the derivative instruments market, the financialisation of the economy and the globalisation of financial markets.

However, such an approach seems insufficient to understand the deeper causes of the present crisis. It doesn't give answers to the questions: what was the reason that subjective mistakes and institutional imperfections, which were indicated as reasons for the crisis, could accumulate so much? And why, nearly 70 years after the Great Depression of the 1930s, did conditions recur that allowed a world financial and economic crisis to take place?

Finding answers to such questions requires a focus on the premises of the crisis that are connected not only with imperfections of functioning of financial and economic mechanisms, but also with the structure and the mechanisms of the functioning of the modern capitalistic world economy.

Proponents of the neo-liberal doctrine dominating the economic mainstream in recent decades have come up against a barrier in their research, resulting from a dogma that they cannot counter: this is that it is the market that must lead the economy to a state of long-term balance at its optimum level. This means that any aberration from this state should be treated only as a short-term disturbance of the perfectly functioning market mechanisms.

So research into the systemic and structural reasons for the present crisis has been undertaken mainly outside the main stream. In addition, the structural and system approach explaining the origins of the present crisis is interesting because, in contrast to mainstream economists, its supporters were unsurprised by the occurrence of the crisis. On the contrary they could understand it as the realisation of previously presented forecasts and warnings.[3] One of directions of research of structural explanations for the present crisis is to revive the works of Marxist theoreticians from the beginning of the 20th century, especially Rosa Luxemburg's *The Accumulation of Capital* (Gorz, 2008; Bauman, 2009a and 2009b; Kowalik, 2011; Bellofiore and Passarella, 2009), which was particularly fundamental. In her book, Luxemburg shows that the key structural source of crises in a capitalistic economy is its inability to provide a dynamic balance. This results from insufficient domestic demand that does not allow capitalists to realise the surplus value. The mentioned inability leads to the necessity of external expansion; in other words, expansion in a non-capitalistic economy is the only way to achieve a balance.

However, it is 100 years since the work of Rosa Luxemburg was published. During this time enormous technical and technological progress has taken place, and methods and institutions of functioning in the capitalistic economy have changed. The balance of political power in the world has changed significantly as well. The capitalistic economy has manfiested both a very great ability to adapt to changing conditions, and a skill in achieving long-term growth. Finally, during the 20th century the world witnessed the rise and fall of socialist economies, which as it turned out in the long term were unable to provide more effective management than capitalism.

In this situation it seems reasonable to ask once again whether Rosa Luxemburg's ideas can indeed serve as a basis for explaining the origins and the course of the current economic crisis. However, in view of the fact that the fundamental concept of Luxemburg is the inability of the capitalistic economy to grow without crises, the present chapter contains an attempt to consider the thesis on the inevitability of economic crises and the presumptive possibility of preventing crises in a market economy.

10.2 Luxemburg's interpretation of the essence and sources of the crisis

Rosa Luxemburg wrote her work on the problems of reproduction and accumulation of capital in order to explain more clearly the course of the process of reproduction and accumulation of capital in conditions of a capitalist market economy, and to ascertain answers to the questions of whether there are objective historical limits to the accumulation and, if so, why. Luxemburg had observed and understood the phenomena of economic fluctuation and the appearance of cyclical crises in the economy; she assumed crises to be the most striking characteristics of capitalistic reproduction. However, she accepted another starting point for her work: not searching for reasons and mechanisms creating economic crises, but studying conditions and the course of average (normal) processes of reproduction,[4] without taking into account the cyclical fluctuations that do occur (Luxemburg, 2011: p. 74).

As an aside, we can suggest that Luxemburg's methodological approach should be brought to the attention of those scientists who are currently studying the present economic crisis. Only when the analysis of the 'normal' reproduction process shows that the economy has the potential to maintain balance in this process is it possible to consider the reasons for deviations from this state which result in crises. However, if the analysis of the normal processes of growth leads us to the conclusion that it produces structural or institutional imbalance, our deliberation on the direct reasons for any particular crisis might only make our picture of the situation less clear and might hamper the identification of the primary sources of its appearance; this is the basic defect of these attempts to explain the present crisis within the so-called main stream (Tomidajewicz, 2010).

At the beginning of the 20th century Luxemburg sought to verify whether the capitalist market economy is able to guarantee balanced processes of growth (accumulation and increased reproduction of capital). Her attempt was a contribution to contemporary discussions led by Marxist economists on the problems related to the interpretation of the contemporary stage of development of capitalism; Tugan-Baranowski, Kautsky and Lenin took significant stands in this discussion.

From today's perspective, the discussion between Luxemburg and her contemporary opponents is, of course, not very important. However, the relevant thing is what she said in *The Accumulation of the Capital* about conditions for sustainable growth in the capitalist economy. She started her analysis from the two-sector schemes of enlarged reproduction introduced by Marx, and she pointed at the fact that the basic problem of the process of expanded reproduction came from the fact that the surplus value requires a demand for goods produced so that it can be realised. The remuneration of the workers cannot provide this demand, because they form the demand for the part of production equivalent to the expenditure on the variable capital (workers can buy only a part of production that refers to their share in work inputs in the total value of the production). Therefore, this demand must come from capitalists, who create it on basis of the surplus value they have obtained. In addition, Luxemburg accepted that the part of the surplus value assigned to the consumption of capitalists does not encounter any difficulties in realisation; meanwhile, she pointed at the inability to realise the part of the surplus value directed to capital accumulation within the capitalist class itself. As a result, the part of the surplus value which is not dedicated to consumption of capitalists cannot be realised within this economy, because of lack of effective demand.

Luxemburg concluded from this reasoning that in order to provide stable growth of the capitalist market economy, it is necessary to find external sources of effective demand which enable the realisation of the surplus value produced in this economy (Luxemburg, 2011: pp. 427–428). In order to attain sustained growth, the economy must find or create new external (that is, non-capitalist) fields for the realisation of the surplus production. Luxemburg based her reasoning on Marx's two-section schemes of reproduction, where the dominant presumption is the lack of mobility of means between the sphere of consumption and investment. She also consistently applied the assumption that the one global capitalist economy is the object of the analysis and is treated as a single unit. It seems that both these assumptions became the reason why Luxemburg assumed that the condition of development is the expansion of capitalist production to non-capitalist economies; she dropped these assumptions to a certain extent when she considered militarisation and international loans as ways to create the effective demand lacking in the economy. In both situations, the additional demand (that is the demand that allows the realisation of surplus value) is not external to the capitalist economy, but comes from inside this economy. At one first point not realised accumulation is used for granting credits and creating this additional demand abroad. In the second case, using the agency of the State, it allows creating the direct demand for the 'surplus' production.

However, overruling the second assumption and accepting that the world capitalist economy is not subject of deliberation, but only the national economy of one country, leads to the conclusion that the expansion presented by Luxemburg as a condition necessary to maintain the balance in growth processes can take place not only by expanding non-capitalist forms of economy, but also in capitalist economies in other countries. However, this acceptance transfers the problem of maintaining the balance from the domestic economy to the level of the global economy; in this sense it does not solve the fundamental problem of whether the market economy is itself able to maintain the balance in processes of reproduction. However, the processes of reproduction in specific historical and economic situations can be explained more easily by accepting the possibility that the expansion of the market in other countries expands the limits of this economy to reproduce from the progressive disappearance (of liquidation) of non-capitalist economies to the much more distant situation of the equalisation of development in different capitalist countries.

Leaving aside the assumptions applied by Luxemburg, and allowing limited mobility of production in sectors I and II, means that the inconsistency between the material structure of production and the structure of effective demand is no longer the principal barrier to maintaining a balance. The main barrier is now the size of the total effective demand and the realised production. As Tadeusz Kowalik showed, the ultimate solution to the problem that Luxemburg assumed to obtain was not fully possible on the basis of Marx's two-sector model of reproduction. Only the interpretation by Michał Kalecki of this approach to the theory of aggregate demand revealed conditions that must be fulfilled for providing the continuity of processes of reproduction (economic growth, Kowalik, 2011: pp. 10–11).

Despite the weaknesses of Luxemburg's approach to explaining balanced growth in the capitalist economy, its fundamental theses and assertions still remain important; they point at the following:

1. Growing profits (surplus value) meet the barrier of realisation resulting from insufficient aggregate demand. In other words, there is a tendency to create a surplus of accumulation that has no rational use, or, from the other perspective, to create the demand gap that does not realise the production made.
2. In order to reduce this barrier it is necessary to find, or even create a demand that would realise the production, and thereby capitalist profits. Luxemburg presented examples of forming these (additional) artificial sources of demand: primarily expansion to non-capitalist economies, but also militarisation of the economy and international loan expansion.[5] Tadeusz Kowalik and Zygmunt Bauman show that many mechanisms of the modern economy are being used today for finding (forming) new fields of demand (Z. Bauman calls them 'pastures'); these can be: foreign debt, consumer credits, stock exchange bubble, subprime credits development, and so on (Kowalik, 2011: p. 14; Bauman, 2009a and 2009b).

At the same time we must remember that according to the accepted assumptions, Luxemburg did not usually examine sources or the origins of economic crises. For her such crises were the symptoms and consequences of the fundamental inability of the capitalist economy to realise sustainable development (expanded reproduction). Thus *The Accumulation of Capital* focused on the systemic sources of difficulties in the course of processes of growth (accumulation) of the capitalist economy and was therefore unable to present possibilities and ways of eliminating, or at least mitigating, those aspects of this economy that might lead to crises.

Luxemburg, like other Marxists and indeed Marx himself, believed that the only way to solve the problems of capitalist reproduction was by its transition to a socialist economy. But in considering the socialist economy, Luxemburg did not consider the problem of what conditions should be fulfilled in the division of the surplus product in order to guarantee a sustainable course for the processes of reproduction.

10.3 Problems and questions

The authors mentioned above (Gorz, 2008; Bauman, 2009a, 2009b; Kowalik, 2011; Bellofiore and Passarella, 2009) suggest that Luxemburg's work concerning systemic sources of crises in capitalist economy can be treated as inspiration for research into explanations for the crises in the world economy of the later 20th and early 21st century. However, we must point out these elements of Luxemburg's analysis which are less valid today.

Over the 100 years that have passed since Luxemburg's *The Accumulation of Capital* was published, the capitalist economy has survived several experiences that have had a crucial impact on the modern interpretation of her theory. Without any doubt, the most important experience was the birth, development and fall of the socialist economies. Thereby, the course of the historical processes that took place after the publication of the work of Luxemburg seem to prove how illusory were her hopes that a socialist economy would be able to solve the problems of balanced reproduction that are impossible to solve in a capitalist economy. At the same time the capitalist market economy has shown during the 20th century how well it is able to adapt to changing conditions and, despite the crises that have occurred, can still provide long-term economic development. This leads us to the following question: whether capitalist economic development since the publication of her book has managed to negate the contradiction examined by Luxemburg at the beginning of the 20th century, or whether the capitalist economy was using the possibilities of expansion presented by Luxemburg as well as new ones, appearing later.

The fundamental thesis on the inability to maintain balanced growth in capitalist economy remains important, mainly because during the last 100 years the development of this economy was accompanied by processes of expansion – on an international scale (first through colonialism, then in neo colonialism) and in the specific organisation of the international economic system, which enabled economic expansion of the most developed capitalist countries at the expense of developing countries and within the economy (militarisation, development of consumer credit, appearance of stock exchange bubbles, financialisation, and so on). The fact that along with the development of the capitalist economy we have had economic crises, especially the Great Depression of the 1930s and the current financial and economic crisis, shows that Luxemburg's basic theses are still relevant today.

However, it is important to notice that during the century since the publication of Luxemburg's work, nearly 70 years consisted of a period of relatively stable and sustainable development. This leads us to the following questions: Why did the world crisis on this scale appear only after over 70 years after the last major crisis? What factors prevented the crisis during those 70 years? And hat caused those existing factors to become ineffective after 70 years?

To answer these questions, we must refer to the main thesis formed by Luxemburg, that the very nature of the capitalist economy means that it is unable to create domestic demand sufficient to fully realise the surplus value produced on the market.

If we assume that this thesis is correct, we would have to admit that repeated crises are an indispensable element of the development of this type of economy, and thereby any attempts to eliminate them must fail. Therefore, the conclusion that we could draw would be close to the neo-liberal tenet that the crisis should be treated as a transitional phase of the developmental processes that is required in order to create the conditions for a repeated rise in the economy after the crisis has ended.

However, if it might be possible to show that after fulfilling the conditions for recovery the capitalist market economy is able to maintain balanced reproduction, the search for structural sources of crises and methods of prevention would be justified.

The observation of the historical course of processes of reproduction and the accompanying processes since Luxemburg's work provides arguments supporting both the thesis on the inevitability of crises and that on the ability of the market economy to avoid them.

From the point of view of our question, it is particularly important to discuss the situation in the period between the Great Depression of the 1930s and the financial and economic crisis of the late 2000s. Generally speaking, this 70- year period can be characterised as a time when the occurrence of crises was stopped (at least on a significant scale and in the global dimension). In addition two parallel phenomena appeared in this period.

On the one hand it was a period of vibrant external and domestic expansion of the economies in most developed capitalist countries. Without going into detail, such processes include: colonial and neo-colonial expansion, militarisation of economies connected at first with World War II and later with the Cold War; commercial expansion as a consequence of the liberalisation of the international monetary exchange; financial expansion associated with the coming into existence of the global financial market; and credit expansion allowing the development of domestic markets based on consumer credit.

However, in tandem with that external expansion, this period was also characterised by a specific approach to economic policy connected with structural changes in the mechanisms of the functioning of the economy.[6]

The noticeable change of paradigm in economic policy was expressed particularly in the increase of the role of the State in the creation of the final demand, as well as in highly progressive tax systems and the development of various mechanisms of budget redistribution in favour of the social groups with the lowest incomes. We can assume that the first aspect, the continuous external and domestic expansion of economies of the most developed capitalist countries, confirms Luxemburg's reasoning; the change of economic policy paradigm led to a change in the distribution of production indicating the possibility of achieving balanced reproduction while avoiding, or at least seriously reducing, the risks of economic crises (at least on the global scale). Still, the relatively crisis-free development of the most developed capitalist economies since the end of the Great Depression have resulted from many factors, not just one. The combination of these elements, which were combined in certain historical circumstances, enabled the course of economic processes that we could observe (Kołodko, 2011).

Of course, confirmation of any of these hypotheses would be made possible with suitable empirical studies. However, in view of the fact that many processes take place in tandem, the chances of assigning them weights that would determine their relative influence on the course of processes of reproduction seem small.[7] In this situation, maybe as Kalecki and Keynes suggested, and as was largely realised in the economic policy, changing the distribution of the social product can bring more effective results, and might constitute the premise for limiting and easing crises, a cyclical occurrence that characterises this economy.

In Luxemburg's reasoning, the key reason why the capitalist economy was unable to obtain long-term balanced reproduction was the lack of the final effective demand, which was on the one hand a consequence of tendencies of the capitalists to reduce outlay on wages (in Marxist terms, expenses on the variable capital) and on the other hand, from the necessity to realise profits (surplus value) from the sale of products constituting this surplus that could not be bought by the workers who had produced them; the remuneration (that is, the purchasing power) of the workers was minimised in the processes of production. Also in the investment sphere, finding markets for the products constituting produced profits met the same barrier, consumer demand, except that the barrier was postponed to the period after implementing investment and obtaining its production effect.

This method of presenting the problem leaves us with the open question as to whether the contradiction described here, concerning increasing profits and creating demand for the produced products, occurs independently of the distribution of income between wages and profits. It is a consequence of capitalists taking over the surplus product; or maybe the contradiction appears only when the surplus value taken over by capitalists is greater than the value they would be able to use rationally for increasing their consumption and for making investments justified by the growth of future effective demand. We cannot find direct answers to these questions in Luxemburg, although her analysis (based on two-sector models) seemed to convince her that this contradiction is crucially connected with the nature of the capitalist economy and therefore cannot be removed from it.

10.4 What results from it for possibilities of preventing crises?

In 1933, Kalecki reached conclusions that were to some extent different. Just like Luxemburg, he observed that the means accumulated by capitalists meet the barrier of insufficient demand in their realisation. However, he pointed at the fact that the way to create this demand might be achieved by State spending on public works and investment, and for increased consumption financed by the State with an additional money issue.[8]

The economic development in the main capitalist countries without crises, during the period when economic policy followed the guidelines of Kalecki and Keynes, seems to confirm the accuracy of these theories on the possibility of eliminating, or at least reducing, the principal capitalist contradiction, thanks to interventions of the economic policy, as presented by Luxemburg. Policy would fill the gap in demand that inevitably occurs in the course of free economic processes. The change in the distribution of income obtained via the redistributive role of the State could have been the additional factor here, functioning alongside the creation of the additional demand. In particular the strongly progressive income tax limited the surplus that could accumulate in the hands of capitalists searching for possibilities to invest efficiently. This enabled the State to finance institutions and operations that provided a wide range of social services, and created the necessary domestic demand in the economy.

The crisis-free course of economic development during the period between the Great Depression and the present economic crisis shows both those factors at work: very strong external and domestic expansion and the influence of the economic policy in reducing the gap in demand. The combination of the two factors explains the relatively sustainable course of the processes of reproduction during that period.

At the same time, this combination allows hypotheses relating to the return (after the 1970s) of the global economic crisis. We must point out here that from the early 1980s economic policies in most developed capitalist countries gradually started to retreat both from using instruments for stimulating domestic demand financed by additional State spending and from limiting the range and scale of the fiscal redistribution. The first, resulting primarily from monetarist theories, was closely related to the implementation of so-called 'sound' principles of monetary policy and to the independence of central banks and subordinating their monetary policy to retain the stability of money. The second was a consequence of the reduction of taxes for enterprises and the reduction of the tax levels on the highest incomes, as required by the management of demand.

Abandoning the Welfare State politics inspired by theories of Kalecki and Keynes (triggered by developmental problems that occurred in the 1970s and manifested in the phenomenon of Stagflation) initially allowed the countries adopting neo-liberal economic policy to regain their development dynamics. However, in time this led to an increase in the disproportion of incomes inside these economies, and to reduced State intervention in the domestic demand necessary for maintaining balance. Reduced State intervention in most developed capitalist countries required the use of the second mechanism – external and domestic expansion had to be strengthened and widened.

Observing from this perspective the course of processes of reproduction in the period of domination of the neo-liberal paradigm in the economic policy, we might state that from the 1970s an increase in exports related to the liberalisation of the international exchange became more and more important in the processes of growth. Next, because of the liberalisation of the international financial markets, credit and capital expansion became stronger. At the same time, facing the risk of domestic demand shrinking due to reduced income redistribution, demand started being supported by the development of the consumer credit. As a result, the potentially widening gap between the growing accumulation (savings) and the relatively decreasing domestic consumer demand was filled by the development of production for export stimulated by foreign credit and by the creation of additional investment opportunities for profits in domestic and international financial markets. The growth of foreign investment in instruments of the international and domestic financial market involving the development of new technologies, or so-called emerging markets, as well as the development of domestic consumer credit (including home loans), all constituted ways to fill the growing gap between rising accumulation and the insufficient development of final demand. Thanks to these mechanisms, and despite the withdrawal from demand management policies, the economies in most of the developed capitalist countries retained their ability to maintain a balance in the processes of reproduction for the following 30 years, until the onset of the current global economic crisis,.

However, it is important to notice here that external and domestic expansion can efficiently produce balanced processes of development, but only under the condition that the expected profits are realised. In the situation in which the expansion takes place through a simple development of exports, this drains the markets of the importing countries. This causes the impoverishment of these countries, and it means that the expansion of the most developed countries takes place at the cost of the countries at an earlier stage of development. This situation corresponds best to the expansion of capitalist economies in their non-capitalist environment as described by Luxemburg. However, the possibilities of such expansion are obviously limited because of the restricted range of and resources possessed by these economies. In this situation, facing an insufficient absorption of domestic markets, it is necessary to stimulate external markets through investment and credit expansion, in order to maintain the expansion. This solves for a certain amount of time the problem of scarcity of external demand. However, in this case, too, the expansion meets the barrier of the ability to obtain the required rate of return from the invested capital. In situations where the expected rates of return cannot be achieved, a more or less violent withdrawal of invested capital takes place, and then a local financial and economic crisis takes place. The last 30 years of domination of the neoliberal model witnessed many such crises in, for example, Argentina, Mexico, Russia and Indonesia. Also, so-called 'stock exchange bubbles' were arising and bursting. They were related to the exaggerated commitment of capital assets to chosen sectors and directions of investment. The dotcom bubble is the most typical example; its bursting in 2000 initiated a new stock exchange crisis.

A method of creating demand in developed countries was the development of consumer credit. The fact that in 2007 the average debt of an

American citizen (without counting mortgage debt) was over US$16,000 (Ciszewski, 2008) illustrates the scale of the phenomenon. It could be said that the facing of the reduction of the redistributive function of the State to create incomes that might stimulate domestic demand was replaced by a private credit system. Yet, comparing that with the redistribution of incomes, offering credit for consumption has the disadvantage that credit must be paid off. This might cause on one hand the reduction of demand in future, which means renewed difficulty in the process of development of the economy resulting from insufficient demand – but on the other hand, when consumers renege on contracted credit, the profitability of conducting the credit business falls and owners of surplus of funds lose a crucial location for investment. These weaknesses of the credit mechanism in stimulating the economy were revealed very clearly, in the case of the American mortgage debt market. Its crisis initiated the global financial and economic crisis. While the redistribution of incomes by the State gives a definite boost to demand, the stimulation of demand by consumer credit is a mechanism that renews imbalance.

10.5 Conclusion

It is possible to construct the following hypotheses concerning the principal reasons for the appearance of crises, as well as the possibilities of providing balance in the processes of reproduction in the capitalist economy:

1. The capitalist economy, in its liberal and neo-liberal version, matches Luxemburg's analysis of the capitalist economy, in which there is, due to the lack of effective demand, an inevitable contradiction between the capitalist tendency to maximise profits and the possibility of realising them. This contradiction leads to cyclical outbreaks of economic crises, which, in the processes of reducing the production and bankruptcies, 'eliminate' the part of the economic activity that had developed on the basis of the accumulation that had been unable to find a market. This process might be stopped or tempered as a result of finding external and domestic fields of market expansion. However, this expansion has some structural and natural limits, which may only postpone the crises; then they have a correspondingly greater scale and range, so they become global crises.
2. The possibility of overcoming the fundamental contradiction in the development of the capitalist economy occurs if we constrain the free market model (liberal and neo-liberal) to functioning through

state economic intervention. This is especially so if this intervention constitutes an active monetary and budget policy that creates both an additional domestic demand 'from nothing' and the redistribution of incomes limiting excessive accumulation (over-accumulation), increasing the effective consumer demand, and eliminating the contradiction between the capitalist aspiration to the maximisation of profits (surplus value) and the limited growth of effective demand. Therefore, during the period when in most developed market economies the model of interventionist welfare state dominated, it seemed that the theory developed by Luxemburg had lost its topicality and had become part of the history of economic theory. Yet it regains its timeliness in the situation where the economic policy of these countries has been dominated by the neo-liberal paradigm and the State has lost its ability to eliminate the basic contradiction stated by Rosa Luxemburg.

Notes

1. It is important to notice that the present crisis is the first global crisis of this scale since the Great Depression of the 1930s. Until more or less the end of the 1980s, it was only periods of economic slowdown that manifested the cyclical character of the development of the economy; in the 1990s and shortly after the year 2000 there occurred certain crisis phenomena, but they were limited from the geographic and sector side. (The Argentine, Mexican and Indonesian economic crises, as well as the IT sector depression, are the most popular examples.)
2. W. Szymański indicates: growth of the money supply on the global market, uncertainty and greed, irresponsible financial innovations and the weakness of the surveillance system and the control as direct reasons of the crisis (Szymański, 2009: pp. 85–108).
3. The text of André Gorz: 'The exit from Capitalism has Already Begun', written in September 2007, that constitutes an introduction to the manifest of the French social movement UTOPIA, can be an example. In this text, A. Gorz wrote among others: 'The real economy became an addition to financial bubbles. A very high profitability of equities of companies would be necessary so that a stock exchange bubble, frugality blown up with the constant rise of estate prices and depositing into mortgage certificates, doesn't burst– because its bursting will threat the banking system with a sequence of the bankruptcy and for the real economy – a long recession'. We find another example of the announcement of the current crisis in a document published by European economists acting within the group 'Euromemorandum' in December 2007 (EuroMemorandum Group, 2007). In this paper they state: 'In an increasingly fragile financial system the probability of disruption rise over time although it is not always possible to predict which particular assets will be affected or when and which part of the economy will be touched by it'.

4. Luxemburg used the term 'reproduction' to mean expanded reproduction, and this might be translated into the language of modern economics as 'economic growth'.
5. 'The accumulation in an environment exclusively capitalist is not possible. Therefore, since the very beginning of the capitalist development of the tendency to expand, to broaden capitalism to non-capitalist social groups and countries, there is the ruin of the craft and peasantries and the proletarianisation of the middle classes, hence the colonial policy and the policy of "open door", hence the export of capital' (Luxemburg, 2011: p. 696).
6. It is not possible to consider here all the sources and components of the observed change of economic policy paradigm. Most often the changes related to the development of economic theories that supported interventionism of the state in the capitalist economy (in particular the theories of Kalecki and Keynes) and the growing political pressure to present welfare effects of the capitalist economy, which resulted at the time from the competition between systems.
7. Results of the majority of this type of econometric research strongly depends on accepted statistical measures for examined processes and on the model assumptions in use. Therefore, one might fear that results obtained from accepted assumptions and measures might be contradictory and the solution of the fundamental problem will not be possible.
8. 'In theory, the most rational form of cyclical intervention is inflationary financing of public work. The government takes credits in the issuing bank and uses funds obtained from it for realization of for example: buildings of the public utility [...] it is possible to simplify this intervention, that is inflationary financing instead of public work – jobseekers' allowance. The economic effect would be the same. The issue is not on what the state spends its money, but the fact that it spends the money at all, taking it from the issuing bank instead of taxes' (Kalecki, 1933a: p. 9).

11
Capitalism, Crisis, Growth and Ecology

Pat Devine

11.1 Introduction

The present global crisis of capitalism, the worst for 100 years, or at least since the Great Recession of the inter-war years, has affected all varieties of capitalism. The response to the crisis from the right has been to insist on austerity to deal with deficits, together with supply side measures to create the conditions for renewed growth. The response from the left has been to emphasise the demand side through fiscal stimulus, relying on growth to deal with the deficits. In both cases there has been an unquestioned assumption that growth is a good thing, albeit from the left sometimes green growth, through a green new deal.

However, this emphasis on growth, whether from right or left, fails to take account of the impact of growth on non-human nature, on the environment and the earth's ecosystems. One way of capturing this is the Global Footprint Network's estimate of the global ecological footprint, which measures the impact of human activity on the earth's ecosystems (Global Footprint Network, 2013). This footprint can then be compared with global biocapacity, which measures the resources available from these ecosystems. The most recent data, for 2008, suggest that human activity is currently using ecosystems equivalent to one and a half times the earth's carrying capacity, which is clearly unsustainable. The inescapable conclusion is that, at least in the rich countries, we need to move rapidly towards a steady-state economy, or even a period of de-growth.

11.2 Environmental exploitation

The first decade of the 21st century ended with the first fully global crisis of capitalism. Even the Great Depression of the 1920s and 1930s, between the 20th century's two world wars, was not fully global; the Soviet Union had escaped from the global reach of capitalism, was industrialising and growing rapidly, and was seen by many at the time as an inspiring socialist alternative to a capitalism that appeared to be on its last legs. However, Roosevelt's New Deal and the Second World War pulled capitalism away from the abyss, and this led to the post-war Golden Age of the Keynesian social democratic welfare state, from 1945 until the 1970s. This unprecedented period of full employment resulted in a profit squeeze and mounting inflationary pressure, which culminated in the 1970s in a Gramscian organic crisis that was ultimately resolved in favour of capital, ushering in the globalised neoliberal era that is still with us. At the same time, problems were accumulating in the Soviet bloc, and 'actually existing socialism' lost its allure as the human cost and oppressive character of its regimes became more widely known. With the collapse of 'communism' in Eastern Europe and the Soviet Union in 1989–1991 and the end of the cold war, capitalism emerged triumphant, and the 'end of history' was proclaimed.

And yet all was not well. On the one hand, evidence accumulated that higher material standards of living in the developed capitalist countries (GDP per head) did not in general improve people's level of well-being, while in the poorer countries of the world hunger, illness and general deprivation continued to be endemic. On the other hand, rapidly developing evidence of accelerating environmental and ecological degradation, most prominently but by no means only the issue of climate change caused by human activity, placed the issue of society's relationship with non-human nature firmly in the public domain. The past 20 years have seen a flourishing of grass roots and NGO activity promoting aid and fair trade, and engaging in a variety of forms of protest and pressure on environmental issues. Alongside this there has been a continuous stream of policy announcements and financial commitments by governments and international organisations aimed at ending global poverty and 'saving the planet'. Yet, despite all this activity, the state of the world, in terms of both social justice and environmental sustainability, seems to get no better, and in many ways is getting worse.

The argument of this chapter is that the underlying cause of this unhappy and intolerable state of affairs is the capitalist system itself, with its fundamental dynamic of endless growth based on the ruthless exploitation of both labour and non-human nature. Policies to deal with the dysfunctional consequences of capitalism are like policies to treat the symptoms of illness; they are certainly worth having, but they should not be allowed to divert attention away from the need to get rid of the illness and prevent it from occurring in the first place. We need to understand the anatomy of capitalism in order to grasp why reforms, however worthwhile they may be, will always sooner or later be subverted by the dysfunctional contradictions of the system's essential structure and dynamic.

11.3 The two contradictions of capitalism

For Marx, the dominant contradiction within the capitalist system is that between the forces of production (capital equipment and material inputs – the 'means of production', plus the workers who design and operate the production process), and the relations of production (fragmented ownership and control of the means of production by a minority class of property owners which employs the majority class of workers who can only live by working for an employer to obtain an income). Production is a social process, but the means of production entering into this social process are privately owned, and the use made of them is decided atomistically by their separated owners, who compete against each other. These fragmented private decisions are coordinated through the operation of market forces, with those successful in the competitive struggle of all against all prospering, and the unsuccessful going to the wall. This is what gives rise to capitalism's relentless pressure to innovate and reduce labour costs, and to its inherent instability due to a lack of planning what is an integrated social process – Schumpeter's 'creative destruction' and Marx's 'anarchy of production'.

Marx concentrated on analysing this fundamental contradiction of capitalism, showing how the capitalist system is based on exploitation, with workers receiving less than the full value of what they produce, and how it is subject to periodic and unavoidable economic crises, with all the misery and insecurity they cause. It is these characteristics of capitalism that gave rise to the trade union, labour and socialist movements that developed as capitalism took hold in the 19th century, in order to struggle against the exploitation and oppression of labour and the inhuman conditions in which workers lived – and, in some cases, to see beyond the need for reforms, and work towards the overthrow of capitalism and its replacement by a new socialist or communist society.

Whereas Marx focused on the effects of capitalism on labour, O'Connor, a century later, while fully accepting what he called Marx's first contradiction of capitalism, shifted the focus from labour to land – the effects of capitalism on non-human nature and the environment – through what he called the second contradiction of capitalism. This is the contradiction between capitalist forces and relations of production taken together as a whole – the entire ensemble of the capitalist mode of production, on the one hand, and the non-human natural conditions on which capitalist, or indeed any, production depends, on the other. This second contradiction consists in the inherent tendency for the capitalist mode of production to degrade and undermine the underlying environmental and ecological conditions on which it depends for its continued existence.

It is the growing awareness of the consequences of this second contradiction, according to O'Connor, that has led to the environmental social movements of today. These 'green' movements are concerned with promoting policies to mitigate the worst effects of capitalism on the environment and on global ecologies. But, as in the case of the 'red' labour movements, there is also a strand within these green movements that recognises that such reforms, while necessary, are addressing symptoms rather than dealing with the underlying cause, capitalism. This, then, creates the basis for an alliance seeking to transcend capitalism between the labour movement, as a response to the first contradiction of capitalism, and the environmental movement, as a response to the second. It holds forth the prospect of a red–green alliance, a movement for a democratic, participatory eco-socialism.

11.4 The environmental and ecological crisis

There is now near universal agreement that climate change due to human activity is occurring at an accelerating rate and that in order to contain it at a manageable level there must be a reduction of 80–90 per cent in greenhouse gas emissions by 2050 compared with 1990. In addition to the compelling scientific evidence, people on a daily basis experience or hear about increasingly severe weather – droughts, unprecedented flooding, retreating glaciers and melting ice-caps. Yet despite this agreement, very little has been done to tackle the problem. Negotiations to allocate the necessary reduction in emissions between countries, notably between the developed and the developing countries, have effectively broken down. Following the Cancun climate change conference in December 2010, the Secretary General of the United Nations, Ban Ki-moon, abandoned the attempt to reach international agreement on binding national targets for reducing greenhouse gas emissions, in favour of encouraging each country to adopt its own national plan for promoting clean, more efficient energy, and sustainable growth and development. The fact that collective social action has so far been largely ineffective, and on present trends seems likely to remain so, with the UN's Rio+20 Sustainable Development Conference in 2012 ending in abject failure, is a setback that has reinforced the already dominant emphasis on market-based policies focused on decentralised individual and institutional behaviour.

Market-based measures aim to promote energy efficiency and non-fossil fuel energy generation, and to persuade people to modify their individual behaviour in ways that save energy, by altering the pattern of prices and subsidies to which profit-seeking firms and individuals respond. The best known such measure is the carbon trading scheme, which allocates permitted allowances for emissions to firms and allows those with unused allowances to sell them to firms that exceed their allowances. Such schemes, however, have so far failed to reduce emissions since, due to corporate political lobbying, allowances have been set at too high a level. The schemes also contain provisions for offsetting excess emissions by promoting emission-reducing projects in developing countries. However, many of these schemes are of dubious provenance, consisting of projects already under way, which therefore lack 'additionality', thus enabling firms to continue with their polluting business as usual.

More recently, the fall in production resulting from the 2008 economic crisis meant that emissions also initially fell, so that firms had more allowances to pollute than they needed, and the price of permits to pollute collapsed. This experience parallels that of the ex-Soviet bloc countries after 1989–1991, when their economies collapsed and industrial production and fuel consumption declined rapidly. Both highlight the fact that while clean energy and energy efficiency are important, at the moment, and for the foreseeable future, it is the absolute level of production that is decisive in determining the level of emissions and their rate of increase.

Although climate change due to human-induced greenhouse gas emissions currently receives most attention, further evidence of pressure on the environment comes from loss of bio-diversity. The impact of human settlement on habitat from mining and chemically-based agribusiness, through deforestation and over-fishing, to atmospheric and marine pollution, has had a devastating effect. And this is accentuated by the rapid rate of urbanisation and shanty town development, with their associated demands on water supplies and waste disposal.

The unending economic growth of the capitalist global economy, albeit repeatedly interrupted by the collapse of financial bubbles and crises of overproduction, coupled with rising global population, is producing more and more signs of resource scarcity. And this is exacerbated by the reckless policies of unsustainable agricultural irrigation, and unsustainable development in desert areas like Las Vegas and the Gulf States. Struggles over access to land, water, oil, gas and minerals underlie many of the regional conflicts in the world today, and resource wars may be expected to increase in the future. A new 'scramble for Africa' is already well under way, with China playing a prominent part. Although long-term trends are difficult to identify and predict, not least because they are interrupted by speculation and cyclical variations in the level of economic activity, the prices of fossil fuels and other primary commodities on the world market, including food, are likely to be subject to long-term increases.

There is still uncertainty over whether peak oil production has yet been reached (peak oil refers to the point of maximum production, not to falling reserves and potential supply), but most experts agree that even if it has not, it is not far off. However, there remain plentiful reserves of coal around the world, and global coal production is still increasing. And of course, if the price is high enough, oil and gas that is very costly to extract and even more ecologically damaging, as from the tar sands in Canada and Venezuela, or deeper and deeper underwater oil drilling, such as led to the BP Deepwater Horizon disaster in the Gulf of Mexico and is now being extended to the Arctic Circle and the Falkland Islands, becomes economically viable. The recent development of 'fracking' to extract hydrocarbons trapped in shale rocks, with vast reserves having already been discovered, postpones any absolute decline in non-renewable energy availability, but it is extremely expensive and very environmentally damaging. So while the post-war cheap fossil fuel growth economy is clearly at or approaching an end, continued dependence on now dearer fossil fuels may well be possible for some time, which highlights dramatically the contradiction between economic growth and environmental and ecological sustainability.

11.5 The social crisis

Of course, material growth in the South will have to continue for a long time to create the infrastructure and productive capacity required to meet the basic human needs of its growing population. But for this necessary growth to be ecologically sustainable it will have to be based on technology systems and production techniques that incorporate a qualitatively different relationship between materials/energy flows and human needs from that which has so far underpinned the fossil fuel-dependent growth of the capitalist, and previously the Soviet bloc, countries.

The only morally defensible approach to this problem compatible with social justice and ecological sustainability is to adopt the objective of moving towards an equal ecological footprint, including an equal carbon emission allowance, for the entire global population. This would have to be at a level which is compatible with the sustainable global carrying capacity. The unavoidable implication of this is that there will have to be a major redistribution of resource use, from rich to poor countries and from rich to poor within countries. A study by the UN found that between 2000 and 2006, notwithstanding the rapid rate of growth of China with its 20 per cent of world population, greenhouse gas emissions in the developing countries rose by only 2.3 per cent, compared with a rise of 10 per cent in the already developed countries. This again highlights the contradiction between the relentless dynamic of unending capitalist growth and the developmental model needed for a socially just and ecologically sustainable world.

Faced with the enormity of the ecological challenge confronting the world today, it is perhaps understandable that the 'common sense' of the age is rapidly becoming the need to achieve sustainable growth and development within a reformed 'green' capitalism. The possibility that growth and sustainability are completely incompatible and that capitalism depends on growth rarely gets a hearing. As Fredric Jameson has reminded us: for most people 'it is easier to imagine the end of the world than to imagine the end of capitalism'. However, an alternative and more radical strand within the green movement argues that the transformations required, particularly when one takes account of the need for the poorer countries to grow in order to satisfy the basic needs of their populations, will necessarily involve severe austerity in the rich countries, with an unavoidable deterioration in the quality of life – what is sometimes called the 'hair shirt' or 'austerity' approach.

Whether or not this approach was ever convincing, it is certainly not so today. Over the past decade evidence has accumulated, brought to wider public notice by Richard Layard's book, *Happiness* (Layard, 2005), that once a society has reached a certain threshold level of real income, further increases in real income are not associated with increases in overall human happiness or well-being, which may even decline. The reason is fairly obvious. Once people's basic needs for food, clothing and shelter, together with health and education, have been met, human flourishing depends not on the accumulation and consumption of material things but on the quality of personal relationships with family and friends, the degree of job satisfaction, the level of security people experience, and the extent of social cohesion – the extent to which people see themselves as citizens with a sense of shared purpose wider than their own narrow self-interest. There is also mounting evidence that human well-being is positively associated with active engagement with the non-human natural world.

In the developed capitalist countries, therefore, the material conditions for the good life, what Kate Soper has called an 'alternative hedonism', have existed for some time. Yet the people in these countries, to a greater or lesser extent, are in fact becoming increasingly unhappy and dysfunctional. This is most evident in the US and the UK where sometime in the 1970s the link between GDP per capita and well-being was broken; GDP per capita continued to increase but the various indices of well-being levelled off or went into reverse. This break coincided with the start of the neoliberal era at the end of the 1970s, with its privatisation and deregulation, rampant consumerism, and the growth of the 'me, me [...] because I deserve it' culture. The preceding long-term trend for a reduction in inequality was reversed, inequality rapidly increased, social mobility stalled, and people's economic security was undermined.

In their influential book, *The Spirit Level* (2009), Richard Wilkinson and Kate Pickett marshal a vast body of evidence showing that among the developed capitalist countries, the more unequal the society the more dysfunctional it is. In all societies the rich do better than the poor; but in general, the more unequal a society, the more troubled are both rich and poor. Their findings are summarised in a graph plotting a composite 'index of health and social problems' against the degree of income inequality in each country. Japan and the Scandinavian countries, with the lowest levels of income inequality, have the lowest incidence of health and social problems across the society; the US, Portugal and the UK, the most unequal countries, have the highest incidence. And the relationship holds also for those countries in the middle range. While there is obviously room for debate about the strength of the relationships examined, the evidence presented is overwhelming. In every case – community life and social relations, mental health and drug use, physical health and life expectancy, obesity, educational performance, teenage births, violence, imprisonment and punishment, and social mobility – the more unequal the society, the worse the performance (the one exception being suicide).

Wilkinson and Pickett (2009) suggest that the reason inequality gives rise to these dysfunctional outcomes is the anxiety associated with what they call 'social evaluative threat' – an underlying lack of confidence in oneself, one's place in the world, how one is seen by others. The more unequal the society, once it has surpassed the threshold below which material deprivation is the most urgent problem, the greater are the actual and perceived differences between people, and the greater is the fear of falling back, whatever one's current position in the social hierarchy. The consumerist capitalism of today's rich countries generates discontent – someone may be doing better than you, may have the latest fashionable or trendy product which you do not have, may have their children in a better school, or have a better doctor. Richard Sennett has described the anxiety created by neoliberalism's emphasis on competition and consumerism as a form of 'ontological insecurity', a free-floating anxiety about what might happen, even when there is nothing specific in the offing to fear. And, of course, to this ontological insecurity, since 2008 in Europe there has been added the insecurity, misery, and inhumanity arising from the savage but completely unnecessary austerity policies imposed by governments and international financial institutions. These policies are said to be necessary to appease the financial markets, and look set to continue for a decade or so. They are in fact an open declaration of class war.

Of course, capitalism preceded the neoliberal era, and earlier periods in its history had their own hardships and insecurities. However, what is distinctive about the neoliberal period is that its individualism, marketisation, and commodification have eroded the social institutions that underpin community, have undermined previous senses of social cohesion. The 'social security' of the welfare state has given way to 'welfare benefits', or 'scroungers'. Economic growth in the developed capitalist countries since the 1970s has not improved people's quality of life. Movement towards a less materialistic way of life in these countries is not only essential for the achievement of ecological sustainability; it would also improve the quality of our lives. But this is not yet the case for the majority of the world's population in the poor countries, where growth and increases in the material standard of living will be necessary for some time if basic needs are to be met. Even there, however, a developmental model that does not seek to replicate the growing inequalities and profligacy of capitalist consumerism – a new model, based on equality and social justice, and a different metabolism between human activity and non-human nature – would be more ecologically sustainable and produce a better life. The obstacle is the global capitalist system.

11.6 Sustainable capitalism?

There are two strands within the conventional mainstream 'common sense of the age' response to the growing environmental and ecological crisis. The first, the overwhelmingly dominant response, espouses some form of technological modernisation, a 'techno-fix' enabling everything to continue on the basis of business and growth as usual. However, the historical record lends no support to the argument that technical change resulting in greater efficiency of resource use will be sufficient to offset the combined effect of population growth and rising levels of per capita income on carbon emissions. The second, very much minority, response accepts that growth is incompatible with sustainability but completely fails to address the question of whether zero growth, let alone de-growth, is compatible with capitalism.

The case for sustainable growth is that by moving towards more efficient energy generation, increasingly from renewable sources, and reducing energy use through more energy-efficient techniques of production and marginal changes in consumption habits, growth can be combined with reduced greenhouse gas emissions. And the same argument is used with respect to other scarce non-renewable resources. This is the process known as 'relative decoupling' (a reduction in emissions, or resource use, per unit of energy used or GDP produced). However, so far although there has been relative decoupling, there has been no 'absolute decoupling' (a reduction in total emissions or resource use). Relative decoupling has been more than offset by growth, an increase in the number of units produced, with the result that total emissions continue to increase.

Angus Maddison in his book, *Contours of the World Economy, 1–2030 AD: Essays in Macro-Economic History* (2007), gives estimates of total world energy consumption, carbon emissions per unit of energy consumed, fossil fuel carbon emissions per US$1000 of GDP in real terms (that is, at constant prices), per capita income in real terms, per capita fossil fuel carbon emissions, world population, world fossil fuel emissions and world GDP in real terms. World energy consumption rose over 48-fold between 1820 and 2003, during which period the proportion of world energy consumption accounted for by fossil fuels rose from 6 per cent to 80 per cent. Carbon emissions per unit of fossil fuel energy consumed peaked in 1913 and have been falling since, but in 2003 were still ten times the 1820 level. Fossil fuel carbon emissions per US$1000 of GDP also peaked in 1913 and had more than halved by 2003, but world per capita income rose more than fourfold over the same period, with the result that world per capita carbon emissions doubled. And to this must be added the three-and-a-half-fold increase in world population. The result was an increase in fossil fuel carbon emissions from 534 metric tons in 1913 to 4271 metric tons in 2003, an eightfold increase, with the reduction in emissions per $1000 GDP swamped by the increase in world GDP from £2733 billion in 1913 to US$40,913 billion in 2003, due to the combined effect of population increase and increasing income per head.

The figures are, of course, estimates and depend on assumptions that may be challenged, but the overall picture is clear enough. Of course, capitalism had been developing slowly for around two centuries before 1820, but it really took off at the beginning of the 19th century. Since then, capitalism and fossil fuel-based energy and technology have co-evolved. The technological modernisation / techno-fix case has to be judged in the context of current projections for population and per capita income growth, together giving world GDP growth. Maddison (2007) estimates that between 2003 and 2030, population will increase from 6279 million to 8175 million; average per capita income will increase in real terms from US$6516 to US$11,814; and as a result, world GDP will increase from US$40,913 billion to US$96,580 billion.

The UK Labour Government's Sustainable Development Commission (now abolished by the Conservative-Liberal Democrat Coalition) reaches much the same conclusion. Chapter 5 of its report, *Prosperity without growth?*, is titled 'The Myth of Decoupling' (Sustainable Development Commission, 2009). Global energy intensity (energy use per unit of output) is estimated to have fallen by a third since 1970, and global CO_2 intensity (CO_2 emissions per unit of output) by almost a quarter in the past 25 years. Yet total global CO_2 emissions have increased by 80 per cent since 1970 and by 40 per cent since 1990, and until the current crisis had been increasing at 3 per cent per annum since 2000. Between 1990 and 2007, carbon intensity decreased by 0.7 per cent per annum, population increased by 1.3 per cent per annum, and per capita income increased by 1.4 per cent, giving an increase in carbon emissions of 2.0 per cent per annum (1.3 + 1.4 – 0.7), or 40 per cent over 17 years. The IPCC's Fourth Assessment report (2007) estimates that up to 2050 global population will increase at 0.7 per cent per annum, and global per capita income at 1.4 per cent pa. To achieve a 450 ppm target for 2050, it estimates that CO_2 emissions will need to fall by 4.9 per cent per annum, which means a reduction of carbon intensity of 7.0 per cent per annum (0.7 + 1.4 + 4.9) – ten times faster than the 0.7 per cent per annum decrease since 1990. There is not the remotest possibility that this, and all the other pressing ecological challenges, can be met on the basis of a return to growth and business as usual.

The Sustainable Development Commission (2009) recognised this and argued that society needs to move to a zero-growth, steady-state economy, arguing correctly that it is possible to have 'prosperity without growth'. Its report also recognised that historically capitalism and growth go together: 'there is as yet no credible, socially-just, ecologically sustainable scenario of continually growing incomes for a world of nine billion people [...] it is entirely fanciful to suppose that "deep" emission and resource cuts can be achieved without confronting the structure of market economies' (ibid: p. 57); 'Profit is the key to the system' (ibid: p. 61); 'there is no macroeconomics for sustainability and there is an urgent need for one' (ibid: p. 10). However, although the Commission echoed Marx, 'Accumulate, accumulate! That is Moses and the prophets!' (Marx, 1976: ch. 24), identifying the underlying growth dynamic of the capitalist mode of production (often euphemistically referred to as the 'market economy'), it did not address the corollary that in order to meet the challenge of climate change and the other pressing ecological issues we must go beyond capitalism.

11.7 Conclusion

This chapter has argued that ecological sustainability is incompatible with global growth and that we therefore need to move away from quantitative growth and consumerism towards qualitative improvements in human well-being. However, since all varieties of capitalism depend on growth, the unavoidable conclusion is that the world urgently needs to move towards an eco-socialist system which would enable a self-governing society consciously to control the economy and mediate its relationship with non-human nature through a process of participatory democratic planning. Measures to deal with the current crisis, therefore, need to focus on redistributing wealth, income and work, restructuring consumption and the economy, overcoming the democratic deficit, and improving the quality of life. This would give them a transformatory dynamic towards 'another world' which we must insist 'is indeed possible'.

12

Trend and Cycle: On the Timeliness of Grossman's Breakdown Theory

Paul Mattick

12.1 Introduction

Marx's theory of capitalist accumulation, as Henryk Grossmann was the first 20th-century writer to point out, both proposes an explanation of the business cycle as a normal feature of capitalism and predicts an inherent limit to this social system's development – a 'breakdown,' in Grossmann's words. On the one hand, thanks to factors counteracting the tendency of the rate of profit to fall that Marx put at the centre of his theory of capitalist dynamics, every crisis is a means to producing a new prosperity. On the other, Marx clearly suggests that the 'historical tendency of capitalist production' points to an end of the system and its replacement by a new form of society. While stressing that the abolition of capitalism would have to be the conscious act of a revolutionary working class, Grossmann claimed to be maintaining an essential element of Marxian theory when he insisted that the work of revolution cannot be expected from the spontaneous appearance of a conscious rejection of capitalism on ethical or rational grounds, but is comprehensible only as a response to the actual difficulty of capitalism's self-reproduction – its breakdown. But how can this idea coexist within one consistent theory with that of regular alternation of prosperity and depression?

During the long period since the Second World War, both these elements of Marx's outlook largely disappeared from the centre of attention within Marxist theorising.[1] With the decline of the Socialist and Communist left, the issue of the end of capitalism receded from political discussion. Above all, the economic Golden Age that followed the war, and the apparent taming of the business cycle by Keynesian manipulations, resulted in a loss of interest in Marx's focus on breakdown and crisis, as well as in earlier bourgeois cycle theory. The dramatic financial collapse of 2007 and the continuing global depression, however, have already provoked a revival of attention to such issues, to which I wish to contribute.

12.2 The theory in Marx

According to Marx, capital accumulation, once set in motion on a large scale, leads both to the global extension of modern socialised production and distribution and, over time, to 'a constant decrease in the number of capitalist magnates, who usurp and monopolize all the advantages of this' system of production, so that 'the mass of misery, oppression, slavery, degradation, and exploitation grows' (Marx, 1976: p. 929). This is what he called the 'historical tendency' of capitalist development. Marx's expectation, or at least hope, was that the negative aspect of this tendency would produce a growing revolt of the working class, which would finally put an end to its sufferings by 'expropriating the expropriators' and creating a new social system based on conscious social cooperation.

The chief force driving this process, in Marx's view, was what he called 'the most important law of modern political economy', the law of the tendency of the rate of profit to fall. This law is a consequence of the requirement to expand forced upon each capital entity by the need to competitively appropriate as much as possible of the surplus value produced by the system as a whole. Expansion – capital accumulation – would involve, Marx predicted, a tendential increase of capital invested in means of production relative to that invested in labour power. From the point of view of the individual firm, this is a means to lower costs; with regard to the system as a whole, it (directly or indirectly) decreases the value of labour power and so raises the rate of exploitation, increasing the quantity of value appropriable by capital entities as profit. The long-term effect must, however, Marx argued, be a decline in the surplus value produced per unit of capital invested, since value is produced only by labour and 'the compensation for the reduced number of workers provided by a rise in the level of exploitation of labor has certain limits that cannot be overstepped' (Marx, 1981: p. 356). Thus 'the rise in the rate of surplus-value and the fall in the rate of profit are simply particular forms that express the growing productivity of labor in capitalist terms' (ibid: p. 347). In Marx's view, this process is self-reinforcing: even apart from the competitiveness inherent in a system of independent firms each of which is striving to maximise profitability, the tendential decline, relative to total capital investment, of the total surplus value available for division between those firms exerts pressure on each of them to increase profitability by cost cutting.

There is a long history of criticism of this idea of Marx's. The commonest objection to his prediction is what seems the commonsense observation that if the rate of surplus value is the ratio of surplus value to the value of labour power $\frac{s}{v}$, and the rate of profit is the ratio of surplus value to total capitalist investment $\frac{s}{c+v}$ then the downward pressure on profitability caused by an increase in the organic composition of capital, $\frac{c}{v}$, can be effectively counteracted by an increase in $\frac{s}{v}$, despite Marx's description of these changes as facets of the same process.[2] (This is obvious once we rewrite $\frac{s}{c+v}$ as $\frac{s}{v}/\frac{c}{v}+1$).

The distinguished line of objectors in this vein includes Joan Robinson (1966) and Paul Sweezy (1946); a recent reviver of this critique is Michael Heinrich, who follows his illustrious forebears in insisting that it is impossible to prove that the rate of profit must fall, because 'there exists no general relationship between a determinate increase in productivity and the magnitude of the increase in the value composition necessary to accomplish it' (Heinrich, 2006: p. 70). As he makes the same point elsewhere:

In order to prove that the rate of profit necessarily falls, it is not sufficient to prove that $\frac{c}{v}$ increases. One must also show that $\frac{c}{v}$ increases *by a certain degree*; namely so strongly, that the condition [that the value composition increases faster than the rate of surplus-value] is fulfilled And here lies the fundamental difficulty for every proof of the 'law of the tendency of the rate of profit to fall': A general statement about the *degree of increase* for $\frac{c}{v}$ is not possible. (Heinrich, 2006: p. 95)

We owe to Mario Cogoy a particularly clear explanation of the error involved in this argument. As he pointed out in an article first published in 1974, in the passages that are the basis for everyone's discussion of this question, Marx uses $\frac{c}{v}$ to symbolise the value composition of capital because he is assuming a constant rate of surplus value; under this assumption, because *v* represents a given number of workers, an increase in $\frac{c}{v}$ will always mirror a change in the technical composition of capital, which is how Marx defines the 'organic' composition (to distinguish such changes, representing a long-term trend, from the effect on the value composition of momentary increases or decreases of raw materials costs). 'If, on the other hand, one begins with a rising rate of surplus value,' as Marx believes typifies the capitalist long term,

> *one can no longer express the organic composition by* $\frac{c}{v}$. This is because an increase in this ratio can express not only an increase of constant capital relative to the quantity of labor, but also a simple reduction in the value of labor power, or both at the same time. If we assume a rising rate of surplus value then only the ratio $\frac{c}{v+s}$ is of significance for the organic composition [...] because an increase of this ratio *is not affected by a decrease in the value of labor power but only by an increase of constant capital relative to the quantity of labor.* [...] All the contradictions that Sweezy and Robinson have found in Marx's treatment of the law of the tendency of the rate of profit to fall are thus easily resolved and attributable to these authors' incomprehension of Marx's method. (Cogoy, 1987: p. 61)

And on the basis of this representation of the organic composition, in fact, Cogoy demonstrates mathematically that 'the increase in the rate of surplus value cannot ultimately compensate for the rise in the organic composition' (ibid: p. 64).

As has been pointed out by various authors (Rosdolsky, 1977: pp. 398–411), Marx anticipated the Robinson–Sweezy objection, especially because he held that the nature of capital accumulation compels continual efforts to raise the rate of surplus value. In Volume I of *Capital* he stresses that

> The absolute limit of the average working day – this being by nature always less than 24 hours – sets an absolute limit to the compensation for a reduction of variable capital by a higher rate of surplus-value, or for the decrease of the number of workers exploited by a higher degree of exploitation of labor-power. (Marx, 1976: pp. 419–420)

Further, within the absolute limit set by the working day, the advance of labour productivity makes it increasingly difficult to increase the rate of surplus value by decreasing the part of the day in which the labourers work for themselves. As Marx expanded on this idea in the *Grundrisse*,

> The greater the surplus value of capital *before the increase in productivity*, i.e. the greater the quantum of surplus labor or surplus-value of capital presupposed, or the smaller the fraction of the working day which constitutes the equivalent of the worker and expresses necessary labor, the smaller is the growth of surplus-value accruing to capital from increased productivity. [...] The self-valorization of

> capital becomes more difficult to the extent to which it is already valorized. (Marx, 1986: pp. 265–266)

This argument, of course, seems as much a matter of intuition as the idea that the effect on the profit rate of growth in $\frac{c}{v}$ can always be compensated by an increase in $\frac{s}{v}$.

Heinrich explains the problem clearly. For Marx, what is decisive for capitalist development is not the rate of surplus value *per se* but the mass of surplus value generated by the number of workers performing surplus labour at this rate.

And 'the compensation for the reduced number of workers provided by a rise in the level of the exploitation of labor has certain limits that cannot be overstepped; this can certainly check the fall in the profit rate, but it cannot cancel it out' (Marx, 1981: p. 356).

In Heinrich's words, 'if the number of employees declines beyond a certain critical mass, then at some point the amount of surplus-value produced also declines, regardless of how strongly the rate of surplus-value increases'. According to Marx, this means that its ratio to total capital invested also declines. But Heinrich insists that 'this isn't the case. A declining mass of surplus-value *s* only indicates a fall in the rate of profit with certainty when the total capital $c + v$ required for the production of this surplus value has not also fallen but has at least remained constant.' And this, given the decline in *v*, implies that 'it is not sufficient for the constant capital *c* to increase; rather, it must increase by a certain amount, namely, it must increase by the same amount that the variable capital has been reduced.' But 'we don't know whether the productivity increase has been implemented with a lot or a little additional constant capital' (ibid: p. 96).[3]

The big issue that is in this formulation too is not the increase of the rate of surplus value but the growth of the composition of capital. It is clear that Marx *assumed* a tendential increase of constant relative to variable capital, over time, sufficient to reduce the profit rate. One reason this assumption seems reasonable, we have already seen: the consideration that, to use Fred Moseley's formulation, 'the elasticity of surplus value per worker with respect to productivity diminish[es] over time and the elasticity of capital per worker with respect to productivity is assumed to remain more or less constant', since there is no obvious factor to cause it to decline (Moseley, 1991: p. 19). Another, as Marx emphasised, is that if a decline in profitability due to the decline in the amount of labour performed relative to the size of capital investment is to be overcome,

> the capital must grow in a higher ratio than that in which the profit rate falls. In other words, if the variable component of the total capital is not just to remain the same in absolute terms, but rather to grow, even though its percentage falls as a proportion of the total capital, then the total capital must grow in a higher ratio than that at which the percentage of variable capital falls. (Marx, 1981: p. 329)

This condition is likely to be realised both because increased productivity of labour involves great increases in the quantity of raw materials utilised, as well as in the size of fixed capital and because a given level of capital investment requires expansion not at any rate but at a technically determined one. One cannot simply add one welding station to a car factory.

In addition, the growth of the organic composition of capital over the first three-quarters of the 19th century seemed to Marx so obvious that, as he put it, what had to be explained is not a fall in the profit rate but 'why this fall is not greater or faster' (ibid: p. 339). Moseley seems to be following in Marx's footsteps when he asserts that his law of the tendency of the rate of profit to fall can be taken as valid or not 'for a particular historical period', its validity thus becoming 'an empirical question' (Moseley, 1991: p. 25). As Grossmann insisted, however, it cannot be an empirical question of this sort, and for two reasons: first of all, as Marx's law is formulated as governing a long-term trend characteristic of capitalist development, its validity is consistent with periods of rising as well as of falling profitability. Secondly, the terms in which Marx formulates his law are not those of empirical price data but of abstract labour-time values, which are not to be identified with empirical data series.

This is a necessity not just because of the enormous complexity of the economic system, which already calls for simplifying assumptions, but specifically because (even if we assume commodity money, as Marx does, in conscious contradistinction to reality) 'there are,' as Grossmann insisted, 'no [...] constant reference points for gold as the measure of value', so that 'there is no exact measure possible of the value fluctuations of commodities' (Grossmann, 1929, p. 88). Accordingly, Marx substituted what he called 'the power of abstraction' for use of the missing constant reference points.

> Thus in order, for example, to be able to determine the influence of alterations in the productivity of labor on the formation of value and surplus-value, Marx was forced to carry out his investigation under the presupposition of a 'constant value of money' (ibid: p. 89).

The model of the capitalist system formulated in these terms – as, again, Grossmann was the first theorist to point out – is not intended as a depiction of the actual historical process of economic development, but as a simplified representation of forces operating throughout that process. Grossmann described Marx's procedure as one of approximation, the addition of more specific features – such as the difference between mercantile and industrial capital – making the less abstract representation more phenomenally descriptive.[4] But there are problems with this approach – not only the lack of a clear definition of 'approximation' in this context but also the fact that this mode of speech suggests misleadingly that for Marx the value calculations employed in the first two volumes of *Capital* are approximations of the price calculations that structure real-life economic affairs. It may be more illuminating to borrow a concept from the philosophy of physics and speak of Marx's employment of *ceteris paribus* laws in his analysis.

Ceteris paribus laws, in Nancy Cartwright's explication, are 'generalizations that hold only under special conditions, usually ideal conditions' (Cartwright, 1983: p. 45). She gives the example of Snell's Law governing the refraction of light as it crosses media, which appears in all physics textbooks but actually holds only under special conditions (when the two media involved are optically isotropic). In fact, these conditions rarely obtain, but physics students must still learn Snell's Law because it signals 'that the same kind of explanation can be given even for some anisotropic media. The pattern of explanation derived from the ideal situation is employed even where the conditions are less than ideal; and we assume that we can understand what happens in nearly isotropic media by rehearsing how light rays behave in pure isotropic cases'. (ibid: p. 48)

Similarly, describing his procedure in the 1861–1863 draft of *Capital*, Marx explains:

> Here we need only consider the forms which capital passes through in the various stages of its development. The real conditions within which the actual process of production takes place are therefore not analyzed. It is assumed throughout, that the commodity is sold at its value. We do not examine the competition of capitals, nor the credit system, nor the actual composition of society, which by no means consists only of two classes, workers and industrial capitalists, and where therefore consumers and producers are not identical categories. [...] Nevertheless [...] the examination of the general nature of

> capital, even without going further into the actual relations which all constitute prerequisites for the real process of production, reveals [the possibility of crisis...] clearly. (Marx, 1989: p. 124)

In application to real world situations, Marx's theoretical schema must be understood as replaced by historically specific constellations of social relations in which the value relations fundamental to Marx's 'law of motion' – in particular, the relation of surplus labour performed to the labour necessary to reproduce capital investment – can be identified conceptually, though not in terms of quantitative data. This does not mean that the theory is not an empirical one. The test of such a model is its conformity with the actual long-term course of events – for example, as we will see, with the continued recurrence of the alternation of prosperity and depression.

While excluding many major complicating factors from consideration throughout *Capital*, Marx mentioned a number of them, without much elaboration, in a list of factors taken over from J. S. Mill (1848),[5] counteracting his law of declining profitability: the temporary effects of productivity increases, the reduction of the value of labour power, the cheapening of constant capital, foreign trade, and even the unproductive use of capital in speculation. It is because of these factors that 'the law operates [...] as a tendency, whose effect is decisive only under certain circumstances and over long periods' (Marx, 1981: p. 346).

In speaking of 'long periods' Marx means that the counteracting factors cause the developmental path of capitalism to fluctuate around the trend defined by the tendential fall of the profit rate. That trend should still lead, therefore, to what Marx called 'an absolute overproduction of capital', which would be reached at the moment when the mass of surplus value produced at the new low rate of profit would be insufficient for further accumulation given the existing scale of investment. At this point, therefore, 'no further capital could be employed for the purposes of capitalist production', that is, of producing accumulable surplus value. This moment would mark the end of capitalism as a social system governed by the drive to accumulate.

The story is more complicated, however, because, according to Marx, the long-term trend is inflected not only by the counteracting factors but by systemic crises. Here Marx's analysis is, as we would expect, clearer and bolder than Mill's. For Mill, 'the waste of capital in periods of over-trading and rash speculation, and in the commercial revulsions by which such times are always followed,' is both 'a consequence of the [...] tendency of profits' to fall, and chief among the circumstances counteracting that tendency. But Mill derives the fatal tendency from a Ricardian argument that capitalist development leads inevitably to an increase in wages which, by the supposed laws of distribution, drives down profits.[6] For Marx, in contrast, there is no inherent conflict between profitability and stable, or even increasing, real wages. This, in fact, is why he presented his law on the assumption of a constant rate of surplus value, so as to derive the decrease in profitability endogenously from the process of accumulation itself. Looked at in abstraction from the complexity of the economic system, this process leads to the long-term 'historical tendency' discussed above. But the actual 'circumstances' under which the process takes place produce near-term manifestations of the tendency.

These 'circumstances', which will be different at different historical moments, have in common, in Marx's analysis, that they are manifestations of a conflict between the development of labour productivity to which capital is driven in the struggle for surplus value, and the need to maintain the capital value already invested, even while it is being devalued as a result of the continuing progress of productivity. The ongoing devaluation of capital 'disturbs the given conditions in which the circulation and reproduction process of capital takes place, and is therefore accompanied by sudden stoppages and crises in the production process' (ibid: p. 358). Some firms continue to make sufficient profits under these circumstances, while others, unable to meet demands from creditors or to see produced goods at sufficiently high prices to continue operations, go under.

Similarly, a crisis restores a higher average profitability not, as in Mill, simply by sweeping away quantities of uninvestable capital but by altering the value relations that dominate the process of accumulation. 'The portion of capital that exists simply in the form of future claims on surplus-value and profit [...] is devalued simultaneously with the fall in revenues on which it is reckoned.' Money 'lies idle and does not function as capital'. The sale of commodities at prices below their original sales prices likewise represents a devaluation of the capital that produced them, since it cannot be reconstituted. And in the same way 'the elements of fixed capital are devalued' (ibid: pp. 362–363). All this, by lowering the composition of capitals, makes possible an increase of profitability and a resumption of capitalist growth. A crisis, although experienced by capitalists and workers alike as a calamity, is thus a solution (however temporary) to the underlying problem of insufficient profitability, at least for those firms that survive.

The latter point is particularly significant, as can be seen if we consider the same subject in terms of Marx's concept of 'organic composition' of capital. He defines the 'technical composition' as the relation between quantities of use-values – specific types of means of production, on the one hand, and particular types of labour, on the other – involved in the production process, and the 'value composition' as the relation between the quantities of money invested in production goods and labour power. To capture the close historical relationship between the two, he calls 'the value-composition of capital, in so far as it is determined by its technical composition and mirrors the changes in the latter, the organic composition of capital' (Marx, 1976: p. 763). To the extent that a period of depression, through such phenomena as bankruptcy sales, lowers the cost of means of production (along with that of produced goods) it decreases the value composition of capital independently from the technical composition. This, so to speak, resets the value relations of capital, so that the tendential increase in the organic composition (which continues to occur in depression periods, normally characterised by technologically induced increases in the productivity of labour) starts again from a lower level.

In this way, as Grossmann puts it, 'the breakdown as the natural "basic tendency" of the capitalist system decomposes into a series of cycles apparently independent of each other, in which the breakdown tendency sets in anew only *periodically*, like the natural growth process of wool, which is broken by every shearing only to begin again' (Grossmann, 1929: p. 140). Grossmann's metaphor is not in accord with the diagram of the crisis cycle included in his book, in which the starting-point of each upturn from a level of capital investment lowered by crisis-induced devaluation is nevertheless higher than the one before.

But why should this be? A negative answer to this question is proposed, for example, by Andrew Kliman (2012):

> The destruction of capital value through crises is a recurrent phenomenon. The restoration of profitability that this destruction brings about is therefore a recurrent phenomenon as well. Because of this, the rate of profit does not have a determinate secular trend throughout the entire history of capitalism, and efforts to deduce or predict such a trend are futile.

Specifically, if 'capital value has been destroyed on a massive scale, the peak rate of profit in the boom that follows is likely to be *higher* than the previous peak' (Kliman, 2012: p. 25).

This opinion, of course, is also a pure speculation. One can just as well guess – as Marx and Grossmann did – that the continual rise in the technical composition of capital since the inception of the industrial revolution has been so gigantic, in all major industries, that periodic devaluations, even on the large scale of recent depressions, could hardly return the total capital investment, against which the rate of profit must be measured, to the levels holding at the start of the previous upswing. Kliman suggests that 'if major slumps become increasingly frequent, the tendency for the rate of profit to fall between slumps has less and less time in which to operate, so it is as likely that trough rates of profit rise over time' (ibid). But an increasing frequency of slumps may also suggest an insufficiency of slump-induced devaluation – in fact, I believe something like this is likely to have been true in the years since the mid-1970s – and so a failure of the profit rate to recover significantly.

Luckily, we are not reduced to guesses based on common sense or theory, since numerous researchers have attempted to trace changes in the capital/labour ratio through the history of capitalism, despite the inherent limitations of economic statistics and the particular problem of defining a standard of price measurement holding over long periods and different national currencies. And of course all such estimates are made in terms of prices, not in the terms of the values on the basis of which Marx's theory is constructed. Nevertheless it is surely significant that all such researchers agree that the ratio has steadily increased. This can be seen clearly, to take only one, particularly authoritative, example in Table 12.2., 'Stock of Machinery and Equipment and Non-Residential Structures per Person Employed, Six Countries, 1820–1992,' in Angus Maddison (1995), *Monitoring the World Economy, 1820–1992*. Maddison concludes from his data that there 'seems no doubt that high rates of capital accumulation, and high and increasing levels of capital per worker were a necessary condition for the productivity increases achieved in the capitalist epoch' (Maddison, 1995: p. 36).

The empirical data, such as they are, thus seem in agreement with Marx's prediction of a long-term increase in the value composition of capital. From this follows, as we have seen, a long-term tendency of the rate of profit to fall. The crisis cycle, with its recurrent periods of breakdown and recovery, is the empirical history predicted and explained by the abstract value-theoretic analysis that culminates in the tendency. It follows from this account that the long-term prospect of capitalism must be one of increasing severity of crisis and increasing difficulty in overcoming it, as lower profit rates make it difficult to accumulate the sums of value necessary for expansion.

While declining profits, market gluts, and bankruptcies are the real-life forms in which capitalists experience Marx's value-theoretic breakdown tendency most sharply, that tendency affects the working class directly in the form of what Marx calls 'the progressive production of a relative surplus population'. Both sets of effects are aspects of the continuing accumulation of capital, which involves 'a progressive qualitative change in composition, i.e. [...] a continuing increase of its constant component at the expense of its variable component' (Marx, 1976: p. 781).

Despite the continuous increase of the employed population, its numbers fall relative to total capital investment. This process is most visible at moments of crisis, as 'the path characteristically described by modern industry [...with] periods of average productivity, production at high pressure, crisis, and stagnation, depends on the constant formation, the greater or less absorption, and the re-formation of the industrial reserve army or surplus population' (ibid: p. 785). But this cycle too is the manifestation of a trend, towards the increase of the 'industrial reserve army' of unemployed:

> The same causes which develop the expansive power of capital also develop the labor-power at its disposal. The relative mass of the industrial reserve army thus increases with the potential energy of wealth. But the greater this reserve army in proportion to the active labor army, the greater is the mass of a consolidated surplus population, whose misery is in inverse ratio to the amount of torture it has to undergo in the form of labor. The more extensive, finally, the pauperized sections of the working class and the industrial reserve army, the greater is official pauperism. *This is the absolute general law of capitalist accumulation.* (ibid: p. 798)

While Marx's theory, making neither specific quantitative nor temporal predictions, does not forecast a timespan for capitalism, it does imply that the 'historical tendency' should make itself felt over a long enough span of time, while suggesting that the period since the start of the 19th century ought to be a sufficiently long one. Has it?

12.3 From the 20th century

It was Grossmann's opinion that the falling rate of profit, a phenomenon of the global capitalist system, manifested itself serially in different countries, with its effects visible in the 18th century in Holland, in the 1820s in England, and in the 1860s also in France (Grossmann, 1929: p. 530). The United States was, in his view, similarly affected after the

First World War, and surely Grossmann saw the Great Depression, which broke out in the US in the same year as his magnum opus was published, as a confirmation of this judgement. At the same time, given the ever closer integration of the world's nations into what gradually emerge as a world market for commodities and capital investment, the international character of crises became stronger. Eighty-odd years after the end of the Great Depression, is there any evidence of a continuing effect of this predicted trend?

The idea that world capitalism entered a period of decline in the course of the 20th century was not peculiar to Marxists: Werner Sombart wrote in 1927 of contemporary capitalism as declining into 'late capitalism', and in 1952 Josef Steindl, focusing on the United States, saw lower rates of accumulation after 1899 (Steindl, 1952: p. 156). The theme of stagnation as characteristic of the American economy reappeared in heterodox economic literature after the 1970s, with the advent of stagflation and relatively low growth rates following the recession of 1974–1975 (for example, Coates, 2000). At one time it was fashionable to contrast the poor performance of the American economy with the dynamism of the Japanese, but the depression gripping Japan since the 1990s has put an end to that.

Despite the particular features of the Great Depression, and most importantly the war into which it opened, the post-1945 revival of the capitalist economy followed, in broad outline, the pattern set in previous episodes of economic collapse and regeneration. The depression had been long-lasting and the level of physical and economic destruction of capital unusually high; it is not surprising, therefore, from a Marxian point of view, that the revival led to an exceptionally long prosperity. At the same time, however, as Angus Maddison observes, a 'major feature of the golden age was the substantial growth in the ratio of governmental spending to GDP' which 'rose from 27 per cent of GDP in OECD countries in 1950 to 37 per cent in 1973' (Maddison, 1995: p. 69). These numbers were, of course, well below the levels of government spending during World War II itself, but they show that the capitalist economy proper – the private enterprise system – was, even after the profit-restoring effects of a crisis lasting from 1929 to 1945, not by itself able to produce a level of well-being sufficient, in the eyes of social decision makers, to achieve a politically desirable level of social contentment. Thus, for example, when a Republican government, acting on its anti-New Deal, pro-free enterprise ideology, cut defence spending after the end of the Korean War in 1953 without adding offsetting increases in domestic expenditure, the United States experienced a sharp drop in production and a correspondingly sharp increase in unemployment. Despite its wishes, the Eisenhower administration quickly acted to lower interest rates and increase government spending, including on public works (on the scale of the interstate highway system) as well as on directly military projects. In the United States, in fact, political economist Joyce Kolko noted in 1988, 'roughly half of all new employment after 1950 was created by state expenditures, and a comparable shift occurred in the other OECD nations' (Kolko, 1988: p. 19).

Thus the prosperity made possible by the economic and physical destruction effected by the Great Depression and the Second World War was, even at its highest point, the late 1950s, insufficient to obviate the need for government stimulus. Government spending, on the other hand, was not able to eliminate 'official pauperism', as the failure of the American 'War on Poverty' demonstrated. Exactly as Marx's value-theoretic model suggests, the increased productivity of labour making possible the post-war growth of private capital continued to involve a displacement of labour from employment. This feature of capitalist development was accentuated when the postwar Golden Age came to a definitive end in the mid-1970s, leading to a durable increase in unemployment in Europe and a tendential weakening in the American labour market. As a specialist on the topic observed more than a decade ago, the 'perceptible rise in unemployment in the mid-1970s marked the beginning of a new phase' in which 'elevated unemployment rates are the reflection [...] of the definite decline of the [post-war] epoch of full employment' (Pugliese, 1993: p. 15). The current downturn has brought these conditions to the United States, as well as raising levels of unemployment throughout the world.

If we attend specifically to the workers involved in Marx's theoretical model, which focuses on those whose labour is given social definition as value and surplus value, 'the last 30 years have witnessed a global stagnation in the relative number of industrial workers'. It is only 'a low-wage service sector' that 'has made up the difference in the high GDP countries alongside an unparalleled explosion of slum-dwellers and informal workers in the low GDP countries' (Benanav and Endnotes, 2011: p. 34). As the authors of the insightful text just cited also observe, this 'deindustrialization' – which has involved not so much a decline in industrial production as in the numbers of workers relative to capital investment, needed to perform it – has been an international tendency, operating in the underdeveloped as well as the developed countries. To take the most spectacular example, 'the latest statistics show that *China did not create any new jobs in manufacturing between 1993 and 2006*', both because the development of its new export-oriented sector was accompanied by the dismantling of older state industries and because Chinese industrialisation, like that elsewhere in the developing world, has involved 'the incorporation of existing labor-saving innovations' (ibid: p. 49).

At the same time, the economic growth made possible by the increases in the rate of exploitation achieved by the combination of lowered global wage levels and technologically enhanced labour productivity has clearly not involved a growth in profits sufficient to employ increasing numbers of the masses of people being thrown onto the mercies of the labour market or to satisfy their needs unproductively. In the words of a recent survey,

> Between 1973 and the present, economic performance in the U.S., Western Europe, and Japan has, by every standard macroeconomic indicator, deteriorated, business cycle by business cycle, decade by decade (with the exception of the second half of the 1990s). Equally telling, over the same period, capital investment on a world scale, and in every nation except China, even including the East Asian [Newly Industrialized Countries] since the middle 1990s, has been growing steadily weaker. (Brenner, 2009: p. 62)

As a result, according to the United Nations' *Human Development Report 2004*, 'an unprecendented number of countries saw development slide backwards in the 1990s' –before the current depression. 'In 46 countries people are poorer today than in 1990. In 25 countries more people are hungry today than a decade ago' (Davis, 2006: p. 163). To take only one example of this trend, the mass pauperisation of the population in the formerly 'socialist' countries after 1989 led, by one estimate, to an increase of those living in extreme poverty from 14 to 168 million (ibid: p. 106).

Alongside these surplus people we find surplus capital – that is, capital that cannot be profitably invested in the production of new surplus value. Here again, Grossmann's analysis, formulated on the basis of economic history up to the early 20th century, has been strikingly vindicated by developments of the most recent period. Speaking of 'unemployed capital' unable to find investment opportunities, he observed that 'because it cannot be utilized within the sphere of production, capital is exported or – from the viewpoint of production – directed towards "internal export," the streaming of unemployed money into speculation' (Grossmann, 1929: pp. 536–537). This function of financial speculation – to create 'a profitable "investment" for over-accumulated capital'[7] (ibid: p. 543) is accompanied by speculation in real estate (ibid: p. 541), to which we can now add all the other asset classes on the basis of which bubbles can be developed, from commodity futures and more arcane derivatives to fine art. And just as capital flowed into speculation instead of into productive investment, producing the effect of temporary prosperity by means of a series of bubbles, working-class living standards were maintained by the massive growth of consumer debt, culminating in workers' participation in the mortgage bubble of the early 21st century.

Like the growth of state debt and the welfare state, the difficulty we see today in doing away with them registers the decline of the private enterprise economy. Despite its dynamism and the gigantic increases in the productivity of human labour that it has achieved since the early 19th century, and despite the disappearance of political and social barriers to its spread in the course of the 20th, capitalism has not been able to generate the quantities of profit required to incorporate much of the world's population into its modern industrial form. Instead, more and more profit must be diverted from capitalist purposes to feed the starving, attempt to pacify the rebellious, and manage the insufficiencies of accumulation even in the developed countries.

Whether private, corporate, or public, debt must eventually be repaid out of money made by the profitable production and sale of goods and services. The failure of the non-financial parts of the economy to expand sufficiently showed itself in 2008 in the near-collapse of the whole Rube Goldberg device of cantilevered finance. For the same reason – the insufficient growth of profits – the massive increase in government spending, based on the borrowing of underutilised capital that avoided a return to depression conditions after the mid-1960s, was another step on the way to today's increasingly problematic deficits. From the viewpoint of Marx's theory of capital accumulation, it has been precisely the avoidance of depression conditions that has prevented a new transition to prosperity since the end of the post-war Golden Age. Despite the sense that this is what is needed, evident in the world's rulers' wish to impose austerity on the global working class, they are also clearly afraid of the consequences for social order; hence the political paralysis that today accompanies economic stagnation.

Is this to say that the current crisis cycle has moved capitalism to the point of breakdown, in the sense of self-destruction? No, because today, as at all earlier moments, capitalism's fate ultimately depends on the willingness of human beings to engage in the difficult struggles needed to overthrow existing relations of social power and create new forms of production and consumption. On the other hand, in its current condition capitalism promises economic difficulties for decades to come, with increased assaults on the earnings and working conditions of those who are still lucky enough to be wage earners around the world, with waves of bankruptcies and business consolidations for capitalist firms, and with increasingly serious conflicts among economic entities and even nations over just who is going to pay for the system's survival. The mass unemployment and material deprivation that Marx predicted as the long-term outcome of capitalist development have become features of the world economy that if not permanent will clearly be with us for an extended time. Like its predecessors, today's crisis makes visible, for anyone who cares to see, the historical tendency of capitalist accumulation.[8]

Notes

1. There have been a number of important exceptions to this rule, such as the German 'Krisis' and 'Wertkritik' grouplets, and the occasional writer in English (David Yaffe, Fred Moseley) and German (Mario Cogoy) inspired by Paul Mattick, who himself was an exception that proved the rule, being a survivor from prewar Marxism.
2. I ignore criticisms based on the Okishio Theorem, which some have taken to prove the impossibility of an increase in investment leading to a decrease in profitability, because it is based on a neoricardian variant of equilibrium price theory in direct conflict with Marx's theory of value and price. As Michael Heinrich has observed, it is 'highly controversial' whether the model on which Okishio's argument is based 'can be accepted as a corrected version of Marx's production price theory' (Heinrich, 2006: p. 75). Nobuo Okishio himself, while finding his theorem valid given his assumptions, ultimately decided that those 'assumptions were inappropriate' (Okishio, 2000: p. 493).
3. Fred Moseley (1991) earlier provided a detailed mathematical version of this argument in his *The Falling Rate of Profit in the United States Economy*, pp. 11–20.
4. For a serious attempt to formalise this concept in application to Marx's work, see Nowak 1979.
5. See Book IV, secs. 5–8. To my knowledge, Grossmann was the first to identify Mill as the source of the list of counteracting factors in Volume III of *Capital* (Marx, 1981[1875]).
6. Hence for Mill all the counteracting factors are economic phenomena offsetting a process based on extra-economic facts, in particular the fertility of the soil and population growth, just as he derives the inducements to save and invest, Keynes-style, from human psychology.

7. Grossmann adds that, of course, 'these profits do not arise from actual production, but are transfers of capital from one hand to another', whence arises the inevitable bursting of all such bubbles.
8. For an analysis of the current economic crisis in terms of Marx's theory of accumulation, see Mattick (2011).

13

Macroeconomic Paradoxes with Kalecki and Kaleckians

Marc Lavoie

13.1 Introduction[1]

Post-Keynesian economics is known for the several paradoxes that it uncovers by taking macroeconomics as something else than some aggregated model with micro-foundations. Among these paradoxes is Michał Kalecki's paradox, which we can define as the claim that higher government deficits generate larger profits for the capitalists. Kalecki's paradox can be derived straight from the national accounts, with a couple of simple behavioural assumptions.

This was not Kalecki's only contribution to economics. He also had a deep understanding of political economy, in particular how it applied to capitalist economies. Among the many aphorisms or statements that can be attributed to Kalecki, there is this following sentence, which without a doubt illuminates the current situation, as governments try to come out of the financial crisis by pursuing austerity policies whose purpose is to create confidence among the actors of the financial market. As Kalecki put it in 1943:

> Under a laisser-faire system the level of employment depends on the so-called state of confidence [...]. This gives to the capitalists a powerful indirect control over Government policy: everything which may shake the state of confidence must be carefully avoided because it would cause an economic crisis. The social function of the doctrine of 'sound finance' is to make the level of employment dependent on the 'state of confidence'. (Kalecki, 1971b: p. 139)

This statement is brilliant and is still relevant. Governments in Europe in particular refuse to proceed with expansionary policies, and hence functional finance, on the grounds that expansionary policies would destroy the confidence of the financial markets and of entrepreneurs. Under quite simple assumptions, however, the reality is completely the opposite: expansionary policies would increase the profits of the corporate sector and thus ought to lead to a recovery of confidence. The behaviour of the business class is thus itself paradoxical.

The objective of this chapter is to introduce government deficits within Kaleckian models in a simple manner. It will be shown that the introduction of government deficits yields some results that will appear to be paradoxical, both to mainstream economists and to economists who have been working within the Kaleckian tradition. To a large extent, only short-run results will be examined.

The outline of the chapter is the following. In the first section, I recall a highly simplified Kaleckian model, in a closed economy without government. In the second section, government deficits are introduced into this simple model; it will be shown that opening the economy to foreign trade will yield similar results. In the third section, a slightly more complicated model is introduced, while interest payments on the debt are explicitly taken into account. This will allow us to tackle the issue that has been raised by Tom Palley (1997: p. 340), that is whether deficits could have favourable effects on profits and economic activity in the short run while the accumulated debt would have negative effects in the longer run.

13.2 A simple Kaleckian model

Take the simplest Kaleckian model, as can be found, for instance, in the writings of Sidney Weintraub (1978). Let the value of output (pq) be a simple multiple of the wage costs (wL), where κ is a constant larger than one:

$$pq - \kappa wL \tag{13.1}$$

This implies that profits (P), in real terms, are a constant share of real output, this share being π, where π represents the share of profits seen from the supply side. Profits in real terms are thus:

$$P = \pi q \tag{13.2}$$

On the other hand, we may also consider the share of profits from the demand side. Short-run equilibrium is achieved when saving equals investment. In the simplest model, there are no savings out of wages, and hence:

$$I = S = s_p P \tag{13.3}$$

where s_p is the propensity to save out of profits.

From the above equation, it follows immediately that:

$$P = I/s_p \tag{13.4}$$

that is, the amount of profits in real terms is determined by the level of real investment, which is assumed to be given from past decisions. Taking the share of profits into account, we also get:

$$q = I/(s_p \pi) \tag{13.5}$$

that is, the higher the profit share, the smaller the level of output (and hence of employment), for a given amount of real investment (Lavoie, 1998).

This, according to Andrew Trigg (1994), is the true representation of Kalecki's economics. Trigg claims that changes in the costing margin, or in the profit share π as is the case in our simplified model, will have no impact on the level of profits. As Trigg (1994: p. 97) says, 'The relative share of profits in income must increase in response to the higher degree of monopoly. Since profits are determined by investment [...] the level of profits does not change'. This last sentence is illustrated with the help of Figure 13.1. Changes in the profit share (or in the costing margin, or in the so-called degree of monopoly) have no effect whatsoever on the level of profits. Profits are determined by investment, and this is why the profits curve shown in Figure 13.1 is a simple horizontal line.

On the other hand, it is clear that an increase in the costing margin or in the profit share for a given level of investment leads to a reduction in the level of output. Trigg (1994: p. 98) made it quite clear: 'An increase in monopoly power generates a reduction in output that increases the profit share without changing the absolute volume of profits'. Higher costing margins thus induce lower rates of capacity utilisation for the same level of profits. This is a result that can be directly attributed to Kalecki (1954: p. 71): 'The level of income or product will decline to the point at which the higher relative share of profits yields the same absolute level of profits'. The decreased output and employment which is assumed to accompany a redistribution of income towards profit

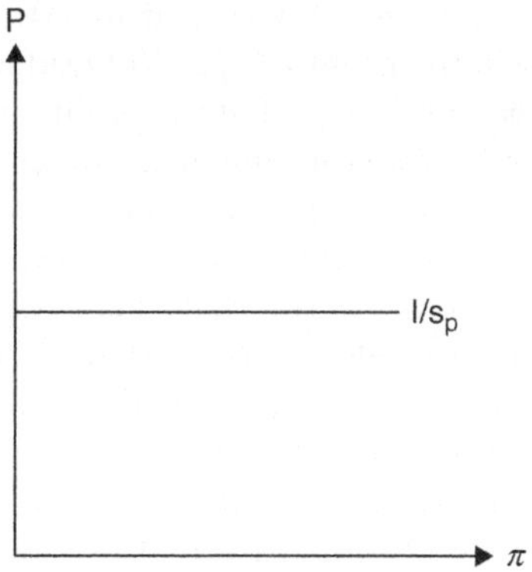

Figure 13.1 Profits and costing margins in a closed economy without a public sector

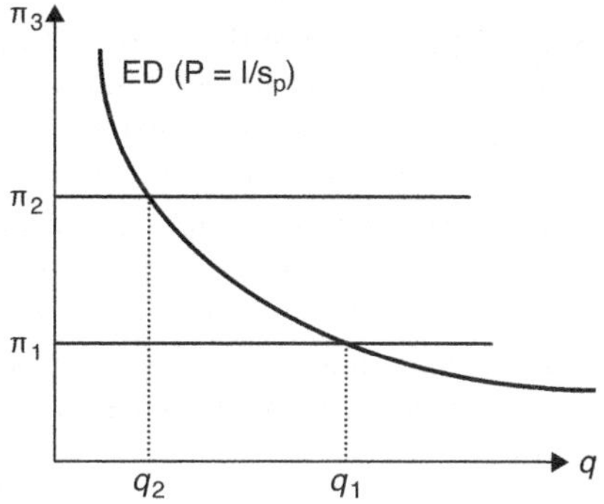

Figure 13.2 A simple Kaleckian model in a closed economy without public sector

earners (or an increase in the bargaining power of firms) is illustrated in Figure 13.2. The effective demand condition given by the last equation above is represented by a rectangular hyperbola to the horizontal axis.

In the present model, investment is assumed not to depend on current conditions. If this were not the case, as in standard Kaleckian growth models, where investment reacts to the current rate of capacity utilisation, a higher costing margin would induce a reduction in investment (or in the rate of accumulation in a growth context), and this would induce a fall in realised profits and the rate of profit. In those Kaleckian models, *higher* profit margins are thus associated with *lower* levels of profit (Lavoie,

1992; Mott and Slattery, 1994). However, if investment is given in the short run, the increase in the profit margin will lead to a fall in the rate of capacity utilisation that will be such that the profit rate remains at exactly the level it had achieved before the change in the profit margin.

This peculiar consequence of macroeconomic identities is still not always perceived by heterodox authors. For instance, Sergio Cesaratto (2012) in his presentation of the Kaleckian model wonders why Kaleckian authors (for example, Lavoie, 2006: p. 118) assume that a reduction in the profit margin at a given investment rate implies no change whatsoever in the profit rate of the economy while the rate of utilisation of capacity increases. Cesaratto (2012), as shown in the quote below, believes that with the increase in the rate of capacity utilisation anything could happen: the profit rate could increase, decrease or remain the same, depending on the values of the parameters.

> On this basis, the NK authors extend the Keynesian paradox of thrift to a dynamic setting. Suppose that a rise in real wages causes a fall of the profit share π. This causes a rightward rotation of both g_s and PC curves of figure 1, respectively. At the initial growth rate $g_w = \alpha$, the lower capacity savings determine a higher degree of capacity utilisation u_a^0 (point B). The higher rate of extraction of profits out of a given capital stock may (less than, more than) compensate the fall in the profit share, so that the resulting profit rate can be – depending on the shape of the function – equal, lower, higher than the initial one. In the uncertainty (and following Lavoie, 2006: figure 5.2), we keep it equal. (Cesaratto, 2012)

While Cesaratto makes use of the equation that arises from the definition of the profit rate, noting that the profit rate r is such that $r = \pi u/v$ where u is the rate of utilisation of capacity and where v is the capital to full-capacity ratio, he forgets the other equation that defines the actual profit rate, the equation that arises from the macroeconomic condition that investment must equal saving, which is that when there is no saving out of wages, the profit rate is simply $r = g/s_p$, where g is the rate of accumulation. Hence, as long as there is no change in the propensity to save out of profits and no change in the level of investment and hence in the rate of accumulation decided by firms, the profit rate remains constant, as shown in Figure 13.3, which reproduces the figure to which Cesaratto alludes. The economy moves from point A to point B in Figure 13.3. Thus, putting Trigg's statement into a dynamic setting, this implies that

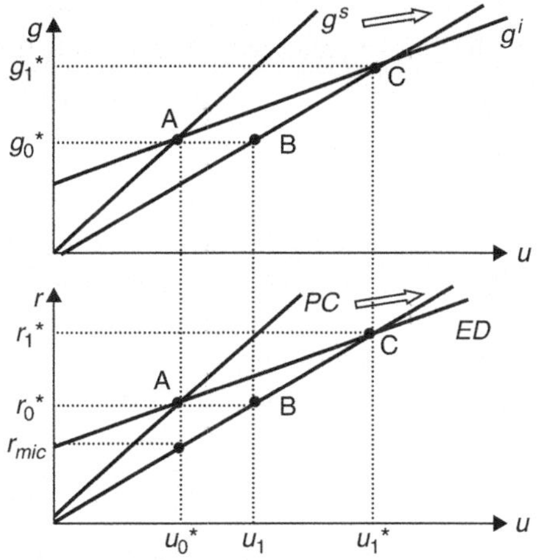

Figure 13.3 The profit rate in a Kaleckian growth model

the change in the profit margin embedded in the pricing procedure will have no impact on the profit rate.[2] By contrast, as already mentioned, if the rate of accumulation depends on the rate of capacity utilisation, as is assumed in the canonical Kaleckian growth model and as assumed in Figure 13.3, the reduction in profit margins will drive the economy towards point C, thus attaining a higher growth rate and a higher profit rate. This is the Kaleckian paradox of costs – higher real wages lead to higher profit rates![3]

13.3 Adding government deficits to the simple model

Let us now see whether these simple results (with a given investment level) still hold when the public sector (or the foreign sector) is introduced. Let us first add the public sector. Let us assume that the deficit of the public sector is equal to:

$$\Delta D = G - \tau q \tag{13.6}$$

where ΔD is the change in public debt, that is the government deficit, while G and τ represents overall government expenditures and the overall tax rate on revenues (net of transfer payments including interest payments on debt).

In the simplified framework of the previous section, the effective demand condition linking overall saving to overall investment is the following:

$$s_p P = I + (G - \tau q) \tag{13.7}$$

Solving for q, the equilibrium level of output is still an inverse function of the costing margin (here the profit share π), as it was in the closed economy. As one would expect from a standard Kaleckian or Keynesian model, output (or employment) depends positively on government expenditures and negatively on the tax. We have:

$$q = (I + G)/(s_p\pi + \tau) \tag{13.8}$$

Looking now at profits, it is clear that, as Kalecki (1971b: p. 85) would put it, a budget deficit 'permits profits to increase above the level determined by private investment and capitalists' consumption'. On the other hand, when taking changes in costing margins into consideration, profits do not behave in the manner that most Kaleckians would expect. The level of profits is now given by the equation:

$$P = (I + G)/(s_p + \tau/\pi) \tag{13.9}$$

The above equation clearly shows that in contrast to what occurred in the simple model of Figure 13.1, any increase in the costing margin π leads to an increase in the level of profits P, as illustrated in Figure 13.4. Not only are profits sensitive to the costing margin, which was not the case in Kalecki's own model, but in addition profits move in a direction which is the exact opposite of what occurred in Kaleckian growth models, where investment was sensitive to capacity utilisation.

The economic logic of the above result is simple. When firms decide or manage to increase their costing margins, effective demand is reduced and this leads to a decrease in income and output. The fall in income induces a fall in the yield of taxation, thus leading to an increase in the public deficit, assuming there is no change in government expenditures. The increase in government deficit, for a given level of private investment, thus generates in the end an increase in corporate profits.[4] The redistribution of income towards profit earners is thus achieved through the accumulation of debt by the public sector. Profit earners are targeting higher profits, and are achieving those. But the situation was different in a closed economy without government; there, capitalists

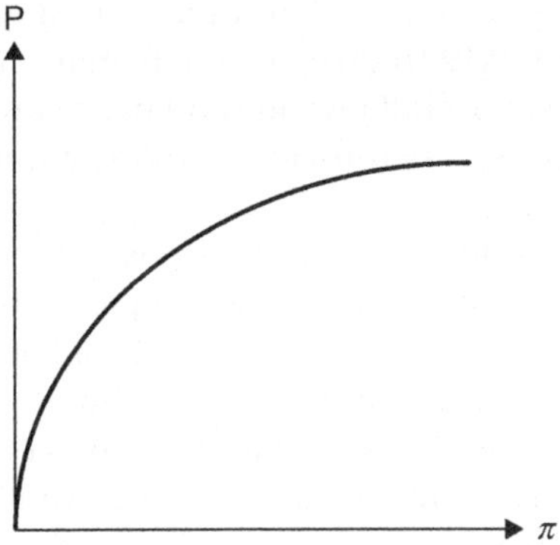

Figure 13.4 Profits and costing margins with an endogenous budget or trade balance

could only realise these higher profits by increasing investment and private debt. With the existence of the public sector, the higher profits can be achieved instead by an endogenous increase in the debt of the public sector.

In the present model, it has been assumed that only government revenues were a function of overall output. Alternatively, we could have assumed as well that government expenditures are an inverse function of output and employment, taking into account, for instance, unemployment insurance support programmes, as do Bougrine and Seccareccia (1999: p. 11).

A very similar result would be achieved in an open economy. Assume that exports are exogenous ($X = X$), while imports depend on the level of income ($M = mq$). Equating injections and leaks of the monetary circuit, we have:

$$I + G + X = s_p\pi q + \tau q + mq \qquad (13.10)$$

or

$$q = (I + G + X)/(s_p\pi + \tau + m) \qquad (13.11)$$

and hence, since $P = \pi q$, the level of profits fulfilling the effective demand condition would be:

$$P = (I + G + X)/\{s_p + (m + \tau)/\pi\} \qquad (13.12)$$

where again realised profits would respond positively to an increase in the costing margin. With higher costing margins, internal demand is reduced, which reduces overall revenue and hence imports, thus leading to an increase in net exports (provided exports are not affected by the higher costing margins).

Figure 13.5 helps to understand why the positive relationship between profits and costing margins occurs. What happens is that while the effective demand constraint is again represented by a rectangular hyperbola in the (q, π) axes, as was the case in the simple model of Figure 13.2, the hyperbola is now rectangular with respect to the $-(m + \tau)/s_p$ horizontal line rather than to the horizontal axis as such. It follows that the level of profits, at high costing margins, must be larger than profits at low costing margins.

It is clear that introducing a public sector, with an endogenous budget deficit, does change the fundamental results of the Kaleckian model.[5] Where as the profitability constraint, sometimes called the reproducibility constraint, plays no role in the simple Kaleckian model of employment, profitability becomes a concern in a model that includes a foreign sector or a government sector. In the simple model, higher real wages, through higher effective demand, can always improve employment. However, once the budget deficit is made endogenous to economic activity, or once savings out of wages are introduced, the profitability constraint may become binding. At some point, increases in real wages become impossible because they would induce non-positive corporate profits. This arises from Kalecki's well-known profit equation,

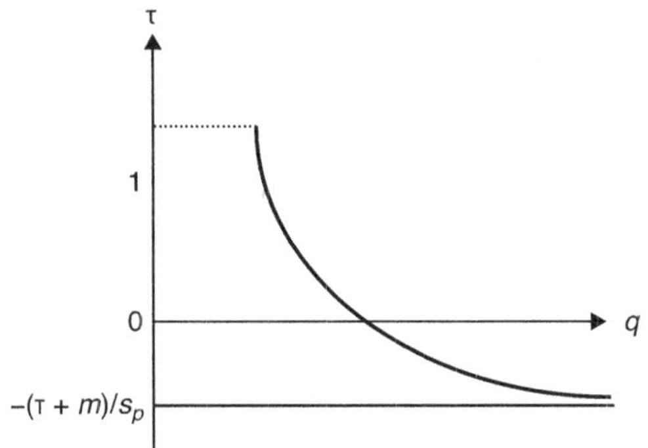

Figure 13.5 The Kaleckian model with an endogenous budget deficit and trade balance

where profits are equal to investment expenditures, plus government deficit, plus consumption out of profits, minus saving out of wages. In a demand-led Kaleckian growth model, where investment is a function of the rate of capacity utilisation, Edward Amadeo (1986: p. 94) shows that with saving out of wages, a decrease in the costing margin may lead to a decrease in the realised rate of profit, even though the rate of capacity utilisation rises in all cases. This can be assessed in our little model, by adding saving out of wages. With s_w the propensity to save, we get:

$$I + G + X = s_p\pi q + \tau q + mq + s_w(1 - \pi)q \qquad (13.13)$$

$$q = (I + G + X)/\{(s_p - s_w)\pi + \tau + m + s_w\} \qquad (13.14)$$

$$P = (I + G + X)/\{(s_p - s_w) + (m + \tau + s_w)/\pi\} \qquad (13.15)$$

Thus a reduction increase in the costing margin leads to an increase in aggregate demand and demand-determined employment; however, with a given investment level, the decrease in the costing margin also leads to a reduction in overall profits as long as wage-earners save part of their income.

13.4 Taking explicit account of interest payments on public debt

The surprising results achieved above are to be found, under a slightly different guise, in an article of Thomas Palley (1997: p. 337), who notes that they contrast with 'the standard Kaleckian result'. In his paper, Palley takes explicit account of the interest payments that the government must make on its public debt. The advantage of such a representation is that taxes on these interest payments, which are not part of gross domestic product in the standard national accounts, can now explicitly be taken into consideration. Palley assumes that there are different tax rates for wage income on the one hand, and for profit and interest income on the other hand, but we can as well assume that all kinds of income are subject to the same tax rate.

The budget deficit now is:

$$\Delta D = (G - T) + iD = Def + iD \qquad (13.16)$$

where G are still programme expenditures only, while T is the overall amount of revenues collected by government (now excluding negative) interest payments, i is the real rate of interest (since everything else is measured in real terms) and D is the public debt stock (again in real terms). The primary deficit, before interest payments, is Def.

Let us again consider the leaks from and the injections into the circuit. Let us assume again, for simplification, that there are no savings out of wages (and no saving (nor taxes) out of transfer income, besides interest payments). With τ the rate of taxation on all other sorts of income, we have:[6]

$$s_p(1 - \tau)(P + iD) = I + Def + iD \tag{13.17}$$

Solving for P, the level of profits, we obtain:

$$P = \{Def + I + iD[1 - s_p(1 - \tau)]\}/\{s_p(1 - \tau)\} \tag{13.18}$$

It is clear again that for a given level of private investment and a given primary deficit the increase in interest payments on the public debt will have a positive impact on the level of profits.

Now Palley (1997: p. 340) argues that the deficit initially has favourable effects on profits, but that ultimately, in the long run, these effects become negative because of the rising debt which becomes unacceptable, thus forcing governments to cut on deficits and thus forcing them to run operating primary surpluses rather than deficits. In the example given by Palley, while the debt and the interest payments are growing, the overall deficit, ΔD, remains constant, thus implying that ultimately the primary deficit necessarily becomes negative, leading to a primary surplus. Is this necessary?

Suppose government officials decide that they do not want the debt level to rise any more. This implies that the overall deficit is zero, or $\Delta D = 0$. As a consequence, the primary surplus must be exactly equal to the interest payments on the debt, or $Def = -iD$. Substituting Def for this value in the above profits equation, one obtains:

$$P = \{I - iD[s_p(1 - \tau)]\}/\{s_p(1 - \tau)\} \tag{13.19}$$

Then, very clearly, under this self-imposed constraint, past deficits have a negative effect on present profits ($dP/dD < 0$). As Palley would put it, 'the cumulative effect of persistent deficits' on the economy becomes negative: 'There is no longer an expansionary flow (deficit) dimension to the budget, but the contractionary stock (debt) dimension remains'. This resembles the present situation in Canada, where the federal government is targeting an overall balanced budget (or at least is claiming to do so).

Now consider the case where the overall deficit is allowed to grow at a rate g, which is consistent with the growth rate of real output. This implies that government officials are willing to keep the debt ratio at a constant level, that is, at the level achieved for historical reasons.[7] This implies that:

$$\Delta D/D = g \tag{13.20}$$

We then have:

$$Def = gD - iD \tag{13.21}$$

With the appropriate substitutions, we obtain:

$$P = \{gD + I\}/\{s_p(1 - \tau)\} - iD \tag{13.22}$$

Taking the derivative, it follows that:

$$dP/dD > 0 \text{ if } g > is_p(1 - \tau) \tag{13.23}$$

Even when the rate of growth g of the economy is lower than the real rate of interest i, or even lower than the rate of interest net of taxes $i(1 - \tau)$, it is still possible for the long-term effects of government deficits to have a favourable impact on corporate profits, provided the above condition is fulfilled.

What if we assume, as do Godley and Lavoie (2007), that households consume part of their wealth?[8] The wealth of household is the sum of public debt D and the value of capital K, assuming that the capital of firms is approximately valued at its replacement cost. The equation equating saving to investment then becomes:

$$s_p(1 - \tau)(P + iD) - c_W(K + D) = I + Def + iD \tag{13.24}$$

where c_W is the propensity to consume out of wealth. Solving again for P, the level of profits, we obtain:

$$P = \{Def + I + c_W K + D[c_W + i(1 - s_p(1 - \tau))]\}/\{s_p(1 - \tau)\} \tag{13.25}$$

Assuming again that $Def = gD - iD$, we get:

$$P = \{gD + I + c_W(K + D)\}/\{s_p(1 - \tau)\} - iD \tag{13.26}$$

And taking once more the derivative, we get:

$$dP/dD = \{(g + c_W)/ s_p(1 - \tau)\} - i \tag{13.27}$$

so that $dP/dD > 0$ when $(g + c_W) > is_p(1 - \tau)$.

The condition is more easily fulfilled when households consume part of their wealth, and hence it is more likely that deficits will have a favourable effect on profits, both in the short and the long run.

13.5 Conclusion

Making simplifying assumptions sometimes makes no difference to the results achieved. In the present case, introducing government deficits that are responsive to economic activity does change some of the better-known results achieved with simple demand-led Kaleckian models. With endogenous government deficits, an increase in the costing margin (in the 'degree of monopoly') may lead to an increase in aggregate profits, something that was impossible in the simpler Kaleckian model without a government or with a given deficit to output ratio or deficit to capital ratio. Furthermore, with saving out of wages, a decrease in the costing margin will increase output but reduce aggregate profits, thus introducing a profitability constraint that did not exist in the simplified Kaleckian model with no foreign sector, no endogenous government deficit, and no saving out of wages.

In addition, we have shown that, in contrast to what some authors claim, past deficits keep having a favourable impact on current profits, so that the favourable impact of government deficits on profits occurs both in the short run and in the long run.

Notes

1. This chapter develops parts of Lavoie (2000).
2. In the revised version, after I had pointed this out, Cesaratto (2012) wrote: 'In practice, the higher rate of extraction of profits out of a given capital stock precisely compensates the fall in the profit share, so that the resulting *actual* profit rate is equal to the initial one.'
3. In Figure 13.3, assuming that the initial rate of utilisation u_0 is the normal rate of utilisation, firms would be facing a new costing margin such that the

realised rate of profit at the normal rate of capacity utilisation would be r_{mic}. This would be the rate of profit that would be consistent with microeconomic analysis, if a firm were to act in isolation. However, if all firms face a reduced costing margin, the rate of utilisation will move up to u_1 and the realised profit rate will remain at r_0^*; while if all firms in addition react positively to their higher rate of capacity utilisation, the realised profit rate will itself increase to r_1^*.

4. In the Kaleckian growth model of Lavoie (1992: p. 310), a public sector is introduced, but the government budget deficit (relative to the stock of capital) is assumed to be exogenously given, and hence none of the results obtained here are to be found.
5. It was recently brought to my attention, by Eckhard Hein, that Asimakopulos (1988) had already pointed out that the presence of a budget deficit and of saving out of wages made overall profits a positive function of the costing margin.
6. A similar equation can be found in the Kaleckian growth model of You and Dutt (1996). Their model goes into the details of the long-run dynamics of public debt. A stock-flow consistent model that takes into account the corporate sector has recently been set up by Ryoo and Skott (2013).
7. Palley (1997: p. 340) does not seem to realise that the variable that he calls *b*, and which plays a crucial role in his final equation, is the inverse of the growth rate of public debt.
8. Kalecki (1954: p. 53) believes that the consumption of capitalists includes a term which 'is a constant in the short run although subject to long-run changes'. This term could be consumption out of wealth.

14

Revisiting the Socialist Calculation Debate: The Role of Markets and Finance in Hayek's Response to Lange's Challenge

Paul Auerbach and Dimitris P. Sotiropoulos

14.1 Introduction

Theoretical and political debates on the character of socialist planning and the so-called 'law of value' under socialism had emerged at the end of the 19th century and became an issue of significance in the wake of the Bolshevik Revolution in the 1920s. The issues raised soon attracted the attention of the liberal thought of the period; in an essay published in 1920, Ludwig von Mises challenged socialist and engineering-technocratic schema, stating that every attempt to abolish markets and money would result in economic disaster: the construction of a viable socialist economy was an impossible task.[1] In fact, the aim of Mises' theoretical and political intervention was not focused solely upon the nature of socialist economies; he was also concerned with all forms of state intervention, including that which was taking place in Austria and Germany at the time (though he approved of state subsidies to the opera). It was not, however, until the 1930s ,when Friedrich Hayek re-circulated Mises' article, that the socialist calculation debate actually started. The most famous reply came from two eastern European economists: the Romanian Abba Lerner and the Polish Oskar Lange. This chapter will not go through the details of this debate but focus on the reasoning of two of the protagonists: Lange and Hayek.

Lange took up the challenge of Mises' claim of the impossibility of constructing a socialist economy. He readily acceded to the need for efficiency calculations to be made in value terms rather than using purely natural or engineering criteria, but claimed that these values could emerge along lines consistent with neoclassical value theory, without the need for a market in capital goods and without private ownership over the means of production. Lange drew heavily upon the dominant neoclassical tradition to defend socialism, or at least to defend a version of it that he considered appropriate. Lange's argument was that the neoclassical static form of equilibrium can be easily replicated by the socialist economy. The version of socialism he chose to refer to as his standard was in facta type of capitalism without capital markets. In this regard, Lange managed implicitly to set out two important arguments. First, he showed that a version of mainstream thinking that underestimates the role of capital markets in capitalism can be utilised to defend the paradigm of central planners. Second, a system that had abolished private property over the means of production and therefore capital markets and finance not only could replicate the much advertised efficiency of capitalism but also would enhance economic stability. We must not forget that the debate took place in the 1930s, when the consequences of the great depression were central in everyone's mind; taming the financial instability of the capitalist system without sacrificing economic efficiency would seem an appealing alternative to the free market system in a period when the latter was generating many unresolved contradictions.

Hayek, along with the other Austrians, understood very well the message of this critique. How could a liberal economist respond to a 'neoclassical' defence of the state ownership of the means of production? There was only one way out of this uncanny encounter: the conceptualisation of the capitalist economy must be clearly differentiated from the neoclassical universe of perfect competition and static equilibrium. This departure was never clearly stated in the writings of Mises and Hayek, and never properly emphasised. Hayek's argument stressed the dynamic aspects of competition in the context of the capital market: market competition is to be seen as a discovery procedure wherein production possibilities must not be taken for granted but emerge from the process of competition in the context of the capital market. Thus, socialist calculation is impossible because of the absence of those markets for capital and risk that evaluate the success or failure of different investment decisions under capitalism. Efficient economic calculation is unthinkable in the absence of disequilibrium prices for capital and risk.

But here we encounter an unexpected twist. While Lange degraded socialism to a mere replication of capitalism's efficiency achievements, Hayek implicitly realised the danger of undermining functional capitalist behaviour and therefore the nature of capitalist relations. If we see economic behaviour in capitalism as the outcome of capitalist social relations of power, then Hayek's perspective renders capital markets a central arena in the organisation of capitalism as a system of exploitation. He also perceived every movement towards collective ownership of the means of production as a real threat to the reproduction of the logic of capitalism. In this sense, he implicitly ended up giving an unexpected endorsement to socialism that is much deeper and sophisticated than the superficial 'defence' of Lange: every serious state intervention in the capital market threatens to eliminate the capitalist spirit, making the existence of the system vulnerable in the context of the reproduction of its power relations. This last point gives us the chance to revisit the socialist calculation debate, interpreting finance as *trauma* for mainstream discussions.

14.2 The background of the debate: the so-called 'market socialists' and the initial intervention of Mises in 1920

The debate between the supporters of socialism and those of capitalism, long before the Bolshevik Revolution of 1917, was interlinked to another theoretical dispute: the one between the labour ('objective') and the 'subjective' theories of value. Nevertheless, this connection was not as straightforward as one might think: the defenders of socialism drew upon both theoretical traditions. In order to understand this, we must have in mind two different issues.

On the one hand, as we shall see below, the established version of socialism in these debates (in the first decades of the 20th century at least) was a society with state ownership of the means of production.[2] If we assume that saving and borrowing take place only within the capitalist class (that is, labourers do not save nor borrow), then this rather awkward version of socialism is close to a capitalism without capital markets, that is to say capitalism without finance.

On the other hand, traditional Marxism (though not Marx himself) argued that the labour theory of value is prior to every possible type of economic and social organisation (Section 14.2.1); market socialists put forward the very same idea with regard to the neoclassical theory of value (Section 14.2.2). Both of these traditions argued for an *ontological primacy* of each theory of value over the institutional configuration of society. Taking that for granted, the above-mentioned model of socialism could, at least in principle, replicate the workings of capitalism because the equilibrium conditions could be specified and met without any reference to the price of capital. This was in fact the meeting point between the two different defences of this type of socialism, with their common focus on static theories of value; they both understated the role of finance in capitalism and implicitly accepted that there can exist institutional conditions which would enable the replication of capitalist economic efficiency in the absence of finance (that is, without any reference to the valuation of capital). In fact, the key issue in these discussions was not socialism but capitalist finance.

14.2.1 Socialism and labour theory of value: Mises vs. traditional Marxism

The Marxist tradition with few exceptions[3] had adopted the viewpoint of the labour theory of value. This set up a specific perspective on both socialism and capitalism. Without going through the details of numerous analytical interventions we shall summarise the basic idea, referring primarily to the argument of Hilferding (1949).[4] Traditional Marxism perceived capitalist social relations as extrinsic to labour itself; the latter thus retained ontological priority in the context of any type of social organisation. From this point of view, traditional Marxism came to resemble a radical reading of Classical Political Economy (Smith and Ricardo), having abandoned Marx's project to criticise it. Labour was understood as a transhistorical source of value pertaining to every possible social configuration, even to socialism itself. The only difference is that while in capitalism the value-creating character of labour remains hidden, in socialism it is openly manifested. 'The difference between socialism and capitalism, then, aside from whether private ownership of the means of production exists, is understood essentially as a matter of whether labour is recognised as that which constitutes and regulates society – and is consciously dealt with as such – or whether social regulation occurs nonconsciously' (Postone, 1993: pp. 60–61). With the transhistorical ontology of the labour theory of value taken for granted, the elimination of markets for the means of production does not actually pose any significant problem for the organisation of economic life: the price system is still viable thanks to labour time calculations.

With that in mind, we can understand why Mises' reaction in 1920 was fired mainly at the proponents of the labour theory of value, especially in the German-speaking world. In his thinking, he had offered a thorough validation of every kind of radical state interventionist social experiment against the free market. And the problem for him was not just Bolshevik Russia, but the very fact that these state intervention issues were gaining ground in Germany and Austria as well (see Hayek,

1935a: p. 122). Therefore, the main theoretical enemies that appeared in the pages of Mises' paper were: Marx, Engels, Lenin, Trotsky, Kautsky, Neurath and Bauer; in other words, the 'fathers' of Marxism, the Bolshevik leaders and the leading authors of German Social Democracy.

Mises' idea was simple. Following the established pattern in the literature, he equated socialism to the ownership of the means of production by the state. This was the dominant perspective on socialism, not only in heterodox discussions of the period but also in the debates in the years to come. Dwelling upon the Austrian tradition of Böhm-Bawerk, he argued that any movement towards socialism would be a disaster. Why? Because 'rational production becomes completely impossible' as soon as one gives up the conception of a freely established monetary price for the means of production (Mises, 1935: p. 104). In other words, 'every step that takes us away from private ownership of the means of production and from the use of money also takes us away from rational economics. [...] Socialism is the abolition of rational economy. [...] There is only groping in the dark' (ibid). From this point of view, finance (which coincides with capital markets in the absence of other forms of credit) is a *sine qua non* for capitalism: the latter cannot function properly unless there is a price for capital.

According to Mises, economic rationality and efficiency is associated with the existence of a 'price' for capital. This price is a valuable economic parameter for the making of efficient choices between alternative economic plans. For Mises, markets are not perfect; monetary calculation, especially in the case of capital, 'has its inconveniences and serious defects, but we have certainly nothing better to put in its place' (ibid: p. 109). However, economic life cannot afford to part with this type of imperfection – it cannot be conceived in the absence of the capital market. It is meaningless to speak of prices in general and economic action when there are no indicators of expected profitability. The latter presupposes a market for capital and therefore finance. Hence, the crucial role of finance is not only to channel saving to investment; even more importantly, its role is to measure the efficiency of capital when the future is not known.[5]

14.2.2 Market socialists: neoclassical theory of value as defence of socialism

As we shall see below, Lange's intervention did not rely upon the labour theory of value, but was rather heavily influenced by the so-called early 'market socialists'. Before discussing his viewpoint in Section 14.3., we shall briefly mention two well known market socialists: Friedrich von

Wieser and Enrico Barone. Both wrote at the end of the 19th century. Neither of them was a socialist, and socialism was not their central analytical preoccupation. Their interventions were mostly critiques directed at the labour theory of value and not at the possibility of realising a central-planned economy (Lavoie, 1985: p. 83). While they followed different methodological approaches, they both came to the same conclusion. They believed that the newly founded subjective or marginalist theory of value had a validity that was independent and transcended any established social regime. In this sense, they adopted the same analytical premise as their opponents: they also believed that their value theory retained ontological priority over any institutional organisation or type of society.

Accordingly, the neoclassical theory of value must not be seen as a bourgeois apologia; it is not an enemy but an ally of the revolution. In Wieser's words, the marginalist approach to value is so little 'a weapon against socialism, that socialists could scarcely make use of a better witness in favour of it' (cited in Lavoie, 1985: p. 82). Or to use Barone's formulations, 'it is obvious how fantastic those doctrines are which imagine that production in the collectivist regime would be ordered in a manner substantially different from that of "anarchist' production"' (Barone, 1935: p. 289). Although both authors made it clear that they did not write for or against socialism, they expressed serious doubts about the workability of a socialist system (Lavoie, 1985: p. 83). They both put forward the notion that there exists a 'formal similarity' (ibid: p. 48) in the general logic of laws and choices that applies to either capitalism or socialism. This is the very same idea of similarity, coming from a different perspective this time, as the one we saw above with regard to the proponents of the labour theory of value.

This perspective sets forth the belief that socialism is just a peculiar form of 'capitalism' governed by the same 'laws' of production and value. The only difference comes from the different structure of ownership over capital. Such conceptions of capitalism and socialism fail to grasp the most important aspect of capitalist societies, namely the nature of social power relations. Of course, some might argue that the 'collective' ownership of capital by itself amounts to a striking institutional shift in the organisation of society. But does this shift challenge the nature of the capitalist relations of exploitation and political domination? The answer is definitely no. The Soviet Union (like other manifestations of 'real-existing socialism') never ceased to be a class society. The ruling class was comprised of a layer of higher state and party officials on the one hand (who staffed both the political and the administrative-control mechanisms of the 'planned' economy that secured the collective/state- capitalist appropriation of surplus value), and on the other, the managers of the state enterprises.[6] The essential question surrounding socialism is not with the status of the ownership of capital but the nature of worker control over the social conditions of production and reproduction. We do not intend here to elaborate more on this question. But since the issue of the nature of capitalist power was left untouched in these discussions, the debate over capital as 'collective property' was not actually concerned with the building of socialism *but indirectly touched upon the very role of capital markets and finance in capitalism.* From this point of view, *the main contributors in the socialist calculation debate were in fact discussing the importance of finance for capitalism in the name of central planning.* In what follows we shall revisit the debate from this viewpoint.

In this regard, the real achievement of the market socialists was to defend the neoclassical theory of value against the labour value version of it and *implicitly raise the issue of finance.* They unintentionally questioned the status that finance retains in the newly established neoclassical paradigm. And their initial answer underestimated this role; it rendered finance redundant and insignificant for the efficiency of production. After all, wasn't this the major outcome of the 'formal similarity' position? If the neoclassical law of valuation is independent of the institutional framework of the society, then the regulation of the supply and the demand of savings throughout the economy can be organised by a central planner, at least in principle. As we shall see below, in this line of thought the role of finance is totally redundant and insignificant, since the optimisation conditions must be met without any reference to the price of capital. To use Barone's reasoning, the central planning board can simply replace Walrasian auctioneering in the financial markets (Barone, 1935). In fact, as we shall see below, this is the route followed by Lange.

14.3 Lange's challenge to the mainstream: central planning board in the role of the Walrasian auctioneer

Lange entered the socialist calculation debate in 1936 without actually making any new theoretical contribution. He drew heavily upon the issue of 'formal similarity' between socialism and capitalism from the perspective of market socialists: both presumed an ontological primacy of neoclassical value theory over both capitalism and socialism. In this sense, the neoclassical theory of value becomes a weapon for socialists, and aids in the configuration of the socialist regime. The conception that had led Wieser and Barone 'to doubt that socialism was impractical is extended by Lange to a practical analogy used to show that socialism is as practicable as capitalism' (Lavoie, 1985: p. 124). This point was raised against the Austrian critique. The challenge that Lange put forward against the neoclassical orthodoxy of the mid 1930s was simple but brilliant: *socialism can easily imitate the efficiency of market capitalism if the central planning board is able to supplant the Walrasian tâtonnment process.*[7]

As expected, the version of socialism defended by Lange was a form of economy with competitive markets for labour and consumption goods, but not for capital: 'in the socialist system as described we have a genuine market (in the institutional sense of the word) for consumers' goods and for the services of labour [...] But there is no market for capital goods and productive resources outside of labour' (ibid: p. 61). With the assumption introduced in Section 14.2. above, this is close to a version of capitalism without finance. In that case, the Walrasian trial-and-error process can be carried out even more efficiently by the central planning bureau than by a market process with private property; the bureau can replicate the role of finance in capitalism without giving up the optimisation conditions associated with competitive capitalist markets: 'there is not the slightest reason why a trial and error procedure, similar to that in a competitive market, could not work in a socialist economy to determine the *accounting prices of capital goods and of the productive resources in public ownership*. Indeed, it seems that it would, or at least could, work much better in a socialist economy than it does in a competitive market. For the Central Planning Board has a much wider knowledge of what is going on in the whole economic system than any private entrepreneur can ever have; and, consequently, may be able to reach the right equilibrium prices by a much shorter series of successive trials than a competitive market actually does' (Lange, 1936: p. 67, emphasis added).

We can briefly summarise Lange's argument as follows.[8] In an economy with no capital market, consumers are free to maximise their utility in the genuine markets for consumer goods. Nevertheless, capitalists, or rather managers of public firms, cannot be guided by the standard profit maximisation rule since there is no market 'price' for capital; they have no basis on which to estimate the profitability prospects between alternative uses of a given amount of investment. According to Lange, this maximisation condition can be replaced by two equivalent ones. This is the message of the canonical textbook microeconomics. On the one hand, profit maximisation leads to optimum output when marginal cost

(MC) meets the price (p) of the product (p=MC). This is the first rule to be met by managers. According to neoclassical theory, marginal benefit (p) must not exceed nor fall below marginal cost for the output to reach the optimum level; this rule can be satisfied without any calculation of profitability. On the other hand, the central planning bureau must also instruct the managers to choose a combination of factors that minimises the average cost of production (ATC). In plain terms, this means that there are no profits above or below the normal level that would induce the producers to increase or decrease the level of production (or to induce inflow or outflow of capital from that branch of industry: the market is in equilibrium). Likewise, this condition can also be met without any knowledge of the profit rate and thus in the absence of capital markets.

The above argument has one important implication: the socialist economy of Lange can perfectly replicate the equilibrium position of neoclassical theory without any reference to the prices of capital and without any market for investment and saving. Capital markets and finance are redundant. In this respect, the result would be quite the same from a different theoretical route in the case of labour theory of value. In Lange's socialism there is an equivalent process of consumer's utility maximisation, while the profit maximisation condition can be met by the above-mentioned two complementary rules imposed upon firm managers. The central planner will announce shadow prices to the managers and they will accordingly apply the profit maximisation conditions to production. They will request resources at those prices for the expansion of production. If the result is sub-optimum (it does not clear the market) the central planner will take this into account in the new price announcement. For Lange, the function of prices is a 'parametric' one: 'although the prices are a resultant of the behaviour of all individuals on the market, each individual separately regards the actual market prices as given data to which he has to adjust himself. [...] Market prices are thus parameters determining the behaviour of the individual' (Lange, 1936: p. 59). This parametric function of prices does not change with socialism; it is only the forms of the 'equations' that change. The only difference is that the role of the Walrasian auctioneer will be carried out by the planning bureau, presumably in a more efficient way than under capitalism. The equilibrium values of these parameters will be still determined by the 'objective equilibrium conditions'. As 'Walras has so brilliantly shown this is done by a series of successive trials (tâtonnements). [...] Thus the accounting prices in a socialist economy can be determined by the same process of trial and error by which prices on a competitive market are determined' (ibid: pp. 59, 66).

At the end, Lange's defence of socialism is weak. His conclusion is that the economy outlined in his model can become as efficient as capitalism. Since finance has no role to play in the neoclassical universe, its functioning can thus be replicated by the central planning board leading to the very same outcome. Nevertheless, this is not much of a defence of socialism, since it functions merely as an indirect critique of the canonical neoclassical argument. There could be an alternative reading of Lange's point: since the capital market is insignificant in the organisation of capitalism and the establishment of competitive equilibrium, then socialism as a regime of public ownership of the means of production can become a real economic alternative. In fact *the real contribution of the market socialist approach was not a genuine defence of socialism but a brilliant critique of mainstream thinking, which was unable to grasp the importance of capital markets and finance.* This challenge triggered the reaction from the Austrian economists. In fact, as we shall argue in the next section, Hayek's critique against market socialists was also a way of emphasising the central role of finance in capitalism, which in his view cannot be supplanted by any concentrated bureau or institution. It is this latent aspect of the debate that has passed unnoticed in the literature.

14.4 Hayek's contribution to the debate: why capitalism is unthinkable in the absence of finance

The engagement of the Austrians in the socialist calculation debate in the 1930s gave them an opportunity to refine and publicise their viewpoint with regard to the nature of capitalism. In fact, as Kirzner (1992: p. 100) suggests, this debate was 'important as a catalyst in the development and articulation of the modern Austrian view of the market'. The Austrians, and Hayek in particular, critically distanced themselves from the established neoclassical orthodoxy of the era (the so-called model of perfect competition) while remaining strong proponents of the market system. In a sense, their response to the market socialists was an effort to defend the spirit of capitalism in the era of the 'great transformation' (to use Polanyi's well-known expression; Polanyi, 2001), in which significant state interference with the economy, in its different versions, was becoming a dominant paradigm of governance. In what follows we shall focus solely on Hayek's contribution to the Austrian view of the debate. While the latter continued to emphasise and develop his perspective throughout the post-Second World War period, the socialist calculation debate revealed an aspect of his argumentation that remained, to a significant extent, veiled in his later interventions: the crucial role of finance.

Hayek first continued in the spirit of von Mises' argumentation. Nevertheless, the context of the discussion had changed: it was not labour theory of value any more but the neoclassical value theory that was the fulcrum of debate. The proponents of socialism (in this debate) had adopted the 'tools' of the enemy in order to make their own point. Hayek used Lange's definition of socialism as his point of reference, admitting that 'it is essentially in this form that Marxism has been interpreted by the social-democratic parties on the Continent, and it is the form in which socialism is imagined by the greatest number of people' (Hayek, 1935a: p. 18). His argument can be seen as a wider criticism not only of other 'loose' ideas of socialism (ibid: p. 20)[9] but also of the heart of the neoclassical static conception of equilibrium.

Hayek understood very well that market socialists draw upon the fallacies of the dominant neoclassical paradigm. In fact, it was rather the latter that was the target of his critique. He fully grasped the fact that a thorough defence of an unstable capitalist system cannot come from its elevation in the form of the standard neoclassical model of perfect competition and static equilibrium; the market system is not perfect but it is the only path to meaningful economic organisation. In what follows, we shall reproduce the parts of his reasoning that we consider the most important. The central point is based upon a certain empiricist conception of knowledge: it cannot be aggregated and cannot be 'produced' in the absence of capitalist competition (with emphasis on the second part of the argument). In an alternative formulation, the required knowledge of the existing 'objective' production possibilities will not be available to anyone without competitive capital markets, even if one could collect and aggregate all the decentralised information spread throughout the economy, because it is only through the process of competition that these processes emerge. Hence, every negation of competition will lead to inferior results in terms of efficiency. No other economic regime can replicate or imitate the success of competitive free-market capitalism.[10]

For Hayek, 'maximisation' and 'efficiency' were indeed the basic and proper economic aims but 'the real economic problem which society faces [...] is a problem of the utilisation of knowledge not given to anyone in its totality' (Hayek, 1945: pp. 519–520). The issue involved with the concept information or knowledge is a double one. No economic regime, including a socialist one, ever reaches a static equilibrium. The character of every economic configuration is dynamic, rather that static.

It is indeed characterised by genuine *disequilibrium:* changes are frequent and unpredictable both in capitalism and socialism; and equilibrium is never actually attained. Therefore:

> all action will have to be based on anticipation of future events and the expectations on the part of different entrepreneurs will naturally differ. The decision to whom to entrust a given amount of resources will have to be made on the basis of individual promises of future return. Or, rather, *it will have to be made on the statement that a certain return is to be expected with a certain degree of probability. There will, of course, be no objective test of the magnitude of the risk.* But who is then to decide whether the risk is worth taking? The central authority will have no other grounds on which to decide but the past performance of the entrepreneur. But how are they to decide whether the risks he has run in the past were justified? And will its attitude towards risky undertakings be the same as if he risked his own property? (Hayek, 1935b: pp. 233–234)

According to Hayek, unlike the imaginary neoclassical universe, real life decisions are made upon the basis of expected unknown future incomes. We can attach 'certain degrees of probability' to the latter, but in the end there is no 'objective' measure of risk. This poses a much more difficult economic problem than the one usually acknowledged. It is one thing to address the difficulty the central planner has in collecting the immense amount of information needed in order to carry out the task of effective planning. But there is also 'another problem of even greater importance' (Hayek, 1935b: pp. 210, 154), and obviously more fundamental. The dispersed technical knowledge that the central planner is supposed to collect *does not even exist* in the first instance (ibid: pp. 210–211). It is of course 'absurd' to assume that all this knowledge can be 'concentrated in the heads of one or at best a very few people who actually formulate the equations to be worked out' (ibid). But even if there was a way to collect this knowledge and implant it in a single mind, the more fundamental problem that would be encountered is that 'much of the knowledge that is actually utilised is by no means 'in existence' in this ready-made form' (ibid). In other words, the market competitive process not only disseminates existing decentralised knowledge (dispersal or communication of knowledge) but more importantly it contributes to its very production (the learning or discovery process).[11] In other words, *competition not only helps discovery, but actually generates in the first place much of the knowledge to be subsequently dispersed.* It is usually the dispersal-of-knowledge aspect of Hayek's reasoning that is emphasised in the secondary literature. Nevertheless, it is the first aspect (discovery) that is crucial in the understanding of the full message of Austrian tradition (see Kirzner, 1992: pp. 139–140).

What are the implications of the above reasoning in the case of capitalism without a market for the factors of production? As we have seen in the above passage, future investment choices in any type of economy rely upon expectations of future circumstances, which encompass a certain anticipated return combined with a degree of confidence (probability) in its achievement. No economic action with regard to the future can be undertaken if there does not exist some estimation of risk, which cannot be objectively known. Decisions are thus open to change and revision. Yet market information is the only meaningful indication available to the entrepreneur or anyone else to decide upon future economic events and embark upon investment projects. The entrepreneur's subjective decisions concerning investment and risk taking will thus be made taking into consideration existing prices of capital and risk which, for all their defects, represent the best information available as a basis for decision making.

In this fashion, market prices are *disequilibrium* prices, in the sense that as signals or communicators they are far from optimal performers. This conclusion also holds for prices of capital and for risk. Instead of informing economic actors of the 'correct' path to follow, they offer incentives and disincentives that motivate them to explore and *discover for themselves* the truly profitable alternatives. Basically, prices in competitive markets do not only disseminate information already discovered and given; they motivate the discovery process itself. In their absence, this type of motivation will cease to exist. Therefore, even if someone manages to collect and compact all the existing information at any point in time it will be worthless because the negation of competition will significantly impoverish the real content of that information.[12]

This aspect of Hayek's argumentation was not so clear in his writings of 1930s and 1940s. Probably he was not fully aware of the consequences of his problematic. He may also, for tactical reasons, have hesitated to attack the neoclassical orthodoxy directly and systematically. But Hayek did not entirely fail to emphasise it. The competitive market process is reliant on market data at any particular point of time in the sense that:

> *provisional results from the market process at each stage alone tell individuals what to look for.* Utilisation of knowledge widely dispersed in a society with extensive division of labour cannot rest on individuals

> knowing all the particular uses to which well-known things in their individual environment might be put. Prices direct their attention to what is worth finding out about market offers for various things and services. [...] We shall see that the fact that a high degree of coincidence of expectations is brought about by the systematic disappointment of some kind of expectations is of crucial importance for an understanding of the functioning of the market order. [...] Competition is essentially a process of the formation of opinion [...] It creates the views people have about what is best and cheapest, and it is because of it that people know at least as much about possibilities and opportunities as they in fact do. [...]Yet this knowledge which is assumed to be given to begin with is one of the main points where it is only through the process of competition that the facts will be discovered. (Hayek, 1948a: pp. 106, 95; Hayek, 1978: pp. 181, 185)

In other words, markets do not only disseminate (imperfect) information but primarily motivate economic actors to conform with specific economic behaviour. As Kirzner (1992: p. 160) summarises: 'the importance of prices for coping with the Hayekian knowledge problem does not lie in the accuracy of the information which equilibrium prices convey concerning the actions of others who are similarly informed. Rather, its importance lies in the ability of disequilibrium prices to offer pure profit opportunities that can attract the notice of alert, profit-seeking entrepreneurs. Where market participants have failed to co-ordinate their activities because of dispersed knowledge, this expresses itself in an array of prices that suggests to alert entrepreneurs where they may win pure profits'. In plain terms, economic actors are living in disequilibrium and an uncertain world; the market system is the only tool they have to aid in calculations about the unwritten future, and efficient economic calculation is unthinkable in the absence of disequilibrium prices of capital and of risk. It was this point that had been overlooked by the market socialists when they adopted the conception of perfect competition. In the absence of competitive markets there will cease to exist the capitalist spirit of action. From this point of view any state interference with the market is a serious threat to the latter.

14.5 In the place of an epilogue: finance as 'trauma' in the mainstream thinking

We can summarise the main findings of the above analysis as follows. Lange drew upon the dominant neoclassical tradition, which emphasises the static character of economic equilibrium,to defend socialism. Lange's argument was that this static form of equilibrium can be easily replicated by the socialist economy: it was in fact a type of capitalism without capital markets. Lange had thus managed *implicitly* to set forth two important points. First, he showed that a version of mainstream thinking that underestimates the role of capital markets can be easily utilised to defend the social paradigm of central planners. Second, the abolition of capital markets – and therefore of finance – could not only replicate the much advertised efficiency of capitalism but would also achieve more economic stability. We must not forget that the debate took place in the 1930s, when the consequences of the great depression were central in everyone's mind. Taming the financial instability of the capitalist system without sacrificing economic efficiency would seem an appealing alternative to the free market system in a period when the latter was generating many unresolved contradictions.

We must mention here that in the German-speaking discussions there was an ongoing debate on the role of the stock and commodity exchanges with regard to speculation and instability, at least from the late 1880s. 'Debate in Germany over the nature and social impact of stock and commodity exchanges had first grown acrimonious in the wake of the major economic downturn of 1873–1879, which put an end to the boom times of the Empire's "founding era", as well as the rather spectacular charges of political manipulation and collusion levelled at Bismarck and the German financial elite by a range of conservative and socialist critics' (Lestition, 2000: p. 289). This debate – which opened the road for government legislation and committees of inquiry – attracted the attention of famous scholars: even Max Weber and Frederick Engels became involved (see Weber, 2000; Engels, 1989). The main issue that had dominated public scene at the time was 'whether it was possible or socially useful to regulate the kinds of "speculation" that were carried on at the exchanges' (Lestition, 2000: p. 289). Market regulation, state intervention and socialism were on the public agenda for many different reasons.

Hayek, along with the other Austrians, understood very well the message of these critiques, the most stimulating of which was undoubtedly coming from the market socialists. How could a mainstream liberal economist respond to a neoclassical defence of the state ownership of the means of production? There was one way out of this bizarre encounter: they had to clearly differentiate their view of capitalism from the neoclassical ideal universe of perfect equilibrium. This departure was never clearly stated in the writings of Mises and Hayek (Kirzner, 1992:

p. 111) and never properly emphasised. Both writers were somewhat tentative in pushing their argument to its limits. Nevertheless, their argument amounts to the strongest defence of the market system that can be articulated. For when they defended the free market system they not only responded to the proponents of socialism but also to everyone who had argued for strong state interference in the workings of the economy. It was not just socialism but every alternative 'halfway house' which would negate to some extent the decentralised market system; in other words, it was not just Stalin as a central planner, but also Hitler as a fascist dictator and Roosevelt as a democratic 'New Dealer' who were the objects of this critique. It was not just Lange and Lerner but also Keynes and Kalecki who were to be refuted.

In order to defend the market system, Hayek realised that he had to revise and criticise mainstream theory. Admittedly, the debate on socialist calculation triggered the process of elaboration and clarification of Austrian ideas (ibid). Against the challenge of the market socialists, Hayek actually highlighted the importance of the competitive market system primarily as a *disequilibrium* process. But since socialism, the debated concept, was perceived as a market system without capital markets, the debate implicitly touched upon the role of finance (under the simplifying assumption that only capitalists save and borrow). It was the role of finance in generating prices for risk that was obscured by the dominant neoclassical paradigm of perfect competition. From this point of view, Hayek's argument can be seen as a suggestion that capitalism is unthinkable in the absence of finance, that is, without a market for risk. This is so because the pure market system provides the motives for economic actors to *generate and discover* the knowledge ('alertness to and the discovery of as yet unknown information' Kirzner, 1992: p. 104) which is at the same time to be dispersed and communicated to other parts of the economy.

In that sense, the real alternative to the market system is definitely not a process that can just collect the decentralised knowledge, because even if this were possible it would deprive the economic system of the proper motives to achieve efficient targets: it would not stimulate discovery and economic action according to the norms of the capitalist system. Markets disseminate imperfect information but also motivate discovery and learning; they generate the information to be communicated. From our point of view, although the Austrians never put it that way, *this must be seen as a process of shaping economic behaviour according to the spirit of capitalism.* For discovery and learning are just the outcomes of an active engagement in proper economic actions. *The market system thus motivates a particular way of acting, and it is only as a consequence of these actions that knowledge is discovered.* From this perspective, the real message of Hayek's response to market socialists – an argument that was never properly stated during the period of the debate – was that capitalism needs the capital market to organise proper business behaviour and reproduce itself. With the establishment of central planning there will not be a 'discovery process' on the part of managers, hence no proper capitalist behaviour and therefore no efficiency in capitalist terms. In the end, every serious restriction of capital markets threatens the reproduction of the capitalist spirit.

But here we encounter an unexpected twist. While Lange degraded socialism to a mere replication of capitalism's efficient achievements, Hayek implicitly realised the danger of undermining capitalist behaviour and thus the nature of capitalist relations. If we see capitalist behaviour as the outcome of the capitalist social relations of power, then Hayek's perspective renders capital markets central in the organisation of capitalism as a system of exploitation. He also perceived at the same time every movement towards collective ownership of the means of production as a real threat to the logic of capitalist reproduction. In this sense, he ended up by implicitly giving an unexpected endorsement to socialism that is much deeper and more sophisticated than Lange's superficial 'defence': every thorough state intervention in the markets, and in the capital market in particular, threatens to eliminate the capitalist spirit, making the existence of the system vulnerable in the context of the reproduction of its power relations.

This last point gives us the chance to revisit the socialist calculation debate, interpreting finance as *trauma* for mainstream discussions. We shall use the concepts of Lacanian psychoanalysis as an analogy in order to clarify our point.[13]

Of course, from a radical Marxian point of view, mainstream thinking in all its versions is just a theoretical ideology (using the Althusserian definition of the term; see Althusser and Balibar, 1997): mainstream ideas misinterpret capitalist reality, but not in an arbitrary way; these systematic ideas are always interwoven with particular capitalist exploitation strategies stemming from reality itself. Mainstream theory systematises ideas and perceptions that arise and are held in place by social and economic power relations themselves (the 'given' ideological representations of everyday 'experience') without transforming their ideological content. Nevertheless, there is one more issue involved here. Mainstream economic reasoning always had the problem of properly incorporating finance and thinking seriously about financial instability and crises. It seems that finance besides a mystery has always been a *trauma* for the mainstream economic edifice.

Mainstream thinking offers an interpretation of the capitalist system by symbolising capitalist reality in a particular way. It sets forth and reproduces practices containing particular symbols, ideas, concepts, questions and visions that together comprise what we may call as the symbolic 'misrecognition' of reality. Nevertheless there is one element that resists this symbolisation and will always do so for mainstream analytical speculations: finance. It is not that mainstream thinking does not have theories of finance; it is that these theories are unable to grasp the fundamental aspects of finance, its crisis-prone character and its key role in the organisation of capitalist production. The financial meltdown of the late 2000s is an eloquent indication of this fact. The pre-crisis confidence in the strength of the system was accompanied by a post-crisis unease that led to fatal economic policy mistakes. In order words, finance is the *real* of capitalism, a place that cannot be properly symbolised, a factor that can never be completely absorbed into the mainstream ideological discourse. It will always be left over, unable to find its way into the established economic language, most especially in the contemporary forms of capitalism.

To speak metaphorically, the above argument suggests that finance is a *trauma* for mainstream thinking. The socialist calculation debate manifests this idea very well indeed. Lange's response was a provocative event, perhaps not deeply significant but in any case an important focal point. It should remind mainstream economists that their neglect of finance as an active and creative force in capitalist reproduction can be easily used as an argument for the negation of the market system. The reaction of the Austrians was a result of the existence of this trauma as it was brought back into the conscious memory. But since the unsymbolised *real* cannot intrude into reality without the breakdown of the capitalist apologia, the argument of the Austrians played the role of *fantasy* for the mainstream thinking. It became the last defence against the traumatic encounter with the *real;* that is to say with finance as manifestation of the exploitative and contradictory character of the system. This is the true contribution of the Austrian tradition to mainstream thinking. This tradition will always be mentioned as a defensive argument of last resort for the free market system when the latter is in crisis, an imaginative context for capitalist apologia. It will always be the speculative border which cannot be crossed without serious consequences for the nature of economic reasoning that purports to defend the capitalist system.

Notes

1. We will analyse Mises' argument in Section 14.2. below.
2. This was indeed the dominant perspective, but surely not the only one. Discussions within Marxist revolutionary circles in the period were rich in scope and content. The key issue was not the replication of the efficiency of capitalism but the overcoming of the nature of capitalist political and economic domination. In this line of reasoning, the key problem with socialism is not the role of the central planning bureau but the structure of 'soviets' as forms of workers' democratic control against the power and violence of capital. This issue remains beyond the aims of this chapter.
3. Clearly Rubin and his 'value form' analysis was one of those (see Milios et al., 2002).
4. Here we follow Postone's argument (see Postone, 2003: ch. 2). Hilferding's major work, *Finance Capital* (1910), became a dominant theoretical intervention at the beginning of the 20th century and is still considered a benchmark in discussions of political economy and heterodox financial theory. We refer to his dispute with Böhm-Bawerk on the labour theory of value (see Hilferding, 1949).
5. For a clear summary of the Mises argument see Lavoie (1985).
6. See Milios and Sotiropoulos (2009: ch. 10).
7. In this sense, Lange simply repeated Taylor's earlier point (see Lange, 1936: pp. 56, 66; Lavoie, 1985: pp. 118–119). In 1929 Taylor offered a planning model in which the socialist central bureau could achieve a practical equilibrating solution using a trial and error method (thus resembling the Walrasian auctioning process).
8. See Lange (1936: pp. 60–71), Lavoie (1985), Block et al. (2002: pp. 53–54).
9. These are versions of socialism that lie in between socialism and the free-market system (Hayek, 1945: p. 521).
10. In what follows we shall base our analysis on the following papers: Hayek (1935a, 1935b, 1945, 1948a, 1948b, 1978).
11. For these issues see also Kirzner (1992: chs 6 and 8).
12. See Hayek (1948a, 1978). See also Kirzner (1992: ch. 8), Lavoie (1985).
13. For instance, see Žižek (2006), and Sean (2005).

References

Aghion, P., Braun, M. and J. Fedderke (2006) 'Competition and Productivity Growth in South Africa', in: *CID Working Papers*, no. 132, Center for International Development at Harvard University, Harvard, Cambridge.

Aglietta, M. (1979) *A Theory of Capitalist Regulation*, New Left Books, London.

Alesina, A. and Perotti, R. (1997) 'Fiscal Adjustments in OECD Countries: Composition and Macroeconomic Effects', *Working Paper* 5730, NBER August.

Alesina, A. and Ardagna, S. (2010) 'Large Changes in Fiscal Policy: Taxes versus Spending', in *Tax Policy and the Economy*, vol. 24, University of Chicago Press.

Althusser, L. and E. Balibar (1997) *Reading Capital*, Verso, London.

Amadeo, E. J. (1986) 'Notes on Capacity Utilisation, Distribution and Accumulation', in: *Contributions to Political Economy*, vol. 5, pp. 83–94.

Anderberg, D., Andersson, F. and A. Balestrino (2000) 'Time, Self-Selection and User Charges for Public Goods', in: *FinanzArchiv*, vol. 57, pp. 137–154.

Andersen C. (2008) 'IMF Spells Out Need for Global Fiscal Stimulus', *IMF Survey online,* December 29. http://www.imf.org/external/pubs/ft/survey/so/2008/int122908a.htm

Asimakopulos, A. (1988) 'Post-Keynesian Theories of Distribution', in: A. Asimakopulos (ed.) *Theories of Income Distribution,* Boston, Kluwer, 133-158.

Atkinson, A. and J. Micklewright (1992) *Economic Transformation in Eastern Europe and the Distribution of Income*, Cambridge University Press, Cambridge.

Backhouse, R. E. (2005) 'The Rise of Free Market Economics: Economists and the Role of the State since 1970', in: Medema, S. G. and P. Boettke (eds) *The Role of Government in the History of Economic Thought: Annual Supplement to Volume 37 History of Political Economy*, Duke University Press, Durham, NC.

Baker, D. (2010) *Taking Economics Seriously*, MIT Press, Boston.

Balassa, B. (1973) 'The Firm in the New Economic Mechanism in Hungary', in: Bornstein, M. E. (ed.) *Plan and Market: Economic Reform in Eastern Europe,* Yale University Press, New Haven.

Balcerowicz, L. (1992) 'The "Socialist Calculation Debate" and Reform Discussions in Socialist Countries,' in: Kovács, J. M. and M. Tardos (eds) *Reform and Transformation in Eastern Europe*, Routledge, London.

Balcerowicz, L. (2000) 'Understanding Post Communist Transitions', in: Kostecki, W., Żukrowska, K. and B. J. Góralcyzk (eds) *Transformations of Post-Communist States,* Macmillan, London.

Barone, E. (1935[1908]) 'The Ministry of Production in the Collectivist State,' in: Hayek, F. A. (ed.) *Collectivist Economic Planning: Critical Studies on the Possibilities of Socialism*, Routledge and Kegan Paul Limited, London.

Batini, N., Callegari, G. and Melina, G. (2012) 'Successful Austerity in the United States, Europe and Japan', *Working Paper,* vol. 12, no. 190, Washington D.C., International Monetary Fund.

Bauman, Z. (1994) 'A Revolution in the Theory of Revolutions?', in: *International Political Science Review*, vol. 15, no. 1, pp. 15–24.

Bauman, Z. (2009a) 'Kapitalizm się chwieje' ['The capitalism is faltering'], in: *Le Monde diplomatique – edycja polska*, vol. 3, no. 37, ch. 10.

Bauman, Z. (2009b) 'Koniec orgii' ['End of the orgy'], in: *Gazeta Wyborcza*, 10 February.

Bellofiore, R. and M. Passarella (2009) 'Finance and the Realization Problem in Rosa Luxemburg: a 'Circuitist' Reappraisal', in: Ponsot, J. F. and S. Rossi (eds) *The Political Economy of Monetary Circuits: Tradition and Change in Post-Keynesian Economics*, Palgrave Macmillan, London.

Benanav, A. and Endnotes (2011) 'Misery and Debt. On the Logic and History of Surplus Population and Surplus Capital', in: *Endnotes*, no. 2, available at: http://endnotes.org.uk/articles/1.

Benes, J. and M. Kumhof (2012) 'The Chicago Plan Revisited', in: *IMF Working Papers*, no. 202, International Monetary Fund, Washington.

Bergson, A. (1987) 'Comparative Productivity: The USSR, Eastern Europe and the West', in: *American Economic Review*, vol. 77, no. 3, pp. 342–357.

Bergson, A. (1992) 'Communist Economic Efficiency Revisited', in: *American Economic Review*, vol. 82, no. 2, pp. 27–31.

Berliner, J. S. (1999) *The Economics of the Good Society*, Basil Blackwell, Oxford.

Bernanke, B. S. (2004) 'The Great Moderation', in: *Remarks at the Meetings of the Eastern Economic Association*, Washington, DC, 20 February, available at: http://www.federalreserve.gov/boarddocs/speeches/2004/20040220/

Bernstein, E. (1899) *Die Voraussetzungen des Sozialismus und die Aufgaben der Sozialdemokratie*, available at: http://www.marxists.org/deutsch/referenz/bernstein/1899/voraus/index.html.

Besomi, D. (2006) 'Formal Modelling vs. Insight in Kalecki's Theory of the Business Cycle', in: *Research in the History of Economic Thought and Methodology*, no. 24A, pp. 1–48.

Bevan, A. (1952) *In Place of Fear*, Heinemann, London.

Bhaduri, A. and S. Marglin, (1990) 'Unemployment and the Real Wage: The Economic Basis for Contending Political Ideologies', in: *Cambridge Journal of Economics*, vol. 14, pp. 375–393.

Bivens, J. and Irons, J. (2010) 'Government Debt and Economic Growth' *Briefing Paper* No. 271, July, Washington D.C., Economic Policy Institute.

Black, F. and M. Scholes (1973) 'The Pricing of Options and Corporate Liabilities', in: *Journal of Political Economy*, vol. 81, pp. 637–659.

Blanchard, O. J. (2008) 'Crowding Out', in: Durlauf, N. and L. E. Blume (eds) *New Palgrave Dictionary of Economics*, Palgrave Macmillan, Basingstoke.

Block, W., Barnett II, W. and S. Wood (2002) 'Austrian Economics, Neoclassical Economics, and Finance', in: *The Quarterly Journal of Austrian Economics*, vol. 5, no. 2, pp: 51–66.

Bougrine, H. and M. Seccareccia (1999) 'Unemployment Insurance and Unemployment: An Analysis of the Aggregate Demand-Side Effects of Postwar Canada', in: *International Review of Applied Economics*, vol. 13, no. 1, pp. 5–21.

Bowles, S. (1998) 'Endogenous Preferences: The Cultural Consequences of Markets and other Economic Institutions', in: *Journal of Economic Literature*, vol. 36, pp. 75–111.

Brenner, R. (2009) *What's Good for Goldman Sachs is Good for America: The Origins of the Current Crisis*, available at: http://eschlarship.org/uc/item/osgo782h.

Bridgeman, B., Qi, S. and J. A. Schmitz (2009) 'The Economic Performance of Cartels: Evidence from the New Deal U.S. Sugar Manufacturing Cartel, 1934–74', in: *Federal Reserve Bank of Minneapolis Research Department Staff Reports*, no. 437, Minneapolis.

Brus, W. (1990) 'The 'March to Socialism': Expectations and Reality', in: Flakierski, H. and T. T. Sekine (eds) *Socialist Dilemmas – East and West*, ME Sharpe, Armonk, NY.

Brus, W. and T. Kowalik (1983) 'Socialism and Development', in: *Cambridge Journal of Economics*, vol. 7, pp. 243–255.

Cartwright, N. (1983) *How the Laws of Physics Lie*, Oxford University Press, Oxford.

Cesaratto, S. (2012) 'Neo-Kaleckian and Sraffian Controversies on Accumulation Theory', in: *Working Paper*, no. 650, Dipartimento di Economia Politica, Università di Siena.

Chilosi, A. (1978) 'Socialist and Communist Income Distribution in Marxian and Soviet Marxist Thought', in: *Il Politico*, vol. 43, no. 4, pp. 698–710.

Chilosi, A. (1990a) 'Privatisation through Competition', in: *Jahrbuch der Wirtschaft Osteuropas*, vol. 14, no. 2, pp. 182–184.

Chilosi, A. (1990b) 'Distributional and Redistributional Processes in Soviet-Type Economies and the Distributional Impact of Institutional Change', in: Dagum, C. and M. Zenga (eds) *Income and Wealth Distribution, Inequality and Poverty*, Springer Verlag, Berlin.

Chilosi, A. (1994) 'Comparisons of Income Distribution East and West, Before and After Transition: Some Methodological Issues', in: *Statistics in Transition*, vol. 1, no. 5, pp. 641–653.

Ciszewski, B. (2008) 'Ameryka budzi się na długu' [*America is waking up in debt*], in: *Gazeta Wyborcza*, 3 November.

Coates, D. (2000) *Models of Capitalism: Growth and Stagnation in the Modern Era*, Polity Press, Cambridge.

Cogoy, M. (1987) 'The Falling Rate of Profit and the Theory of Accumulation. A Reply to Paul Sweezy', in: *International Journal of Political Economy*, vol. 17, no. 2, pp. 54–74.

Colletti, L. (1972) *From Rousseau to Lenin*, Monthly Review Press, New York.

Corneo, G. (2001) 'Work and Television', in: *Iza Discussion Paper*, no. 376, available at: http://papers.ssrn.com/abstract=287317.

Crosland, C. A. R. (1956) *The Future of Socialism*, Cape, London.

Crotty, J. and G. A. Dymski (1998) 'Can the Global Neoliberal Regime Survive Victory in Asia? The Political Economy of the Asian Crisis', in: *International Papers in Political Economy*, vol. 5, no. 2, pp. 1–47.

Davidson, P. (1982) *International Money and the Real World*, London: Macmillan.

Davidson, P. (2002) *Financial Markets, Money and the Real World*, Edward Elgar, Cheltenham.

Davis, M. (2006) *Planet of Slums*, Verso, London.

Dos Santos, C. and G. Zezza (2004) 'A Post-Keynesian Stock-Flow Consistent Macroeconomic Growth model: preliminary results', in: *Working Paper*, no. 402, The Levy Economics Institute, New York.

Dube, A. (2013) 'A Note on Debt, Growth and Causality', www.arindube.com/working-papers

Dullien, S. (2011) 'The New Consensus from a Traditional Keynesian and Post-Keynesian Perspective: A Worthwhile Foundation for Research or Just a Waste of Time?', in: *Economie Appliquée*, vol. 44, no. 1, pp. 173–200.

Dymski, Gary A. (2012) 'Can the US Economy Escape the Law of Gravity? A Minsky–Kalecki Approach to the Crisis of Neoliberalism', in: Yagi, K., Yokokawa, N., Hagiwara, S. and G. Dymski (eds) *The Crisis of 2008 and the Future of Capitalism*, Routledge, London.

Eichner, A. S. (1976) *The Megacorp and Oligopoly*, Cambridge University Press, Cambridge, UK.

Ellis, H. S. (1934) *German Monetary Theory, 1905–1933*, Harvard University Press, Cambridge, US.

Engels, F. (1989) 'The Socialism of Mr. Bismarck', in: Marx, K. and F. Engels (eds) *Collected Works*, vol. 24, International Publishers, New York.

EuroMemorandum Group (2007) *Full Employment with Good Work, Strong Public Services, and International Cooperation – Democratic Alternatives to Poverty and Precariousness in Europe*, available at: http://www.memo-europe.uni-bremen.de/euromemo/indexmem.htm.

European Union (2012) *Treaty on Stability, Coordination and Governance in the Economic and Monetary Union*, Brussels, European Union.

Fedderke, J. and G. Szalontai (2005) 'Industry Concentration in South African Manufacturing: Trends and Consequences, 1972–1996', in: *African Region Working Paper Series*, no. 96, School of Economics, University of Cape Town, Cap Town.

Fernie, S. and D. Metcalf (2005) *Trade Unions: Resurgence or Demise?*, Routledge, London.

Frankel, J. (2013) 'On Whose Research is the Case for Austerity Mistakenly Based?', in: Jeff Frankels Weblog, Views on the Economy and the World, available at: http://content.ksg.harvard.edu/blog/jeff_frankels_weblog/2013/05/20/on-whose-research-is-the-case-for-austerity-mistakenly-based.

Frey, B. S. (1978) 'Politico-Economic Models and Cycles', in: *Journal of Public Economics*, vol. 9, pp. 203–220.

Friedman, M. (1968) 'The Role of Monetary Policy', in: *American Economic Review*, vol. 68, no. 1, pp. 1–17.

Garvy, G. (1975) 'Keynes and the Economic Activists of Pre-Hitler Germany', in: *Journal of Political Economy*, vol. 83, no. 2, pp. 391–405.

Giavazzi, F. and Pagano, M. (1990) 'Can Severe Fiscal Contractions be Expansionary? Tales of Two Small European Countries', *Working Paper* 3372, NBER, May.

Giavazzi, F. and Pagano, M. (1996) 'Non-Keynesian Effects of Fiscal Policy Changes: International Evidence and the Swedish Experience', *Working Paper* 5332, NBER, October.

Global Footprint Network (2013) *Data and Results*, available at: http://www.footprintnetwork.org/en/index.php/GFN/page/footprint_data_and_results.

Glyn, A. (2006) *Capitalism Unleashed: Finance Globalization and Welfare*, Oxford University Press, Oxford.

Godley, W. and M. Lavoie (2001) 'Kaleckian Growth Models in a Stock and Flow monetary Framework: A Kaldorian View', in: *Journal of Post-Keynesian Economics*, vol. 24, no. 2, pp. 277–312.

Godley, W. and M. Lavoie (2007) *Monetary Economics: An Integrated Approach to Credit, Money, Income, Production and Wealth*, Palgrave Macmillan, Basingstoke.

Gomułka, S. and J. Rostowski (1988) 'An International Comparison of Material Intensity', in: *Journal of Comparative Economics,* vol. 12, no. 4, pp. 475–501.

Gordon, D., Edwards, R. and M. Reich (1982) *Segmented Work, Divided Workers: The Historical Transformation of Labor in the United States,* Cambridge University Press, Cambridge.

Gordon, R. J. (2000) 'Does the "New Economy" Measure up to the Great Inventions of the Past?', in: *Journal of Economic Perspectives,* vol. 14, no. 4, pp. 49–74.

Gorz, A. (2008) 'La sortie du capitalisme a déjà commencé' [*The exit from Capitalism has Already Begun*], in: *Manifeste Utopia,* Parangon/Vs, Lyon.

Grossmann, H. (1929) *Das Akkumulations- und Zusammenbruchsgesetz des kapitalistischen Systems,* C. L. Hirschfeld Verlag,, Leipzig.

Grunzel, J. (1902) *Über Kartelle,* Verlag von Duncker & Humblot, Leipzig.

Guajardo, J., Leigh, D. and Pescatori, A. (2011) 'Expansionary Austerity: New International Evidence', *Working Paper,* vol. 11, no. 158, Washington D.C., International Monetary Fund.

Hall, P. A. and D. Soskice (2001) 'An Introduction to Varieties of Capitalism', in: Hall, P. A. and D. Soskice (eds) *Varieties of Capitalism: The Institutional Foundations of Comparative Advantage,* Oxford University Press, Oxford.

Hancké, B. (ed.) (2009) *Debating Varieties of Capitalism: A Reader,* Oxford University Press, Oxford.

Hayek, F. A. (1935a) 'The Nature and the History of the Problem', in: Hayek, F. A. (ed.) *Collectivist Economic Planning: Critical Studies on the Possibilities of Socialism,* Routledge, London.

Hayek, F. A. (1935b) 'The Present State of the Debate', in: Hayek, F. A. (ed.) *Collectivist Economic Planning: Critical Studies on the Possibilities of Socialism,* Routledge, London.

Hayek, F. A. (1945) 'The Use of Knowledge in Society', in: *American Economic review,* vol. 35, no. 4, pp. 519–530.

Hayek, F. A. (1948a[1946]) 'The Meaning of Competition', in: Hayek, F. A. (ed.) *Individualism and Economic Order,* The University of Chicago Press, Chicago.

Hayek, F. A. (1948b[1940]) 'Socialist Calculation III: The Competitive Solution', in: F. A. Hayek (ed.) *Individualism and Economic Order,* The University of Chicago Press, Chicago.

Hayek, F. A. (1978[1968]) 'Competition as a Discovery Procedure', in: Hayek, F. A. (ed.) *New Studies in Philosophy, Politics, Economics and the History of Ideas,* Routledge, London.

Hein, E. (2012a) *The Macroeconomics of Finance-Dominated Capitalism – and Its Crisis,* Edward Elgar, Cheltenham.

Hein, E. (2012b) 'Wage- and Profit-led Regimes', in: King, J. E. (ed.) *The Elgar Companion to Post Keynesian Economics,* Edward Elgar, Cheltenham.

Heinrich, M. (2006) 'Begründungsprobleme. Zur Debatte über das Marxsche "Gesetz vom tendenziellen Fall der Profitrate"', in: *Marx-Engels-Jahrbuch 2006,* Akademie Verlag, Berlin.

Helwig, M. (2008) *Systemic Risk in the Financial Sector: An Analysis of the Subprime-Mortgage Financial Crisis,* Research on Collective Goods, Max Planck Institute, Bonn.

Herndon, T., Ash, M. and Pollin, R. (2013) 'Does High Public Debt Consistently Stifle Economic Growth? A Critique of Reinhart and Rogoff', *Working Paper* No. 566, University of Massachusetts at Amherst.

Hilferding, R. (1910) *Finanzkapital, Eine Studie über die jüngste Entwicklung des Kapitalismus*, Verlag JHW Dietz, Berlin.
Hilferding, R. (1949[1904]) 'Böhm-Bawerk's Criticism of Marx', in: Sweezy, P. M. (ed.) *'Karl Marx and the Close of His System' by Eugen Böhm-Bawerk and 'Böhm-Bawerk's Criticism of Marx' by Rudolf Hilferding*, Kelley, New York.
Hobsbawm, E. (1994) *Age of Extremes: The Short Twentieth Century 1914–1991*, Michael Joseph, London.
Horvat, B. (1991) 'Review of "The Road to a Free Economy" by János Kornai', in: *Journal of Economic Behavior and Organization*, vol. 15, pp. 407–410.
Howard, M.C. and J. E. King (1992) *A History of Marxian Economics: Volume II, 1929–1990*, Macmillan, London, and Princeton University Press, Princeton, NJ.
Howard, M.C. and J. E. King (2008) *The Rise of Neoliberalism in Advanced Capitalism: A Materialist Analysis*, Palgrave Macmillan, Basingstoke. http://www.federalreserve.gov/boarddocs/speeches/2004/20040220/.
IMF (2007) 'World Economic Outlook, October 2007, Globalization and Inequality', in: *World Economic and Financial Surveys*, International Monetary Fund, Washington.
Kaldor, N. (1956) 'Alternative Theories of Distribution', in: *Review of Economic Studies*, vol. 23, no. 61, pp. 94–100.
Kaldor, N. (1982) *The scourge of Monetarism*, Oxford University Press, Oxford.
Kalecki, M. (1932) 'The Influence of Cartelization on the Business Cycle', in: Osiatyński, J. (ed.) (1990) *Collected Works of Michał Kalecki, Volume I, Capitalism: Business Cycles and Full Employment*, Clarendon Press, Oxford.
Kalecki, M. (1933a) 'Nakręcanie koniunktury światowej (Obecna faza kryzysu światowego' ['Stimulating the World Business Cycle (The Present Phase of the Global Crisis)'], in: *Polska Gospodarcza*, no. 1, p. 9.
Kalecki, M. (1933b) 'Stimulating the World Business Upswing', in: Osiatyński, J. (ed.) (1990) *Collected Works of Michał Kalecki, Volume I, Capitalism: Business Cycles and Full Employment*, Clarendon Press, Oxford.
Kalecki, M. (1933c) *Próba teorii koniunktury*, Instytut Badania Koniunktur Gospodarczych i Cen, Warszawa.
Kalecki, M. (1935) 'The Essence of the Business Upswing', in: Osiatyński, J. (ed.) (1990) *Collected Works of Michał Kalecki, Volume I, Capitalism: Business Cycles and Full Employment*, Clarendon Press, Oxford.
Kalecki, M. (1937) 'The Principle of Increasing Risk', in: *Economica*, vol. 4, no. 13, pp. 440–447
Kalecki, M. (1939) *Essays in the Theory of Economic Fluctuations*, George Allen and Unwin, London.
Kalecki, M. (1943) 'Political Aspects of Full Employment', in: *Political Quarterly*, vol. 14, no. 4, pp. 322–331, reprinted in: Osiatyński, J. (ed.) (1990) *Collected Works of Michał Kalecki, Volume I, Capitalism: Business Cycles and Full Employment*, Clarendon Press, Oxford.
Kalecki, M. (1944a) 'The White Paper on Employment Policy', in: *Bulletin of the Oxford University Institute of Statistics*, vol. 6, no. 8, pp. 137–144.
Kalecki, M. (1944b) 'Three Ways to Full Employment', in: Oxford University Institute of Statistics (1944) *The Economics of Full Employment*, Blackwell, Oxford.
Kalecki, M. (1945) 'The Maintenance of Full Employment after the Transition Period: A Comparison of the Problem in the USA and the UK', in: *International Labour Review*, vol. 52, no. 5, pp. 449–464.

Kalecki, M. (1954) *Theory of Economic Dynamics: An Essay on Cyclical and Long-Run Changes in Capitalist Economy*, George Allen and Unwin, London.

Kalecki, M. (1968) 'Trend and Business Cycle Reconsidered', in: *Economic Journal*, vol. 78, pp. 263–276.

Kalecki, M. (1971a) 'The Class Struggle and the Distribution of National Income', in: *Kyklos*, vol. 24, pp. 1–8.

Kalecki, M. (1971b) *Selected Essays on the Dynamics of the Capitalist Economy*, Cambridge University Press, Cambridge.

Kalecki, M. (1999) 'Workers' Councils and Central Planning', in: Sawyer, M. (ed.) *The Legacy of Michal Kalecki, Volume 2*, Edward Elgar, Cheltenham.

Kalecki, M. And T. Kowalik (1971) 'Observations on the "Crucial Reform"', in: Osiatyński, J. (ed.) (1990) *Collected Works of Michał Kalecki, Volume I, Capitalism: Business Cycles and Full Employment*, Clarendon Press, Oxford.

Karwowski, E. (2009) 'The Significance And Distinctiveness Of Islamic Banking in Malaysia', in: *Levy Economic Institute Working Papers*, no. 555, Levy Economics Institute, New York.

Karwowski, E. (2012) 'Financial Operations of South African Listed Firms: Growth and Financial Stability in an Emerging Market Setting', *Conference Paper 6, III Conferência do IESE*, Instituto de Estudos Sociais e Econónomicos (IESE), Maputo.

Keynes, J. M. (1936) *The General Theory of Employment, Interest and Money*, Macmillan, London.

Kimball, M. and Wang, Y. (2013) 'After crunching Reinhart's and Rogoff's data, we've concluded that high debt does not slow growth' *QUARTZ* 29 May.

King, J. E. (2003) 'Non-Marxian Socialism', in: Biddle, J., Davis, J. B. and W. J. Samuels (eds) *The Blackwell Companion to the History of Economic Thought*, Blackwell, Oxford.

King, J. E. (2012a) *The Microfoundations Delusion: Metaphor and Dogma in the History of Macroeconomics*, Edward Elgar, Cheltenham.

King, J. E. (2012b) 'The Future of Neoliberalism', in: Cahill, D., Stilwell, F. and L. Edwards (eds) *Neoliberalism: Beyond the Free Market*, Edward Elgar, Cheltenham.

Kirzner, I. M. (1992) *The Meaning of Market Process: Essays in the Development of Modern Austrian Economics*, Routledge, London and New York.

Klein, L. (1947) *The Keynesian Revolution*, Macmillan, London.

Kliman, A. L. (2012) *The Failure of Capitalist Production. Underlying Causes of the Great Recession*, Pluto Press, London.

Kolakowski, L. (1978) *Main Currents of Marxism: Its Origins, Growth and Dissolution, Volume 2: The Golden Age*, Oxford University Press, Oxford.

Kolko, J. (1988) *Restructuring the World Economy*, Pantheon, New York.

Kołodko, G. W. (2011) *How Things Happen: Economic Processes – What Science, by Policy' in: Truth, Errors, and Lies: Politics and Economics in a Volatile World*, Columbia University Press, New York.

Kornai, J. (1986) 'The Hungarian Reform Process: Visions, Hopes, and Reality', in: *Journal of Economic Literature*, vol. 24, pp. 1687–1737.

Kowalik, T. (1971) 'Kowalik's Rejoinder to Pesenti', in: Osiatyński, J. (ed.) (1990) *Collected Works of Michał Kalecki, Volume I, Capitalism: Business Cycles and Full Employment*, Clarendon Press, Oxford.

Kowalik, T. (1986) 'On Crucial Reform of Real Socialism', *Forschungsberichte*, no. 122, Wiener Institut für Internationale Wirtschaftsvergleiche, Wien.

Kowalik, T. (1987) 'Oskar Lange's Lectures on the Economic Operation of a Socialist Society', in: *Contributions to Political Economy*, vol. 6, pp. 1–2.
Kowalik, T. (1990) 'Toward a Mixed Socialist Economy', in: Flakierski, H. and T. T. Sekine (eds) *Socialist Dilemmas – East and West*, ME Sharpe, Armonk, NY.
Kowalik, T. (1991) 'The Polish Postscript, 1989', in: Mendell, M. and D. Salee (eds) *The Legacy of Karl Polanyi: Market, State and Society at the End of the Twentieth Century*, St. Martin's Press, New York.
Kowalik, T. (1992a) 'Michał Kalecki and Early Attempts to Reform the Polish Economy', in: Knell, M. and C. Rider (eds) *Socialist Economies in Transition: Appraisals of the Market Mechanism*, Edward Elgar, Aldershot.
Kowalik, T. (1992b) 'Reform Economics and Bureaucracy', in: Kovács, J. M. and M. Tardos (eds) *Reform and Transformation in Eastern Europe*, Routledge, London.
Kowalik, T. (1996) 'On the Transformation of Post-Communist Societies: The Inefficiency of Primitive Capital Accumulation', in: *International Political Science Review*, vol. 17, no. 3, pp. 289–296.
Kowalik, T. (1997) 'The Polish Revolution', in: *Dissent*, vol. 44, pp. 26–30.
Kowalik, T. (2001b) 'Why the Social Democratic Option Failed: Poland's Experience of Systemic Change', in: Glyn, A. (ed.) *Social Democracy in Neoliberal Times: The Left and Economic Policy since 1989,* University Press, Oxford.
Kowalik, T. (2003) 'Systemic Variety under the Conditions of Globalization and Integration', in: Kołodko, G. W. (ed.) *Emerging Market Economies: Globalization and Development*, Ashgate, Aldershot.
Kowalik, T. (2011) 'Akumulacja Kapitału R. Luksemburg' ['Rosa Luxemburg's Accumulation of the Capital'], in: Luxemburg, R. (2011) *Akumulacja kapitału* [*The Accumulation of the Capital*], Książka i Prasa, Warszawa.
Krug, B. (2000a) 'Ties That Bind: The Emergence of Entrepreneurs in China', in: *ERIM Report Series*, no. ERS-2000–44-ORG, Erasmus Research Institute of Management, Rotterdam.
Krug, B. (2000b) 'The Interdependence Between Political and Economic Entrepreneurship', in: *ERIM Report Series*, no. ERS-2000–43-ORG, Erasmus Research Institute of Management, Rotterdam.
Krugman, P. (2012) *End This Depression Now*, Norton, New York.
Krzywicki, L. (1957) 'Nowoczesny Prąd Monopolowy', in: Holland, H. (ed.) *Ludwik Krzywicki, Idea a Życie, Z Wczesnej Publicystyki (1883–1892),* Państwowe Wydawnictwo Naukowe, Warszawa.
Lange, O. (1936) 'On the Economic Theory of Socialism', in: *Review of Economic Studies*, vol. 4, no. 1, pp. 53–71.
Lange, O. (1938) 'The Rate of Interest and the Optimum Propensity to Consume', *Economica,* vol. V, no. 17, February, pp. 12–32.
Lange, O. (1941) *Democratic Program for Full Employment*, New America Press, Chicago.
Lange, O. (1973a) *Dziela, Tom 2, Socjalizm*, [*Works, Volume 2, Socialism*], PWE, Warsaw.
Lange, O. (1973b) 'Istota socjalizmu' ['The Essence of Socialism'], in: Lange (1973) *Dziela, Tom 2, Socjalizm*, [*Works, Volume 2, Socialism*], PWE, Warsaw.
Lange, O. (1994) *Economic Theory and Market Socialism: Selected Essays of Oskar Lange,* Edward Elgar, Aldershot.
Łaski, K. (2008) 'Market Economy Needs to Run Budgetary Deficits', in: *The Vienna Institute Monthly Report*, no. 6.

Łaski, K. and L. Podkaminer (2012) *The Basic Paradigms of the EU Economic Policy-making Need to Be Changed*, Cambridge J. Economics, no. 1.

Lavoie, D. (1985) *Rivalry and Central Planning: The Socialist Calculation Debate Reconsider*, Cambridge University Press, New York.

Lavoie, M. (1992) *Foundations of Post-Keynesian Economic Analysis*, Edward Elgar, Aldershot.

Lavoie, M. (1998) 'Simple Comparative Statics of Class Conflict in Kaleckian and Marxist Short-run Models', in: *Review of Radical Political Economics*, vol. 30, no. 3, pp. 101–113.

Lavoie, M. (2000) 'Government Deficits in Simple Kaleckian Models', in: Bougrine, H. (ed.) *The Economics of Public Spending: Debts, Deficits and Economic Performance*, Edward Elgar, Cheltenham.

Layard, R. (2005) *Happiness*, Penguin Books, London.

Le Heron, E. (2007) 'The Dynamic Analysis of Monetary Policy Shock on Banking Behavior', in: McCombie, J. and C. Rodriguez (eds) *Issues in Finance and Monetary Policy*, Palgrave Macmillan, London.

Le Heron, E. (2008) 'Fiscal and Monetary Policies in a Keynesian Stock-Flow Consistent model', in: Creel, J. and M. Sawyer (eds) *Current Thinking on Fiscal Policy*, Palgrave Macmillan, London.

Le Heron, E. (2011) 'Confidence and Financial Crisis in a Post-Keynesian Stock-Flow Consistent Model', in: *Intervention – European Journal of Economics and Economic Policies*, vol. 8, issue 11, no. 2, pp. 361–388.

Le Heron, E. and T. Mouakil (2008) 'A Post Keynesian Stock-Flow Consistent Model for the Dynamic Analysis of Monetary Policy Shock on Banking Behavior', in: *Metroeconomica*, vol. 59, no. 3, 405–440.

Laclau, E. and C. Mouffe (1977) *Hegemony and Socialist Strategy*, New Left Review, London.

Leijonhufvud, A. ([1973]1981) 'Effective Demand Failures', in: *Swedish Journal of Economics*, vol. 75, no. 1, pp. 27–48, reprinted in Leijonhufvud, A. (1981) *Information and Coordination. Essays in Macroeconomic Theory*, Oxford University Press, New York.

Lestition, S. (2000) 'Historical Preface to Max Weber in "Stock and Commodity Exchanges"', in: *Theory and Society*, vol. 29, no. 3, pp: 289–304.

Liefmann, R. (1903) *Schutzzoll und Kartelle,* Verlag von Gustav Fischer in Jena, Jena.

LiPuma, E. and B. Lee (2004) *Financial Derivatives and the Globalisation of Risk*, Duke University Press, Durham, NC.

Lucas, R. E. Jr. (1975) 'An Equilibrium Model of the Business Cycle', in: *Journal of Political Economy*, vol. 83, pp. 113–144.

Lucas, R. E. Jr. (1981) *Studies in Business-Cycle Theory*, The MIT Press, Cambridge, US.

Luxemburg, R. (2011) *Akumulacja kapitału* [*The Accumulation of the Capital*], Książka i Prasa, Warszawa.

Maddison, A. (1995) *Monitoring the World Economy, 1820–1992*, Organisation for Economic Co-operation and Development, Paris.

Maddison, A. (2007) *Contours of the World Economy, 1–2030 AD: Essays in Macro-Economic History,* Oxford University Press, Oxford.

Mann, M. (2004) *Fascists*, Cambridge University Press, Cambridge.

Marglin, S. and J. Schor (eds) (1990) *The Golden Age of Capitalism: Lessons for the 1990s*, Oxford University Press, Oxford.

Marx, K. (1857a[1971]) *Critique of Political Economy*, London: Lawrence & Wishart, 1971.

Marx, K. (1875b) 'Critique of the Gotha Programme', in: *Marx and Engels Collected Works, Volume 3*, International Publishers, New York

Marx, K. (1976) *Capital, Volume I,* translated by B. Fowkes, Penguin, Harmondsworth.

Marx, K. (1981[1875]) *Capital, Volume III,* translated by D. Fernbach, Penguin, Harmondsworth.

Marx, K. (1986) 'Outlines of the Critique of Political Economy (Rough Draft of 1857–58),' in: *Marx and Engels Collected Works, Volume 28,* International Publishers, New York.

Marx, K. (1989) 'Economic Manuscripts of 1861–63', in: *Marx and Engels Collected Works, Volume 32,* International Publishers, New York.

Mattick, P. (2011) *Business as Usual: The Economic Crisis and the Failure of Capitalism,* Reaktion, London.

Megginson, W. and J. Netter (2001) 'From State to Market: A Survey of Empirical Studies on Privatization', in: *Journal of Economic Literature,* vol. 39, pp. 321–389.

Milios, J. and D. P. Sotiropoulos (2009) *Rethinking Imperialism: A Study of Capitalist Rule,* Palgrave Macmillan, New York and Hampshire.

Milios, J., Dimoulis, D. and G. Economakis (2002) *Karl Marx and the Classics, An Essay on Value, Crises and the Capitalist Mode of Production,* Ashgate Publishing Limited, Farnham.

Mill, J. S. (1848) *Principles of Political Economy with some of their Applications to Social Philosophy,* Longmans, Green and Co., London.

Ministry of Reconstruction (1944) *Employment Policy,* Cmnd. 6527, HMSO, London.

Minsky, H. P. (1982) *Can 'It' Happen Again? Essays on Instability and Finance,* M.E. Sharpe, Armonk, NY.

Mises, L. (1935[1920]) 'Economic Calculation in the Socialist Commonwealth', in: Hayek, F. A. (ed.) *Collectivist Economic Planning: Critical Studies on the Possibilities of Socialism,* Routledge and Kegan Paul Limited, London.

Moseley, F. (1991) *The Falling Rate of Profit in the United States Economy,* St Martin's Press, New York.

Mott, T. and E. Slattery (1994) 'The Influence of Income Distribution on Aggregate Demand in a Kaleckian Model: Stagnation vs Exhilaration Reconsidered', in: P. Davidson, P. and J. A. Kregel (eds) *Employment, Growth and Finance,* Edward Elgar, Aldershot.

Nersisyan, Y. (2012) 'Money Manager Capitalism', in: King, J. E. (ed.) *The Elgar Companion to Post Keynesian Economics,* Edward Elgar, Cheltenham.

Nove, A. (1992) 'Soviet Reforms and Western Neo-classical Economics', in: Kovács, J. M. and M. Tardos (eds) *Reform and Transformation in Eastern Europe,* Routledge, London.

Nowak, L. (1979) *The Structure of Idealization: Towards a Systematic Interpretation of the Marxian Idea of Science,* Reidel, Leiden.

Nuti, D. M. (2004) 'Kalecki and Keynes Revisited: Two Original Approaches to Demand-determined Income – and Much More Besides', in: Sadowski, Z. L. and A. Szeworski (eds) *Kalecki's Economics Today,* Routledge, London and New York.

OECD (2011) *Global Forum on Competition, Crisis Cartels,* Organisation for Economic Co-operation and Development, Paris.

Okishio, N. (2000) 'Competition and Production Prices', in: *Cambridge Journal of Economics* vol. 25, no. 4, pp. 493–501.

Osiatyński, J. (1988) *Michał Kalecki on a Socialist Economy,* translated by J. Toporowski, Macmillan Press, London.

Osiatyński, J. (ed.) (1990) *Collected Works of Michał Kalecki, Volume I, Capitalism: Business Cycles and Full Employment,* Clarendon Press, Oxford.

Osiatyński, J. (ed.) (1991) *Collected Works of Michał Kalecki, Volume II, Capitalism: Economic Dynamics,* Clarendon Press, Oxford.

Osiatyński, J. (ed.) (1997) *Collected Works of Michał Kalecki, Volume VII, Studies in Applied Economics 1940–1967; Miscellanea,* Clarendon Press, Oxford.

Oxford Analytica (2001) 'Battered and Cherished: The Private Sector in China', in: *Transition Newsletter,* vol. 11, no. 6, pp. 13–14.

Palley, T. I. (1997) 'Macroeconomics with Conflict and Income Distribution', in: *Review of Political Economy,* vol. 10, no. 3, pp. 329–342.

Patinkin, D. (1982) *Anticipations of the General Theory? And Other Essays on Keynes* Oxford, Basil Blackwell.

Perotti R. (2012) 'The "Austerity Myth": Gain without Pain?' NBER Chapters, in *Fiscal Policy after the Financial Crisis,* pp. 307–354 NBER Inc.

Persky, J. (2000) 'The Neoclassical Advent: American Economics at the Dawn of the 20th Century', in: *Journal of Economic Perspectives,* vol. 14, no. 1, pp. 95–108.

Pesenti, A. (1971) 'A comment', in: Osiatyński, J. (ed.) (1990) *Collected Works of Michał Kalecki, Volume I, Capitalism: Business Cycles and Full Employment,* Clarendon Press, Oxford.

Phillips, A. W. (1958) 'The Relationship between Unemployment and the Rate of Change of Money Wages in the United Kingdom 1861–1957', in: *Economica,* vol. 25, no. 100, pp. 283–299.

Polanyi, K. (2001) *The Great Transformation: The Political and Economic Origins of Our Time,* Beacon Press Books, Boston.

Postone, M. (1993) *Time, Labour, and Social Domination,* Cambridge University Press, New York.

Pugliese, E. (1993) 'The Europe of the Unemployed', in: *International Journal of Political Economy,* vol. 23, no. 3, pp. 13–36.

Quantec (2010) EasyData, available under: http://www.quantec.co.za.

Quiggin, J. (2010) *Zombie Economics: How Dead Ideas Still Walk Among Us,* Princeton University Press, Princeton, NJ.

Reinhart, C.M. and Rogoff, K.S. (2010) 'Growth in a Time of Debt', *American Economic Review,* vol. 100, no. 2, pp. 573–578.

Reinhart, C.M. and Rogoff, K.S. (2013) 'Responding to our Critics', *New York Times* 25 April.

Robinson, J. (1966) *An Essay on Marxian Economics,* Macmillan, London.

Robinson, J. (1976) 'Michał Kalecki: A Neglected Prophet', in: *New York Review of Books,* vol. 23, no. 1, pp. 28–30.

Robinson, J. (1982) 'Shedding Darkness', in: *Cambridge Journal of Economics,* vol. 6, no. 3, pp. 295–296.

Roland, G. (2000) *Transition and Economics,* MIT Press, Cambridge, US.

Ryoo, S. and Skott, P. (2013) 'Public Debt and Full Employment in a Stock-flow Consistent Model of a Corporate Economy', *Journal of Post Keynesian Economics*, vol. 35, no. 4, Summer, pp. 511–528.
Rosati, D. (2010) 'Przyczyny i mechanizmy kryzysu finansowego w USA w latach 2007–09' ['Causes and Mechanisms of the Financial Crisis in the US in 2007–09'], in: Kołodko, G. (ed.) *Globalizacja, kryzys i co dalej?* [*Globalization, crisis and what next?*], Wydawnictwo Poltext, Warszawa.
Rosdolsky, R. (1977) *The Making of Marx's 'Capital'*, Pluto Press, London.
Rothschild, K. W. (1947) 'Price Theory and Oligopoly', in: *Economic Journal*, vol. 57, no. 227, pp. 299–320.
Rothschild, K. W. (2009) 'Neoliberalism, EU and the Evaluation of Policies', in: *Review of Political Economy*, vol. 21, no. 2, pp. 213–225.
Rothschild, K.W. and R. Graber (2009) 'Da hab ich mir gedacht: Habt's mich gern' ['So I Thought to Myself: They Can Get Stuffed!'], in: *Der Standard*, 23 October.
Samuelson, P. A. (1948) *Economics: An Introductory Analysis*, McGraw-Hill, New York.
Sassoon, D. (1996) *One Hundred Years of Socialism*, I. B. Taurus, London.
Sawyer, M. (2011) 'Progressive Approaches to Budget Deficits', in Onaran, O., Niechoj, T., Stockhammer, E. Truger, A. and T. van Treeck (eds) *Stabilising an Unequal Economy? Public Debt, Financial Regulation, and Income Distribution*, Metropolis Verlag, Marburg.
Schumpeter, Joseph A. (1976[1942]) *Capitalism, Socialism and Democracy*, George Allen & Unwin, London.
Sean, H. (2005) *Jacques Lacan*, Routledge, London and New York.
Seccareccia, M. and A. Sharpe (1994) 'Canada's Competitiveness: Beyond the Budget Deficit', in: *Économies et Sociétés*, vol. 23, no. 1–2, pp. 275–300.
Sennett, R. (2006) *The Culture of New Capitalism*, Yale University Press, Yale.
Shapiro, N. (2012) 'Josef Steindl: An Economist of His Times', in: *PSL Quarterly Review*, vol. 65, no. 261, pp. 167–187.
Sharpe, W. (1965) 'A Simplified Model for Portfolio Analysis', in: *Management Science*, vol. 9, pp. 277–293.
Shrcke, M. (2001) 'Preferences for Inequality: East vs. West', in: *Innocenti Working Papers*, no. 89, UNICEF Innocenti Research Centre, Florence.
Skidelsky, R. (2011) 'Recovery Before Reform', in: *Project Syndicate*, 25 October, available at: http://www.skidelskyr.com/site/article/recovery-before-reform.
Steindl, J. (1945a) *Small And Big Business: Economic Problems Of The Size Of Firms*, Basil Blackwell, Oxford.
Steindl, J. (1945b) 'Capitalist Enterprise and Risk', in: *Oxford Economic Papers*, no. 7, pp. 21–45.
Steindl, J. (1952) *Maturity and Stagnation in American Capitalism*, Blackwell, Oxford.
Steindl, J. (1979) 'Stagnation: Theory and Policy', in: *Cambridge Journal of Economics*, vol. 3, no. 1, pp. 1–14.
Steindl, J. (1982) 'The Role of Household Saving in the Modern Economy', in: *Banca Nazionale del Lavoro, Quarterly Review*, vol. 140, pp. 69–88.
Stiglitz, J. E. (1994) *Whither Socialism?*, MIT Press, Cambridge, US.
Stiglitz, J. E. (2010) *Freefall: America, Free Markets, and the Sinking of the World Economy*, W. W. Norton & Company, New York.

Streeck, W. (2009) *Re-Forming Capitalism: Institutional Change in the German Political Economy*, Oxford University Press, Oxford.

Streeck, W. (2011) 'The Crisis of Democratic Capitalism?', in: *New Left Review*, vol. 71, pp. 5–29.

Sturmthal, A. (1944) *The Tragedy of European Labour 1918–1939*, Left Book Club, London.

Sun, L. (2002) 'Fading out of Local Government Ownership: Recent Ownership Reform in China's Township and Village Enterprises', in: *Economic Systems*, vol. 26, no. 3, pp. 249–269.

Sustainable Development Commission (2009) *Prosperity without Growth?*, Sustainable Development Commission, London.

Sweezy, P. (1946) *The Theory of Capitalist Development*, Dobson, London.

Szymański, W. (2009) *Kryzys globalny. Pierwsze przybliżenie [Global Crisis. First Approximation]*, Difin, Warszawa.

Tanzi, V. (2011) *Governments versus Markets: The Changing Economic Role of the State*, Cambridge University Press, Cambridge.

Taylor, J. (1993) 'Discretion versus Policy Rules in Practice', *Carnegie-Rochester Conference Series on Public Policy*, no. 39, pp. 195–214.

The Economist (2012) 'Special Report on State Capitalism', in: *The Economist*, 22 January.

Tobin, J. (1958) 'Liquidity Preference as Behavior Towards Risk', in: *Review of Economic Studies*, vol. 67, pp. 65–86.

Tomidajewicz, J. J. (2010) 'Does the Current Financial Crisis Mean the Crisis of Liberal Capitalism?', in: *Timisoara Journal of Economics*, vol. 3, issue 1, no. 9, pp. 65–68.

Toporowski, J. (1993) *The Economics of Financial Markets and The 1987 Crash*, Ashgate, Aldershot and Edward Elgar, Brookfield, US.

Toporowski, J. (1999) 'Kalecki, Marx and the Economics of Socialism,' in: Sawyer, M. (ed.) *The Legacy of Michal Kalecki, Volume 2*, Edward Elgar, Cheltenham.

Toporowski, J. (2000) *The End of Finance: Capital Market Inflation, Financial Derivatives and Pension Fund Capitalism*, Routledge, London.

Toporowski, J. (2003) 'Kaleckian Economics', in: King, J. E. (ed.) *The Elgar Companion to Post-Keynesian Economics*, Edward Elgar, Cheltenham.

Toporowski, J. (2005a) 'Methodology and Industrial Maturity in Steindl's Capitalism', in: Mott, T. and N. Shapiro (eds) *Rethinking Capitalist Development: Essays on the Economics of Joseph Steindl*, Routledge, London.

Toporowski, J. (2005b) *Theories of Financial Disturbance, an examination of critical theories of finance from Adam Smith to the present day*, Edward Elgar, Cheltenham.

Toporowski, J. (2008) 'Excess Capital and Liquidity Management', in: *Levy Economics Institute Working Papers*, no. 549, Levy Economics Institute, New York.

Trigg, A. B. (1994) 'On the Relationship Between Kalecki and Kaleckians', in: *Journal of Post Keynesian Economics*, vol. 17, no. 1, pp. 91–110.

Tsuru, S. (ed.) (1961) *Has Capitalism Changed?*, Iwanami Shoten, Tokyo.

Varian, H. R. (1992) *Microeconomic Analysis*, W. W. Norton & Company, New York.

Weber, M. (2000[1924]) 'Stock and Commodity Exchanges', translated by S. Lestition, in: *Theory and Society*, vol. 29, pp. 339–371.

Weintraub, S. (1978) *Capitalism's Inflation and Unemployment Crisis*, Addison-Wesley, Reading.

Weisbrot, M. and R. Ray (2011) *Latvia's Internal Devaluation: a Success Story?*, Center for Economic Policy Research, Washington, DC.
White, H. (2012) *The China Choice: Why America Should Share Power*, Black Inc., Melbourne.
Wigham, E. (1973) *The Power to Manage: A History of the Engineering Employers' Federation*, Macmillan, London.
Wilkinson, R. and K. Pickett (2009) *The Spirit Level: Why More Equal Societies Almost Always Do Better*, Allen Lane, London.
Withers, H. (1912) *The Meaning of Money*, E. P. Dutton & Company, Boston.
Woodford, M. (2003) *Interest and Prices: Foundations of a Theory of Monetary Policy*, Princeton University Press, Princeton, NJ.
Wray, L. R. (1998) *Understanding Modern Money*, Edward Elgar, Cheltenham.
Xu, C. (2011) 'The Fundamental Institutions of China's Reforms and Development', in: *Journal of Economic Literature*, vol. 49, no. 4, pp. 1076–1151.
You, J. I. and A. K. Dutt (1996) 'Government Debt, Income Distribution and Growth', in: *Cambridge Journal of Economics*, vol. 20, no. 3, pp. 335–351.
Žižek, S. (2006) *Lacan*, Granta Books, London.

Bibliography of Published Works by Tadeusz Kowalik

Compiled by Ewa Karwowski, Hanna Szymborska, and Jan Toporowski
Translated by Ewa Karwowski

The works listed below are a combination of the works listed by Tadeusz Kowalik in his own list of publications, together with titles discovered in the course of research by Hanna Szymborska and Jan Toporowski. The list does not claim to be comprehensive; Tadeusz Kowalik did not keep a full record of his published works. Two gaps in particular remain to be filled. During the 1970s and the 1980s, Tadeusz Kowalik was active in dissident groups, and wrote articles and memoranda as part of this activity. In the same period there were also articles he wrote that were published under the name of sympathisers who were able to publish more freely than he could; he mentioned Edward Lipinski in particular as a front for his publications.

1 Books and edited books

Brus, W. and T. Kowalik (1967) *Oskara Langego ekonomia i socjalizm* (in Polish: *Oskar Lange's economics and socialism*), SGPiS, Warszawa.

Górski, J., Kowalik, T. and W. Sierpiński (1967) *Historia powszechnej myśli ekonomicznej 1870–1950*, (in Polish: *History of economic thought 1870–1950*), PWN, Warszawa.

Hołda-Róziewicz, H. and T. Kowalik (1976) *Ludwik Krzywicki* (in Polish), Wydawnictwo Interpres, Warszawa.

Kowalik, T. (1958, ed.) *Stanisław Krusiński, Pisma zebrane* (in Polish: *Stanisław Krusiński, Collected works*), Książka i Wiedza, Warszawa.

Kowalik, T. (1959) *O Ludwiku Krzywickim. Studium społeczno-ekonomiczne* (in Polish: *Ludwik Krzywicki. A socio-economic study*), PWN, Warszawa.

Kowalik, T. (1965) *Krzywicki*, Wiedza Powszechna, Warszawa.

Kowalik, T. (1971) *Róża Luksemburg, Teoria akumulacji i imperializmu* (in Polish: *Rosa Luxemburg, Theory of accumulation and imperialism*), Ossolineum, Warszawa-Wrocław, also published in Spanish: Kowalik, T. (1979) *Teoría de la acumulación y del imperialismo en Rosa Luxemburg*, Ediciones Era, México D.F.

Kowalik, T. (1975) *Oskar Lange, Dzieła, Tom 3*, (in Polish: *Oskar Lange, Collected works, Volume 3*), Warszawa.

Kowalik, T. (1977) *Rosa Luxemburg. Il pensiero economico*, (in Italian: *The economic thought of Rosa Luxemburg*), Editori Riuniti, Roma.

Kowalik, T. (1986) *On crucial reform of "real socialism"*, Wiener Institut für Internationale Wirtschaftsvergleiche, Wien.

Kowalik, T. (1991, ed.) *Zachodni spór o socjalizm rynkowy* (in Polish: *The Western dispute about market socialism*), Warszawa.

Kowalik, T. (1992) *Historia ekonomii w Polsce 1865–1950* (in Polish: *The history of economics in Poland 1865–1950*), Ossolineum, Warszawa-Wrocław.

Kowalik, T. (1994, ed.) *Economic Theory and Market Socialism, Selected essays of Oskar Lange*, Edward Elgar, Aldershot.

Kowalik, T. (1995) *From "Self-Governing Republic" to capitalism, Polish workers and intellectuals*, Black Rose Books, Montreal.

Kowalik, T. (1997) *Zmiany systemowe w Polsce (kontekst wewnętrzny i międzynarodowy)* (in Polish: *Systemic changes in Poland (the domestic and international context)*), Polskie Towarzystwo Ekonomiczne, Warszawa.

Kowalik, T. (1997) *Społeczne koszty transformacji* (in Polish: *Social costs of transformation*), Klub Parlamentarny Unii Pracy, Warszawa.

Kowalik, T. (2000) *Współczesne systemy ekonomiczne, powstawanie, ewolucja i kryzys* (in Polish: *Contemporary economic systems, emergence, evolution and crisis*), WSPiZ, Warszawa.

Kowalik, T. (2001, ed.) *Spory wokół Nowej Trzeciej Drogi* (in Polish: *Disputes about the New Third Way*), Wydawnictwo Naukowe Scholar, Warszawa.

Kowalik, T. (2002) *Społeczna gospodarka rynkowa – dekoracja czy program działania?* (in Polish: *Social market economy – decoration or action plan?*), Polskie Towarzystwo Ekonomiczne, Warszawa.

Kowalik, T. (2002, ed.) *Nierówni i równiejsi, sprawiedliwość dystrybucyjna czasu transformacji polskiej* (in Polish: *The unequal and the more equal, distributional justice during the Polish transformation*), Fundacja Innowacja, Warszawa.

Kowalik, T. (2005) *Systemy gospodarcze. Efekty i defekty reform i zmian ustrojowych* (in Polish: *Economic systems. Effects and defects of reform and systemic change*), Fundacja Innowacja, Warszawa.

Kowalik, T. (2009, ed.) *www.Polska Transformacja.pl* (in Polish: *www.Polish Transformation.pl*), Warszawskie Wydawnictwo Literackie MUZA S. A., Warszawa.

Kowalik, T. (2010, ed.) *Stanisław Gomułka i polska transformacja, Dokumenty i analizy* (in Polish: *Stanisław Gomułka and the Polish transformation, Documents and analyses*), Wydawnictwo Naukowe Scholar, Warszawa.

Lange, O., Brus, W., Kowalik, T., and I. Sachs (1972) *Wirtschaftwissenschaft, Hauptströmungen der sozialwisseschaftlichen Forschung, Herausgegeben von der UNESCO*, Ullstein, Frankfurt am Main, also published in English: Lange, O., Brus, W., Kowalik, T., Sachs, I. (1974) *Main Trends of Research in the Social and Human Sciences*, Routledge, London.

2 Book chapters

Bugaj, R. and T. Kowalik (1992) 'Towards a mixed economy', in: *Privatization in Eastern Europe*, Friedrich Ebert Stiftung and Renner Institute, Wien.

Kowalik, T. (1964) 'Biography of Michał Kalecki', in: *Problems of Economic Dynamics and Planning, Essays in Honor of Michał Kalecki*, PWN, Warszawa.

Kowalik, T. (1964) 'R. Luxemburg's theory of accumulation and imperialism', in: *Problems of Economic Dynamics and Planning, Essays in Honor of Michał Kalecki*, PWN, Warszawa.

Kowalik, T. (1964) 'Biography of Oskar Lange', in: *On Political Economy and Econometrics, Essays in Honor of Oskar Lange*, PWN, Warszawa.

Kowalik, T. (1964) 'Three conceptions of political economy of socialism', in: *On Political Economy and Econometrics, Essays in Honor of Oskar Lange*, PWN, Warszawa.

Kowalik, T. (1973) 'Zu Oskar Langes klassischem Model des Sozializmus', in: *Sozialismus, Geschichte und Wirtschaft, Festschrift für Eduard März* (in German: 'Oskar Lange's classical model of socialism', in: *Socialism, History and Economy, Festschrift in Honour of Eduard März*), Europaverlag, Wien.

Kowalik, T. (1974) 'Oskar Lange – tolerancja i uniwersalność', in: Biernacki, A. (ed.) *Portrety uczonych polskich*, (in Polish: 'Oskar Lange – tolerance and universality', in Biernacki, A. (ed.) *Portrays of Polish Intellectuals*), Wydawnictwo Literackie, Kraków.

Kowalik, T. (1975) 'Filozofia społeczna Ludwika Krzywickiego', in: Skarga, B. (ed.) *Polska myśl filozoficzna i społeczna*, (in Polish: 'Ludwik Krzywicki's social philosophy', in: Skarga, B. (ed.) *Polish Philosophical and Social Thought*), PWN, Warszawa.

Kowalik, T. (1980) 'Racjonalność – zasada działania, postulat czy mit', in: Kamiński, B. and A. Łukaszewicz (eds) *Racjonalność gospodarowania w socjalizmie*, (in Polish: 'Rationality – acting principle, postulate or myth', in: Kamiński, B. and A. Łukaszewicz (eds) *Rationality of Planning under Socialism*), PWE, Warszawa.

Kowalik, T. (1983) 'Experts and the working group', in: Kemp-Welch, A. (ed.) *The Birth of Solidarity. The Gdańsk negotiations, 1980*, Macmillan, London.

Kowalik, T. (1987) 'Three attitudes and three dramas', in: Fink, G., Poell, G. and M. Riese (eds) *Economic Theory, Political Power and Social Justice: Festschrift Kazimierz Łaski*, Linzer Universitätsschriften, Springer-Verlag, Wien.

Kowalik, T. (1989) 'Crucial reform of "real socialism"', in: Gabrisch, H. (ed.) *Economic reforms in Eastern Europe and the Soviet Union*, Westview Press, Boulder, Colorado.

Kowalik, T. (1989) 'Toward a mixed socialist economy', in: Flakierski, H and T. Sekine (eds) *Socialist Dilemmas. East and West*, M.E. Sharpe, Armonk, New York.

Kowalik, T. (1991) 'The Polish postscript, 1989', in: Mendell, M. and D. Salee (eds) *The Legacy of Karl Polanyi: Market, State and Society at the End of the Twentieth Century*, St. Martin's Press, New York.

Kowalik, T. (1990) 'Zmiana ustroju – wielka operacja czy proces społeczny', in: Gortat, R. (ed.) *Społeczeństwo uczestniczące, gospodarka rynkowa, sprawiedliwość społeczna*, (in Polish: 'System change – great operation or social process' in: Gortat, R. (ed.) *Participating Society, Market Economy, Social Justice*), Instytut Studiów Politycznych PAN, Warszawa.

Kowalik, T. (1990) 'Prywatyzacja czy gospodarka mieszana', in: Wesołowski, W. (ed.) *Losy idei socjalistycznych i wyzwania współczesności* (in Polish: 'Privatisation or mixed socialist economy' in: Wesołowski, W. (ed.) *The Fate of Socialist Ideas and Contemporary Challenges*), Polskie Towarzystwo in cooperation with the Club of Rome, Warszawa.

Kowalik, T. (1990) 'Piętnaście miesięcy Planu Balcerowicza', in: *Studia i Materiały*, (in Polish: 'Fifteen months of the Balcerowicz Plan' in: *Studies and Materials*), Ośrodek Prac Społeczno-Zawodowych, KK NSZZ Solidarność, Warszawa.

Kowalik, T. (1991) 'Wobec socjalizmu realnego i postulowanego', in: Siciński, A. (ed.) *Sens uczestnictwa. Wokół idei Jana Strzeleckiego*, (in Polish: 'Towards real and postulated socialism' in: Siciński, A. (ed.) *The Sense for Participation. On the Idea of Jan Strzelecki*), Instytut Filozofii i Socjologii PAN, Warszawa.

Kowalik, T. (1992) 'Reform economics and bureaucracy', in: Kovacs, M. and M. Tardos (eds), *Reform and Transformation in Eastern Europe. Soviet-Type Economics on the Threshold of Change*, Routledge, London.

Kowalik, T. (1992) 'Michał Kalecki and early attempts to reform the Polish economy', in: Knell, M. and C. Rider (eds) *Socialist Economies in Transition: Appraisals of the Market Mechanism*, Edward Elgar, Aldershot.

Kowalik, T. (1993) 'Sektor prywatny a prywatyzacja', in: *Polska na rozdrożu* (in Polish: 'The private sector and privatisation', in: *Poland at the Crossroads*), Fundacja Polska Praca, Warszawa.

Kowalik, T. (1993) 'Rysy koncepcji alternatywnej', in: *Stulecie Polskiej Partii Socjalistycznej 1892–1992* (in Polish: 'Outlines of an alternative concept', in: *Centenary of the Polish Socialist Party 1892–1992*), Warszawska Oficyna Wydawnicza, Gryf, Warszawa.

Kowalik, T. (1994) 'Prywatyzacja jako proces społeczny', in: Jakóbik, W. (ed.) *Kontynuacja czy przełom? Dylematy transformacji ustrojowej* (in Polish: 'Privatisation as social process' in: Jakóbik, W. (ed.) *Continuity or Breakthrough? Dilemmas of System Transformation*), ISP PAN, Warszawa.

Kowalik, T. (1994) 'Oskar Lange's market socialism: The story of an intellectual political career', in: Roosevelt, F. and D. Belkin (eds) *Why Market Socialism?* M.E. Sharpe, Armonk, New York.

Kowalik, T. (1994) 'The "Big Bang" as a political and historical Phenomenon: A case study on Poland', in: Berend, I. (ed.) *Transition to a Market Economy and the End of the 20th Century*, Eleventh International Economic History Congress, Südosteuropa Gesellschaft, Milano.

Kowalik, T. (1994) 'Privatization in Poland – social process or another shock?', in: *Privatization in the Transition Process. Recent Experiences in Eastern Europe*, UNDP, Genève.

Kowalik, T. (1994) 'The great transformation and privatization: three years of Polish experience', in: Bryant, C. and E. Mokrzycki (eds) *The New Great Transformation, Change and Continuity in East-Central Europe*, Routledge, London.

Kowalik, T. (1995) 'The free market or a social contract as bases for systemic transformation', in: Hausner, J., Jesop, B. and K. Nielsen (eds) *Strategic Choice and Path Dependency in Post-Socialism. Institutional Dynamics in the Transformation Process*, Edward Elgar, Aldershot.

Kowalik, T. (1996) 'Konserwatywna modernizacja', in: Drozdowski, M. (ed.) *Jałta. Szkice i materiały* (in Polish: 'Conservative modernisation', in: Drozdowski, M. (ed.) *Jalta. Outlines and Materials*), Towarzystwo Miłośników Historii oraz Instytut Historii PAN, Warszawa.

Kowalik, T. (1997) 'Towards a free market or a new mixed market economy', in: Berend, T. (ed.) *Long-Term Structural Changes in Transforming Central & Eastern Europe the 1990s*, Südosteuropa-Gesellschaft in cooperation with the Center for European and Russian Studies, University of California, München and Los Angeles.

Kowalik, T. (1997) 'Transformacja a system docelowy', in: Instytut Rozwoju i Studiów Strategicznych SGH (ed.) *Ustrojowa wizja gospodarki Polskiej* (in Polish: 'Transformation and its destination', in: SGH (ed.) *A Political Vision for Poland's Economic System*), Warszawa.

Kowalik, T. (1997) 'Harmonizacja polityki społecznej i polityki gospodarczej czasu transformacji', in: Belka, M. and W. Trzeciakowski (eds) *Dynamika transformacji polskiej gospodarki* (in Polish: 'Harmonisation of social and economic policies during times of transformation', in: Belka, M. and W. Trzeciakowski (eds) *Dynamics of Polish Economic Transformation*), Polteks, Warszawa.

Kowalik, T. (1997) 'Zmiany w podziale dochodu narodowego w czasie transformacji', in: Belka, M. and W. Trzeciakowski (eds) *Dynamika transformacji polskiej gospodarki* (in Polish: 'Changes in the income distribution during times of transformation', in: Belka, M. and W. Trzeciakowski (eds) *Dynamics of Polish Economic Transformation*), Polteks, Warszawa.

Kowalik, T. (1998) 'Wobec globalizacji nierówności', in: *Praca i polityka społeczna w perspektywie XXI wieku* (in Polish: 'Towards the globalisation of inequality', in: *Work and Social Policy in the 21st Century*), IPISS, Warszawa.

Kowalik, T. (1998) 'Systemowe bariery dla kapitału ludzkiego', in: Mujżel, J. (ed.) *Kapitał ludzki, Stan i perspektywy* (in Polish: 'Systemic barriers to human capital', in: Mujżel, J. (ed.) *Human Capital, Status and Prospects*), Rada Strategii Społeczno-Gospodarczej przy Radzie Ministrów, Warszawa, new version published in: *Przeglądzie Społeczny*, no. 5–6, also published in: Pankowicz, A. (ed.) *Ziemie górskie u progu XXI wieku* (*Mountain Lands on the Brink of the 21st Century*), Związek Podhalan, Zakopane.

Kowalik, T. (1998) 'The experience of ownership transformation of state firms in Poland', in: Ostojic, N.P. and N. Scott (eds) *Experiences and Results of Privatization on the Economies in Transition*, Proceedings of the Second ECPD International Round Table, Belgrade.

Kowalik, T. (1998) 'Konsekwencje społeczne procesu globalizacji', in: Komitet Prognoz PAN (ed.) *Globalizacja gospodarki Światowej a integracja regionalna* (in Polish: 'Social consequences of the globalisation process', in: Forecasting committee PAN (ed.) *Globalisation of the World Economy and Regional Integration*), Warszawa.

Kowalik, T. (1999) 'Privatization and distributive justice, Poland's experience', in: Ostojic, N. P. and N. Scott (eds) *Recent Lessons from Transition and Privatization. Problems of Institutions and Corporate Governance*, ECPD, Belgrade.

Kowalik, T. (1999) 'Polityka kluczem do polskiej transformacji ekonomicznej', in: Jasińska, A. and K. M. Słomczyński (eds) *Władza i struktura społeczna, Księga dedykowana Włodzimierzowi Wesołowskiemu* (in Polish: 'Politics as key to Polish economic transformation', in: Jasińska, A. and K. M. Słomczyński (eds) *Power and Social Structure, Festschrift for Włodzimierz Wesołowski*), Instytut Filozofii i Socjologii PAN, Warszawa.

Kowalik, T. (2000) 'Nowy ład społeczny: ani konieczny ani pożądany', in: Deniszczuk, M. (ed.) *Polska przed nowymi problemami, Barometr społeczno-ekonomiczny 1999* (in Polish: 'New social order: neither necessary nor welcome', in: Deniszczuk, M. (ed.) *Poland Facing New Problems, Socio-Economic Barometer 1999*), Stowarzyszenie Studiów i Inicjatyw Społecznych, Warszawa.

Kowalik, T. (2000) 'Polskie transformacje a emigracja', in: Hausner, J. and T. Kowalik (eds) *Polska ekonomia w świecie* (in Polish: 'Polish transformations and emigration', in: Hausner, J. and T. Kowalik (eds) *The Polish Economy in the World*), PWN, Kraków.

Kowalik, T. (2001) 'Ekonomiści polscy wobec transformacji', in: Wojtyna, A. (ed.) *Czy ekonomia nadąża z wyjaśnieniem rzeczywistości?* ('Polish economists on transformation', in: Wojtyna, A. (ed.) *Does Economics Explain Reality?*), Polskie Towarzystwo Ekonomiczne, Warszawa.

Kowalik, T. (2001) 'The ugly face of the Polish success', in: Blazyca, G. and M. Rapacki (eds) *Poland into the New Millennium*, Edward Elgar, Aldershot.

Kowalik, T. (2001) 'Why the social democratic option failed: Poland's experience of systemic change', in: Glyn, A. (ed.) *Social Democracy in Neo-Liberal Times*, Oxford University Press, Oxford.

Kowalik, T. and D. Tosi, (2001) 'That great glow in the East', in: Brussiere, E., Dumoulin, M. and G. Trausch (eds) *Europa: The European Idea and Identity, from Ancient Greece to the 21st Century*, Mercatorfonds/ Fundación Academia Europea de Yuste, Antwerpen (also published in French).

Kowalik, T. (2001) 'Społeczna gospodarka rynkowa – konstytucyjne wyzwanie dla Polski', in: Toeplitz, K. T. (ed.) *Człowiek, rynek, sprawiedliwość* (in Polish: 'Social market economy – constitutional challenges for Poland', in: Toeplitz, K. T. (ed.) *Man, the Market, and Justice*), Wydawnictwo Naukowe i Literackie, Warszawa.

Kowalik, T. (2001) 'Możliwości wyboru systemu ekonomicznego. Dahrendorf po dziesięciu latach', in: WSPiZ (ed.) *Tworzenie organizacji* (in Polish: 'The possibility to choose the economic system. Dahrendorf ten years later', in: WSPiZ (ed.) *Creating Organisation*), Warszawa.

Kowalik, T. (2002) 'Kapitał globalny a tendencje egalitarne i antyegalitarne', in: Liberska, B. (ed.) *Globalizacja. Mechanizmy i wyzwania* (in Polish: 'Global capital and egalitarian and anti-egalitarian tendencies', in: Liberska, B. (ed.) *Globalisation. Mechanisms and Challenges*), PWE, Warszawa.

Kowalik, T. (2002) 'Sprawiedliwość dystrybutywna – wyzwanie transformacyjne', in: Kołodko, G. (ed.) *Rozwój polskiej gospodarki, perspektywy i uwarunkowania* (in Polish: 'Distributional justice – challenges of transformation', in: Kołodko, G. (ed.) *The Development of the Polish Economy, Prospects and Features*), WSPiZ, Warszawa.

Kowalik, T. (2002) 'Zmiany systemowe ostatniej dekady: spojrzenie ogólne', in: Bowden, E. V., Bowden, J. H., Kabaj, M., Kowalik, T., Noga, A. and J. Wilkin (eds) *Ekonomia – nauka zdrowego rozsądku, podręcznik amerykańsko-polski* (in Polish: 'Systemic changes of the past decade: a general overview', in: Bowden, E. V., Bowden, J. H., Kabaj, M., Kowalik, T., Noga, A. and J. Wilkin (eds) *Economics – Science of Common Sense, American-Polish handbook*), Fundacja Innowacja, Warszawa.

Kowalik, T. (2002) 'Income inequalities in the transition: Poland in comparative perspective', in: Adaman, F. and P. Divine (eds) *Economy and Society. Money, Capitalism and Transition*, Black Rose Books, Montreal.

Kowalik, T. (2003) 'Systemowa różnorodność w warunkach globalizacji i integracji', in: Kołodko, G. W. (ed.) *Globalizacja, marginalizacja, rozwój*, WSPiZ Warszawa, also published in English: 'Systemic variety under the conditions of globalization and integration', in: Kołodko, G. W. (ed.) *Emerging Market Economies*, Ashgate, Aldershot.

Kowalik, T. (2003) 'Społeczna gospodarka rynkowa – dekoracja czy program działania?', in: Mączyńska, E. and P. Pysz (eds) *Społeczna gospodarka rynkowa. Idee i możliwości praktycznego wykorzystania w Polsce* (in Polish: 'Social market economy – decoration or action plan?', in: Mączyńska, E. and P. Pysz (eds) *Social Market Economy. Ideas and Practical Potential in Poland*), PTE, Warszawa.

Kowalik, T. (2003) 'Antyegalitarne tendencje w Polsce na tle literatury światowej', in: Woźniak, M. G. (ed.) *Nierówności społeczne a wzrost gospodarczy, Tom 1* (in Polish: 'Anti-egalitarian tendencies in Poland against the background of the international literature', in: Woźniak, M. G. (ed.) *Social Inequality and Economic Growth*), Uniwersytet Rzeszowski, Rzeszów.

Kowalik, T. (2003) 'Trzecią drogą do centrum, wzloty i upadki socjaldemokracji europejskiej i polskiej', in: Żuk, P. (ed.) *W poszukiwaniu innych światów* (in Polish: On the Third Way towards the centre, flights of fancy and falls of the European and Polish social democracy', in: Żuk, P. (ed.) *In the Search for other Worlds*), Warszawa.

Kowalik, T. (2003) 'Polska – Unia Europejska. W obronie różnorodności', in: *Polska po przejściach, barometr społeczno-ekonomiczny 2001–2003* (in Polish: 'Poland – European Union. Defending diversity', in: *Poland after Change, Socio-Economic Barometer 2001–2003*), SSiIS, Warszawa.

Kowalik, T. (2004) 'Polska rewolucja epigońsko-mieszczańska na drodze do Europy', in: Gardawski J. and J. Polakowska-Kujawa (eds) *Globalizacja, gospodarka, praca, kultura* (in Polish: 'The Polish bourgeois revolution on the way to Europe', in: Gardawski J. and J. Polakowska-Kujawa (eds) *Globalisation, Economy, Labour, Culture*), SGH, Warszawa, also published in: *Przegląd Europy Środkowej i Wschodniej*, no. 1, 2003 and *Belorusskij Ekonomiczeskij Żurnal* no. 2(23)/2003.

Kowalik, T. (2004) 'Oskar Lange – między socjalizmem a kapitalizmem', in: Musiał, G. (ed.) *Twórczość naukowa Oskara Langego i jej znaczenie w teorii ekonomii* (in Polish: 'Oskar Lange – between socialism and capitalism', in: Musiał, G. (ed.) *The Academic Work of Oskar Lange and its Importance for Economic Theory*), Wydawnictwo Akademii Ekonomicznej w Katowicach, Katowice.

Kowalik, T. (2004) 'Globalizacja, integracja, akcesja', in: Etxezarreta M. and T. Kowalik (eds) *Wokół polityki gospodarczej Unii Europejskiej* (in Polish: 'Globalisation, integration, accession' in: Etxezarreta M. and T. Kowalik (eds) *On Economic Policies of the European Union*), SSiIS, Warszawa.

Kowalik, T. (2005) 'Teoria socjalizmu Oskara Langego w konfrontacji z realiami', in: Sadowski, Z. (ed.) *Oskar Lange a współczesność* (in Polish: 'Oskar Lange's theory of socialism confronted with realism', in: Sadowski, Z. (ed.) *Oskar Lange and Contemporary Times*), PTE, Warszawa.

Kowalik, T. (2005) 'Intelektualne źródła polskiej transformacji', in: Bugaj, R. and K. Kulpińska-Cała (eds) *Polska transformacja ustrojowa, próba dyskursu – zarys perspektyw* ('The intellectual origins of Polish transformation', in: Bugaj, R. and K. Kulpińska-Cała (eds) *Polish Systemic Transformation, Attempted Discourse – Outlined Prospects*), Fundacja Innowacja, Warszawa.

Kowalik, T. (2005) 'Własność, właściciele a sprawiedliwość społeczna', in: Galor, Z. (ed.) *Europa Właścicieli* (in Polish: 'Property, property owners and social justic', in: Galor, Z. (ed.) *The Europe of Property Owners*), Wydawnictwo Prodruk, Poznań.

Kowalik, T. (2005) 'Oligarchiczna triada a demokracja i dobrobyt', in: *Dylematy wyboru modelu rozwoju gospodarczego Polski* (in Polish: 'Dilemma triad, democracy and welfare', in: *Dilemmas Surrounding the Choice of an Economic Development Model for Poland*), Wydawnictwo Akademii Ekonomicznej w Krakowie, Kraków.

Kowalik, T. (2005) 'Przyszłość społecznej gospodarki rynkowej w Unii Europejskiej i Polsce', in: Wieteska-Rostek, M. (ed.) *Polska i Ukraina w integrującej się Europie i globalnym świecie XXI wieku* (in Polish: 'The future of social market economy in the European Union and Poland', in: Wieteska-Rostek, M. (ed.) *Poland and Ukraine in an Integrated Europe and the Globalised World of the 21st Century*), Fundacja Innowacja, Warszawa.

Kowalik, T. (2006) 'Jan Drewnowski', in: Kaliński, J. (ed.) *Poczet doktorów honoris causa Szkoły Głównej Handlowej w Warszawie* (in Polish: 'Jan Drewnowski', in: Kaliński, J. (ed.) *Honoris causa doctors of the Szkoła Główna Handlowa in Warsaw*), Oficyna Wydawnicza SGH, Warszawa.

Kowalik, T. (2006) 'Zróżnicowanie i konwergencja ustrojowa w Unii Europejskiej. Czy gospodarki europejskie powinny się amerykanizować?', in: Bieńkowski, W. and M. J. Radło (eds) *Amerykański model rozwoju gospodarczego, istota, efektywność i możliwość zastosowania,* Warszawa, also published in English: Kowalik, T. (2006) 'Convergence and divergence of the European Union: Are the European economies to be "Americanized"?', in: Bieńkowski, W., Brada, C. J. and M. J. Radło (eds), *Reaganomics goes Global. What Can the EU, Russia and other Transition Countries Learn from the USA?*, Palgrave Macmillan, London.

Kowalik, T. (2006) 'Czy polityka pełnego zatrudnienia należy do przeszłości?', in: Kornaś, J. (ed.) *Nowoczesny Lewiatan, studia nad współczesnym państwem* (in Polish: 'Are full-employment policies outdated?', in: Kornaś, J. (ed.) *The Modern Leviathan, Studies of the Contemporary State*), WESiP, Kielce.

Kowalik, T. (2007) 'Państwo opiekuńcze – powstanie, rozwój, kryzys', in: Jankowski, S. (ed.) *Wybrane problemy polityki społeczno-ekonomicznej, podręcznik* (in Polish: 'The welfare state – emergence, evolution and crisis', in: Jankowski, S. (ed.) *Selected Problems in Socio-Economic Policy, Handbook*), Oficyna Wydawnicza Politechniki Warszawskiej, Warszawa.

Kowalik, T. (2007) 'Ekonomiści wobec ruchów społecznych', in: Sadowski, Z. (ed.) *Przełomowy rok 1956 a współczesność* (in Polish: 'Economists on social movements', in: Sadowski, Z. (ed.) *The Critical Year 1956 and Contemporary Times*), PTE, Warszawa.

Kowalik, T. and P. Kozłowski (2007) 'Czy kapitalizm polski może być etyczny?', in: Klimczak, B. and A. Lewicka-Strzałecka (eds) *Etyka i ekonomia* ('Can Polish capitalism be ethical?', in: Klimczak, B. and A. Lewicka-Strzałecka (eds) *Ethics and Economics*), PTE, Warszawa.

Kowalik, T. (2007) 'Intelektualne źródła przemian ustrojowych w Polsce', in: Chałubiński, M. (ed.) *Transformacje systemowe w Polsce i krajach postkomunistycznych. Studia i rozprawy* (in Polish: 'Intellectual origins of Polish systemic change', in: Chałubiński, M. (ed.) *Systemic Transformations in Poland and Post-Communist Countries*), Akademia Humanistyczna im. A. Gieysztora, Pułtusk.

Kowalik, T. (2007) 'Blaski i cienie polskiej transformacji', in: Kaltwasser, M., Majewska, E. and K. Szreder (eds) *Futuryzm miast przemysłowych. 100 lat Wolfsburga i Nowej Huty* ('Light and shade in Polish transformation', in: Kaltwasser, M., Majewska, E. and K. Szreder (eds) *Futurism of Industrial Cities. 100 Years of Wolfsburg and Nowa Huta*), Korporacja Halart, Kraków, also published in German.

Kowalik, T. (2007) 'Przedmowa', in: Holland, H. *Krzywicki nie znany* (in Polish: 'Foreword', in: Holland, H. *The Unknown Krzywicki*), Książka i Prasa, Warszawa.

Kowalik, T. (2007) 'Struktura własności podstawą nierówności', in: Klebaniuk, J. (ed.) *Oblicza nierówności społecznych, studia interdyscyplinarne* ('Ownership structures as basis for inequality', in: Klebaniuk, J. (ed.) *Faces of Social Inequality, Interdisciplinary Studies*), Eneteia Wydawnictwo Psychologii i Kultury, Warszawa.

Kowalik, T. (2008) 'Ekonomia i socjologia a transformacja systemowa', in: Banaszak, S. and K. Doktór (eds) *Problemy socjologii gospodarki* (in Polish: 'Economics, sociology and systemic transformation', in: Banaszak, S. and K. Doktór (eds) *Problems of Economic Sociology*), Wydawnictwo Wyższej Szkoły Komunikacji i Zarządzania, Poznań.

Kowalik, T. (2008) 'Własność a nierówności i bezrobocie', in: Pacho, W. and M. Garbicz (eds) *Wzrost gospodarczy a bezrobocie i nierówności w podziale dochodów* (in Polish: 'Property, inequality and unemployment', in: Pacho, W. and M. Garbicz (eds) *Economic Growth, Unemployment and Distributional Inequality*), SGH, Warszawa.

Kowalik, T. (2008) 'George Blazyca on shock therapy and the third way', in: Myant, M. and T. Cox (eds) *Reinventing Poland. Economic and Political Transformation and Evolving National Identity*, Routledge, London, New York.

Kowalik, T. (2008) 'Czy gospodarka japońska "amerykanizuje" się?', in: Gawlikowski, K. and M. Ławacz (eds) *Japonia na początku XXI wieku* (in Polish: 'Is the Japanese economy "Americanising"?', in: Gawlikowski, K. and M. Ławacz (eds) *Japan at the Beginning of the 21st Century*), Wydawnictwo Adam Marszałek, Toruń.

Kowalik, T. (2008) 'W kierunku realnych utopii', in: Żuk, P. (ed.) *Spotkania z utopią XXI wieku* (in Polish: 'Towards real utopias', in: Żuk, P. (ed.) *Meeting the Utopia of the 21st Century*), Oficyna Naukowa, Warszawa.

Kowalik, T. (2008) 'Hybryda czy nowy system?', in: Pomykało, W. (ed.) *Chiny w globalnym świecie* (in Polish: 'Hybrid or new system?', in: Pomykało, W. (ed.) *China in the World*), Fundacja Innowacja, Warszawa.

Kowalik, T. (2009) 'Kapitalizm kasyna', in: *Kryzys. Przyczyny, analizy, prognozy, przewodnik krytyki politycznej* (in Polish: 'Casino capitalism', in: *Crisis. Origins, Analyses, Forecasts, Handbook of Political Criticism*), Wydawnictwo Krytyki Politycznej, Warszawa.

Kowalik, T. (2009) 'Do Eurolandu? Spieszmy się powoli', in: Sopoćko, A. (ed.) *Polska w strefie euro. Nowe perspektywy wzrostu* ('Towards Euroland? Let us make haste slowly', in: Sopoćko, A. (ed.) *Poland in the Euro Area. New Growth Perspectives*), Wydział Zarządzania UW, Warszawa.

Kowalik, T. (2009) 'Luxemburg's and Kalecki's theories and visions of capitalist dynamics', in: Bellofiore, R. (ed.) *Rosa Luxemburg and the Critique of Political Economy*, Routledge, London.

Kowalik, T. (2010) 'Ekonomia polityczna, Klęski socjaldemokratycznej opcji', in: Morawski, W. (ed.) *Modernizacja Polski. Struktury – agencje – instytucje* (in Polish: 'Political economy, Defeats of the social-democratic option', in: Morawski, W. (ed.) *The Modernisation of Poland. Structures – Agencies – Institutions*), Wydawnictwa Akademickie i Profesjonalne, Akademia Leona Koźmińskiego, Warszawa.

Kowalik, T. (2010) 'Zur Niederlage der sozialdemokratischen Alternative', in: Delheim J. and G. Krause (eds) *Sichtbare Hände – Staatsinterventionismus im Krisenkapitalismus* (in Polish: 'About the defeat of the social-democratic alternative', in: Delheim J. and G. Krause (eds) *The Visible Hand – State Interventionism of Capitalism in Crisis*'), Karl Dietz Verlag, Berlin.

Kowalik, T. (2010) 'Szok jako antyterapia. Jak nie należy budować nowego ładu', in: Kotowicz-Jawor, J. (ed.) *Polska i Rosja. Państwo i gospodarka w perspektywie XXI wieku* (in Polish: 'Shock as anti-therapy. How not to build a new order', in: Kotowicz-Jawor, J. (ed.) *Poland and Russia. State and Economy from the Perspective of the 21st Century*), Wydawnictwo KeyText, Warszawa.

Kowalik, T. (2010) 'Kryzys systemu w perspektywie alterglobalizmu', in: Kołodko, G. W. (ed.) *Globalizacja, kryzys i co dalej?* (in Polish: 'Sytemic crisis in the anti-globalisation perspective', in: Kołodko, G. W. (ed.) *Globalisation, Crisis and What Next?*), Wydawnictwo Poltext, Warszawa.

Kowalik, T. (2010) 'Powtórka z pierwotnej akumulacji kapitału', in: Kozłowski P. and H. Domański (eds) *Po 20 latach. Polska Transformacja z perspektywy ekonomicznej, socjologicznej i prawniczej* ('The repeat of primitive accumulation of capital', in: Kozłowski P. and H. Domański (eds) *20 Years Later. Polish Transformation from an Economic, Sociological and Legal Perspective*), Wydawnictwo KeyText, Warszawa.

Kowalik, T. and P. Kozłowski (2010) 'Reforma i transformacja', in: Instytut Nauk Ekonomicznych Polskiej Akademii Nauk (ed.) *Przeszłość i teraźniejszość* (in Polish: 'Reform and transformation', in: Instytut Nauk Ekonomicznych Polskiej Akademii Nauk (ed.) *The past and the present*), Wydawnictwo KeyText, Warszawa.

Kowalik, T. (2010) 'Kapitalizm niejedno ma imię', in: *Zrozumieć nowoczesność. Księga jubileuszowa Zygmunta Baumana* (in Polish: 'Capitalism has many names', in: *Understanding Modernity. Festschrift for Zygmunt Bauman*), Wydawnictwo Oficyna, Łódź.

Kowalik, T. (2011) 'Systemowe źródła obecnego kryzysu światowego', in: Kieżun, W. (ed.) *Krytycznie i twórczo o zarządzaniu* (in Polish: 'Systemic origins of the current global crisis', in: Kieżun, W. (ed.) *Critically and Creatively about Management*), Wydawnictwa Akademickie i Profesjonalne, Akademia Leona Koźmińskiego, Warszawa.

3 Academic articles

Brus, W. and T. Kowalik (1966) 'Oskar Lange – teoretyk socjalizmu' (in Polish: 'Oskar Lange – theorist of socialism'), in: *Kultura i Społeczeństwo*, no. 2.

Brus, W., Kowalik, T. and I. Sachs (1967) 'Ewolucja ekonomii politycznej a jej miejsce w naukach społecznych' (in Polish: 'The evolution of political economy and its place in social science'), in: *Kultura i Społeczeństwo*, no. 2.

Brus, W., Kowalik, T. and I. Sachs (1967) 'Węzłowe problemy ekonomii współczesnej' (in Polish: 'Key problems of modern economics'), in: *Studia Socjologiczne*, no. 3.

Brus, W., Kowalik, T. and I. Sachs (1967) 'Obszary badań i narzędzia analizy ekonomii współczesnej' (in Polish: 'Areas of research and tools of analysis for modern economics'), in: *Ekonomista*, no. 4.

Brus, W. and T. Kowalik (1970) 'L'économie et le socialisme selon Oskar Lange' (in French: 'Economics and socialism according to Oskar Lange'), in: *Économie et société*, no. 1.

Brus, W. and T. Kowalik (1983) 'Socialism and development', in: *Cambridge Journal of Economics*, no. 3–4.

Bugaj, R. and T. Kowalik (1986) 'Kryzys polski w oczach ekonomistów' (in Polish: 'The Polish crisis in the eyes of economists'), in: *Więź*, no. 10.

Bugaj, R. and T. Kowalik (1991) 'W kierunku gospodarki mieszanej' (in Polish: 'Towards a mixed economy'), in: *Więź*, no. 1, published in German: 'Auf dem Weg zu einer gemischen Ökonomie', in: *Prokla 82 Markt und Demokratie*, March.

Kalecki, M. and T. Kowalik (1971) 'Osservazioni sulla "riforma cruciale"', in: *Politica ed Economia*, no. 2–3, Roma, also published in Polish: Kalecki, M. and T. Kowalik (1980) 'Uwagi o "reformie przełomowej"', in: Kalecki, M., *Dzieła*, Tom 2, (*Collected works*, vol. 2), PWE Warszawa, also published in Spanish: Kalecki, M. and T. Kowalik (1983) in: *Investigación Economica*, no. 42, Mexicó, and in English: M. Kalecki and T. Kowalik (1991), 'Observations on the "Crucial Reform"', in: Osiatyński; J. (ed.) *Collected works of Michał Kalecki*, vol. 2, Oxford.

Kowalik, T. (1955) 'Z historii marksistowskiej myśli ekonomicznej w Polsce (O pierwszych publikacjach Ludwika Krzywickiego)' (in Polish: 'About the history of Marxist economic thought in Poland (Ludwik Krzywicki's first publications)'), in: *Ekonomista*, no. 5–6.

Kowalik, T. (1956) 'Na marginesie polskiego wydania "Historii Ekonomii Politycznej" D. Rozenberga' (in Polish: 'On the margins of the Polish editions of "The History of Political Economy" by D. Rozenberg'), in: *Ekonomista*, no. 2.

Kowalik, T. (1957) 'O Instytucie Gospodarstwa Społecznego' (in Polish: 'The institution of social economy'), in: *Ekonomista*, no. 2.

Kowalik, T. (1958) 'Pisma Ludwika Landaua (recenzja)' (in Polish: 'The works of Ludwik Landau (book review)'), in: *Ekonomista*, no. 5.

Kowalik, T. (1961) 'Z dziejów polskiej myśli społeczno-ekonomicznej' (in Polish: 'History of Polish socio-economic thought'), in: *Ekonomista*, no. 3.

Kowalik, T. (1962) 'Aleksander Łukaszewicz, "Socjalizm ricardianski w historii ekonomii politycznej" (recenzja)' (in Polish: 'Aleksander Łukaszewicz, "Ricardian socialism in the history of political economy" (book review)'), in: *Ekonomista*, no. 5.

Kowalik, T. (1963) 'Teoria ekonomiczna R. Luksemburg w oczach jej krytyków: Włodzimierz Lenin' (in Polish: 'The theory of R. Luxemburg in the eyes of her critics: Włodzimierz Lenin'), in: *Ekonomista*, no. 1.

Kowalik, T. (1963) 'Z prehistorii ekonomii politycznej socjalizmu' (in Polish: 'The prehistory of the political economy of socialism'), in: *Ekonomista*, no. 4.

Kowalik, T. (1964) 'Michał Kalecki' (in Polish), in: *Ekonomista*, no. 3.

Kowalik, T. (1964) 'Oskar Lange' (in Polish), in: *Ekonomista*, no. 3.

Kowalik, T. (1964) 'Socjologia Ludwika Krzywickiego' (in Polish: 'The sociology of Ludwik Krzywicki'), in: *Studia Socjologiczne*, no. 4.

Kowalik, T. (1966) 'Mesjanizm kapitalistycznego uprzemysłowienia: o Józefie Supińskim' (in Polish: 'Messianism of capitalist industrialisation: on Józef Supiński'), in: *Ekonomista*, no. 6.

Kowalik, T. (1967) 'Kapitał Karola Marksa w literaturze polskiej (miscellanea historyczne)' (in Polish: 'Karl Marx's Capital in Polish literature (historical miscellanea))', in: *Ekonomista*, no. 2.

Kowalik, T. (1968) 'Stanisław Szczepanowski – ekspert rozwoju gospodarczego' (in Polish: 'Stanisław Szczepanowski – expert in economic development'), in: *Kwartalnik Historii Nauki i Techniki*, no. 2.

Kowalik, T. (1968) 'Nowy spór o stosunek M. Webera do Karola Marksa' (in Polish: 'New dispute about the relationship of M. Weber to Karl Marx'), in: *Ekonomista*, no. 3.

Kalecki, M., Kowalik, T. and K. Secomski (1969) 'Ekonomia Edwarda Lipińskiego' (in Polish: 'The economics of Edward Lipiński'), in: *Ekonomista*, no. 2.

Kowalik, T. (1969) 'O teorii imperializmu Róży Luksemburg' (in Polish: 'Rosa Luxemburg's theory of imperialism'), in: *Ekonomista*, no. 1.

Kowalik, T. (1969) 'Claude-Henri de Saint-Simon, Pisma wybrane (recenzja)' (in Polish: 'Claude-Henri de Saint-Simon, Selected works (book review)'), in: *Ekonomista*, no. 4/1969.

Kowalik, T. (1970) 'Model socjalizmu Karola Rodbertusa' ('Karl Rodbertus's model of socialism'), in: *Ekonomista*, no. 2.

Kowalik, T. (1970) 'O marksowskim obrazie gospodarki komunistycznej' (in Polish: 'On Marx's image of the comunist economy'), in: *Ekonomista*, no. 4.

Kowalik, T. (1970) 'Oskara Langego wczesne modele socjalizmu' (in Polish: 'Oskar Lange's early models of socialism'), in: *Ekonomista*, no. 5.

Kowalik, T. (1971) 'Wizje socjalizmu w szkole Owena i u Saintsimonistów' (in Polish: 'Visions of socialism in the schools of Owen and the Saint Simonians'), in: *Ekonomista*, no. 2.

Kowalik, T. (1971) 'Jean Jaures, Wybór pism (recenzja)' ('Jean Jaures, Selected works (book review)), in: *Ekonomista*, no. 4.

Kowalik, T. (1971) 'O humanizację ekonomii (recenzja książki E. Lipińskiego: Marks i zagadnienia współczesności, 1969)' (in Polish: 'The humanisation of economics (review of E. Lipiński's book: Marx and contemporary issues, 1969)'), in: *Więź*, no. 3.

Kowalik, T. (1971) 'Młodość i socjalizm Oskara Langego. W poszukiwaniu własnych dróg' (in Polish: 'Youth and socialism of Oskar Lange. In search of his own path'), in: *Kultura i Społeczeństwo*, no. 2.

Kowalik, T. (1971) 'Ekonomia liberalna a program pracy organicznej' (in Polish: 'Liberal economy and the plan of organic work), in: *Kwartalnik Historii Nauki i Techniki*, no. 4.

Kowalik, T. (1971) 'Oskar Lange et la pansée économique' (in Polish: 'Oskar Lange and economic thought'), in: *Perspectives Polonaises*, no. 6 (also published in English and German).

Kowalik, T. (1972) 'Polski spór o ekonomię jako naukę ścisłą w XIX wieku' (in Polish: 'The Polish dispute about economics as hard science in the 19th century'), in: *Ekonomista*, no. 1.

Kowalik, T. (1974) 'Socjologiczny obszar w ekonomii O. Langego' (in Polish: Sociology in the economics of O. Lange'), in: *Studia Socjologiczne*, no. 3.

Kowalik, T. (1975) 'Propozycja socjologii ekonomicznej' (in Polish: 'The proposition of economic sociology'), in: *Ekonomista*, no. 2.

Kowalik, T. (1975) 'Economics and praxiology. Oskar Lange's Political Economy', in: *Organon*, no. 11.

Kowalik, T. (1975) 'Notas sobre la teoría luxemburguiana de la acumulación' (in Spanish: 'Notes on Luxenburg's theory of accumulation'), in: *Materiales. Critica de la cultura*, no. 3.

Kowalik, T. (1976) 'Racjonalność i historyzm' (in Polish: 'Economic rationality and historism'), in: *Ekonomia*, Uniwersytet Warszawski, no. 36.

Kowalik, T. (1978) 'The institutional framework of Dobb's economics', in: *Cambridge Journal of Economics*, no. 2.

Kowalik, T. (1983) 'Próba kompromisu. O Komisji Ekspertów MKS w Gdańsku' (in Polish: 'The attempt of a compromise. About the commission of experts MKS in Gdańsk), in: *Zeszyty Literackie*, no. 2, also published in French: Kowalik, T. (1983) 'Les minutes d'un compromise', in: *Les Temps Modernes*, August–September.

Kowalik, T. (1984) 'Alec Nove, The economics of feasible socialism', in: *Contributions to Political Economy*, no. 30.

Kowalik, T. (1984) 'Review on the economics of feasible socialism (written by Alec Nove, 1983)', in: *Contribution to Political Economy*, vol. 3, no. 1.

Kowalik, T. (1985) 'O Oskarze Langem mniej rocznicowo' (in Polish: 'A few commemorative words about Oskar Lange'), in: *Miesięcznik Literacki*, December.

Kowalik, T. (1987) 'Oskar Lange na nowo odczytywany' (in Polish: 'Oskar Lange reread'), in: *Ekonomista*, no. 5.

Kowalik, T. (1987) 'Oskar Lange's thought reconsidered', in: *Oeconomica Polona*, no. 3/1987.

Kowalik, T. (1988) 'Reforma przełomowa realnego socjalizmu' (in Polish: 'Breakthrough reform of real socialism'), in: *Colloquia Communia*, no. 4–5.

Kowalik, T. (1988) 'Ekonomia i ekonomiści wobec kryzysu' (in Polish: 'Economics and economists on crisis'), in: *Ekonomista*, no. 3–4, 1988, pre-published in: *Zdanie*, no. 12/1987.

Kowalik, T. (1989) 'Michał Kalecki and first attempts to reform the Polish economy', in: *Oeconomica Polona*, no. 2/1989, also published in Polish in: *Nauka Polska*, no. 2.

Kowalik, T. (1989) 'Wiązka praw' (in Polish: 'A bundle of rights'), in: *Zmiany*, no. 1.

Kowalik, T. (1989) Liberałowie i socjaldemokraci, in: *Zmiany*, no. 34–35.

Kowalik, T. (1989) 'Tra l'utopia comunista e l'utopia neo-liberale' (in Italian: 'Between the communist and the neo-liberal utopia'), in: *Problemi del Socialismo*, no. 4/1990.

Kowalik, T. (1991) 'Economia de mercado o economia mixta' (in Portuguese: 'The market economy and the mixed economy'), in: *Jornadas Internacionales de Ciencias Politicas*, July/1991.

Kowalik, T. (1991) 'The costs of "shock therapy", economic transition in Poland', in: *Dissent*, fall.

Kowalik, T. (1991) 'Marketization and privatization: the case of Poland', in: *Socialist Register*.

Kowalik, T. (1992) 'Szwedzkie doświadczenie (w polskiej perspektywie)' (in Polish: 'The Swedish experience (in Polish perspective)'), in: *Przegląd Społeczny*, no. 3.

Kowalik, T. (1992) 'W stronę umowy społecznej' (in Polish: 'Towards a social contract'), in: *Przegląd Społeczny*, no. 1.

Kowalik, T. (1993) 'Can Poland afford the Swedish model?', in: *Dissent*, winter.

Kowalik, T. (1993) 'Socjalizm rynkowy – system czy polityka? Na marginesie ksiażki W. Brusa i K. Łaskiego: Od Marksa do Rynku' (in Polish: 'Market socialism – economic system or politics? On the margins of the book by W. Brus and K. Łaski: From Marx to the market'), in: *Ekonomista*, no. 4.

Kowalik, T. (1994) 'A reply to M. Glasman', in: *The New Left Review*, no. 205.

Kowalik, T. (1994) 'I costi sociali della terapia d'urto' (in Italian: 'The social cost of shock therapy'), in: *Europa, Europe*, Fondazione Istituto Gramsci, no. 2.

Kowalik, T. (1995) 'Skuteczność polityki gospodarczej czy sprawność systemów (O książce Z. Landaua i W. Roszkowskiego, Polityka gospodarcza II RP i PRL)' (in Polish: 'Effectiveness of economic policy or systemic efficiency (About Z. Landau's and W. Roszkowski's book, Economic policies in the Second Polish Republic and the Polish People's Republic)'), in: *Ekonomista*, no. 5–6.

Kowalik, T. (1995) 'W kręgu reformy przełomowej, polityczna "przygoda człowieka myślącego"' (in Polish: 'In the circle of groundbreaking reforms, the political "adventure of the thinking man"'), in: *Ekonomista*, no. 1–2.

Kabaj, M. and T. Kowalik (1995) 'Who is responsible for postcommunist successes in Eastern Europe?', in: *Transition*, no. 7–8.

Kowalik, T. (1996) 'Społeczny charakter ekonomii Edwarda Lipińskiego' (in Polish: 'The social character of Edward Lipiński's economics'), in: *Ekonomista*, no. 6.

Kowalik, T. (1996) 'On the transformation of post-communist societies: the inefficiency of primitive accumulation', in: *International Political Science Review*, no. 3.

Kowalik, T. (1996) '"Wybór" systemu ekonomicznego jako proces społeczny' (in Polish: 'The choice of the economic system as social process'), in: *Roczniki Kolegium Analiz Ekonomicznych (SGH)*, no. 4.

Kowalik, T. (1996) 'Reformy ustrojowe czy rozwiązywanie problemów' (in Polish: 'Systemic reform or problem solving'), in: *Zdanie*, no. 3.

Kowalik, T. (1997) 'The Polish Revolution', in: *Dissent*, spring.

Kowalik, T. (1997) 'Marksizm i skok do królestwa wolności: dzieje komunistycznej utopii (na marginesie książki Andrzeja Walickiego' (in Polish: 'Marxism and the jump into the kingdom of freedom: history of communist utopia' (on the margins of the book by Andrzej Walicki)), in: *Zdanie*, no. 1–2.

Kowalik, T. (1997) 'Czy sprawiedliwość społeczna kosztuje?' (in Polish: 'Is social justice costly?), in: *Ekonomista*, no. 3.

Kowalik, T. (1998) 'Systemowe uwarunkowania polskiej polityki społecznej' (in Polish: 'Systemic conditioning of Polish social policy'), in: *Polityka Społeczna*, no. 1.

Kowalik, T. (1998) 'Kapitał ludzki – polska bariera rozwoju', in: *Przegląd Społeczny*, no. 5–6/1998, also published in English: 'The systemic conditioning of Polish social policy', in: *Labour Focus on Eastern Europe*, no. 59.

Kowalik, T. (1998) 'Wobec globalizacji nierówności' (in Polish: 'Towards the globalisation of inequality'), in: *Zeszyty Naukowe Instytutu Badań Społecznych i Międzynarodowych Fundacji im. K. Kelles-Krauza*, no. 3.

Kowalik, T. (1998) 'Amartya K. Sen – Nobel za badania nierówności' (in Polish: 'Amartya K. Sen – Nobel prize for researching inequality'), in: *Zdanie*, also published in: *Nowe Życie Gospodarcze*, no. 46.

Kowalik, T. (1998) 'Spór o polski ład ekonomiczny' (in Polish: 'Dispute about the Polish economy order'), in: *Przegląd Społeczny*, no. 1–2.

Kowalik, T. (1998) 'Inteligenci jadą do Stoczni Gdańskiej' (in Polish: 'Intellectuals on the way to the Gdańsk shipyard'), in: *Przegląd Społeczny*, no. 3–4.

Kowalik, T. (1998) 'Ewolucja systemu ekonomicznego w USA' (in Polish: 'The evolution of the economic system in the USA'), in: *Przegląd Społeczny*, no. 7–8.

Kowalik, T. (1998) 'W oczekiwaniu na terapię, na marginesie książki G. Kołodki' (in Polish: 'Awaiting therapy, on the margins of the book by G. Kołodki'), in: *Ekonomista*, no. 4/1999.

Kowalik, T. (1999) 'O condicionamento sistêmico da politica social Polonesa' (in Portuguese: 'The systemic conditioning of Polish social policy), in: *Sociedas Em Transformacao*, no. 1.
Kowalik, T. (2001) 'Michał Kalecki, kim był, jakim go znałem i podziwiałem' (in Polish: 'Michał Kalecki, who he was, how I knew and admired him'), in: *Człowiek i Świat*, Fundacja Innowacja, Warszawa, republished in 2006 in: Musiał, G. (ed.) *Twórczość Michała Kaleckiego i jej znaczenie dla teorii ekonomii*, Akademia Ekonomiczna w Katowicach, Katowice.
Kowalik, T. (2003) 'Globalizacja i integracja nie prowadzą do jednego systemu społeczno-ekonomicznego' (in Polish: 'Globalisation and integration do not lead to one socio-economic system'), in: *Studia i Materiały*, no. 4., SSiIS, Warszawa.
Kowalik, T. (2004) 'Olgierd Gedymin: Kapitalizm niemiecki. Szkice o genezie, rozwoju i teraźniejszości, Białystok 2003 (recenzja)' (in Polish: 'Olgierd Gedymin: German capitalism. Outline of its origin, development and present state, Białystok 2003 (book review)'), in: *Ekonomista*, no. 30.
Kowalik, T. (2004) 'Państwo dobrobytu – druga fala' (in Polish: 'The welfare state – second wave'), in: *Problemy Polityki Społecznej, Studia i Dyskusje*, no. 6.
Kowalik, T. (2004) 'Systemic diversity of modern capitalism', in: *Dialogue and Universality*, no. 10–12.
Kowalik, T. (2004) 'America in an age of settling accounts, review of J. Stiglitz's The roaring nineties', in: *Dialogue and Universality*, no 10–12.
Kowalik, T. (2005) 'Własność źródłem wielu niesprawiedliwości' (in Polish: 'Property ownership, the origin of much injustice'), in: *Przegląd Socjalistyczny*, no. 4–5.
Kowalik, T. (2005) 'Od Stiglitza do Keynesa, wywiad przeprowadzony przez Sławomira Sierakowskiego' (in Polish: 'From Stiglitz to Keynes, interview by Sławomir Sierakowski'), in: *Krytyka Polityczna*, no. 9–10.
Kowalik, T. (2005) 'Rola państwa w transformacji' (in Polish: 'The role of the state in transformation'), in: *Przegląd Socjalistyczny*, no. 2–3.
Kowalik, T. (2007) 'Polska transformacja a nurty liberalne' (in Polish: 'Polish transformation and liberal movements'), presentation at the plenary session of the Congress of Polish Economists (Kongres Ekonomsitów Polskich), November 2007, published in: *Ekonomista*, no. 6.
Kowalik, T. (2007) 'Sylwetka laureata Nagrody Nobla z ekonomii 2007 – Leonid Hurwicz' (in Polish: 'Profile of the 2007 economics Nobel Prize winner – Leonid Hurwicz), in: *Problemy polityki społecznej*, no. 10.
Kowalik, T. (2008) 'Czy kapitalizm może być etyczny?' (in Polish: 'Can capitalism be ethical?'), in: *Annales SWSEiZ*, Salezjańska Wyższa Szkoła Ekonomii i Zarządzania, vol. 11, no. 1, Łódź.
Kowalik, T. (2008) 'Euro – kolejny filar ładu społecznego' (in Polish: 'Euro – another pillar of social order'), in: *Studia Ekonomiczne*, no. 1–2.
Kowalik, T. (2009) 'У истоков современного финансового кризиса' (in Russian: 'The origins of the current financial crisis'), in: *Белорусский экономический журнал*, no. 1.
Kowalik, T. (2010) 'Is cooperation of sociologists and economists possible and if so when?', in: *Warsaw Forum of Economic Sociology*, SGH, vol. 1, no. 1.
Kowalik, T. (2010) 'Cięciobsesja' (in Polish: 'Budget cut obsession'), in: *Krytyka Polityczna*, no. 23.

4 Other publications

Kowalik, T. and W. Sadowski (1956) 'O krytyce' (in Polish: 'A critique'), in: *Życie Gospodarcze*, no. 19.
Kowalik, T. (1957) 'Miscellanea radzieckie – Nowy etap dyskusji o prawie wartości w ZSRR' (in Polish: 'Soviet miscellanea – A new phase of discussion about the law of value in the USSR'), in: *Życie Gospodarcze*, no. 29.
Kowalik, T. (1957) 'O socjalizmie bez mistyki' (in Polish: 'Socialism without mysticism'), in: *Życie Gospodarcze*, no. 31.
Kowalik, T. (1957) 'Miscellanea radzieckie – Jeszcze o dyskusjach' (in Polish: 'Soviet miscellanea – More discussions'), in: *Życie Gospodarcze*, no. 32.
Kowalik, T. (1957) 'Swoiste curiosum i obsesje' (in Polish: 'Specific curiosity and obsession'), in: *Życie Gospodarcze*, no. 47/1957.
Kowalik, T. (1958) '"Kapitału" tom trzeci' (in Polish: '"Capital" volume three'), in: *Życie Gospodarcze*, no. 8.
Kowalik, T. (1958) 'Lenin wielki rewolucjonista' (in Polish: 'Lenin, the great revolunionary'), in: *Życie Gospodarcze*, no. 16.
Kowalik, T. (1958) 'Wybitna książka w obronie złej sprawy' (in Polish: 'An outstanding book in defence of the wrong cause'), in: *Życie Gospodarcze*, no. 38.
Kowalik, T. (1958) 'Granice ewolucji poglądów L. Krzywickiego' (in Polish: 'The limits of evolution in L. Krzywicki's views'), in: *Życie Gospodarcze*, no. 49.
Kowalik, T. (1958) 'Pierwszy przełom' (in Polish: 'The first breakthrough'), in: *Życie Gospodarcze*, no. 50.
Kowalik, T. (1960) 'Groźba gospodarczego anschlussu' (in Polish: 'The threat of economic Anschluss'), in: *Życie Gospodarcze*, no. 14.
Kowalik, T. (1960) 'Henryk Grossman, polsko-niemiecki teoretyk ekonomii marksistowskiej' (in Polish: 'Henryk Grossman, Polish-German theoretist of Marxist economics'), in: *Życie Gospodarcze*, no. 18.
Kowalik, T. (1968) 'Rosa Luxemburg', in: Sill, D. L. and R. K. Merton (eds) *International Encyclopedia of the Social Sciences*, vol. 9, Macmillan, New York.
Kowalik, T. (1974) 'Oskar Lange – tolerancja i wszechstronność' (in Polish: 'Oskar Lange – tolerance and universality'), in: *Kultura*, 19 August 1974.
Kowalik, T. (1975) 'Capitale' (in Italian: 'Capital'), entry in *Enciclopedia Einaudi*, vol. 2, Torino.
Kowalik, T. (1978) 'Crisi' (in Italian: 'Crises'), entry in *Enciclopedia Einaudi*, vol. 4, Torino.
Kowalik, T. (1980) *Spory o ustrój społeczno-ekonomiczny w Polsce, 1944–1948*, (wykłady Towarzystwa Kursów Naukowych), (in Polish: *Disputes over Poland's socio-economy system, 1944–1948*, lectures of the Towarzystwo Kursów Naukowych) Niezależna oficyna Wydawnicza "Nowa", Warszawa, republished in 2006 by INE PAN, Warszawa.
Kowalik, T. (1981) 'Z doświadczeń 1956 r. Rady robotnicze i pierwsze reformy' (in Polish: 'The experience of 1956. Workers' councils and first reforms'), in: *Nowa Trybuna Opolska*, no. 3.
Kowalik, T. (1985) 'Spór o racjonalność ciągle otwarty' (in Polish: 'The dispute about rationality remains open'), in: *Nowe Książki*, December/1984.
Kowalik, T. (1986) 'Walczący ślimak (rozmowa o Oskarze Langem)' (in Polish: 'The fighting snail (conversation about Oskar Lange)'), in: *Wprost*, 27 July 1986.

Kowalik, T. (1987–1989) 'Oskar Lange', 'Lange–Lerner model', 'Karl Kautsky', 'Rosa Luxemburg', 'Central Planning', entries in *The New Palgrave Economic Dictionary*, Macmillan, Basingstoke.

Kowalik, T. (1990) 'Destabilizacja gospodarcza czy nowa umowa społeczna?' (in Polish: 'Economic destabilisation or new social contract?'), in: *Życie Gospodarcze*, no. 28.

Kowalik, T. (1992) 'Misja Kuronia' (in Polish: 'Kuroń's mission'), in: *Życie Gospodarcze*, 12 May 1992.

Kowalik, T. (1994) Comment on the presentation by Drygalski, J., 'Pakt o przedsiębiorstwie państwowym a tempo i kierunek prywatyzacji' ('Pact on state enterprises and the pace and direction of privatisation'), in: *Prywatyzacja w Polsce. Szanse i Zagrożenia*, Instytut Gospodarki Światowej, Warszawa.

Kowalik, T. (1994) 'Is a social contract a utopia?', in: conference proceedings from the conference *Negotiations as the way to social contract*, IPiSS and Friedrich Ebert Stiftung, Warszawa.

Kowalik, T. (1995) 'Rola państwa w procesie transformacji' (in Polish: 'The role of the state in the transformation process'), in: *Gospodarka Narodowa*, no. 4.

Kowalik, T. (1996) 'Społeczny charakter ekonomii Edwarda Lipińskiego', in: *Społeczne aspekty rozwoju gospodarczego Polski*, Konferencja naukowa dla uczczenia 10 rocznicy śmierci prof. Edwarda Lipińskiego (in Polish: 'The social character of Edward Lipiński's economics', in: *Social aspects of Poland's economic development*, conference in honour of the 10th anniversary of Edward Lipiński's death), PTE, Warszawa.

Kowalik, T. (1996) 'Biegun nierówności' (in Polish: 'Polarising inequality'), in: *Gazeta Wyborcza*, 1 October 1996.

Kowalik, T. (1996) 'Sierpień – epigońska rewolucja mieszczańska' (in Polish: 'July – the bourgeois revolution of the latecomers'), in: *Nowe Życie Gospodarcze*, no. 37.

Kowalik, T. (1997) 'Dzielenie wzrostu' (in Polish: 'Distributing growth'), in: *Gazeta Bankowa*, 26 January 1997.

Kowalik, T. (1997) 'Jak komuch o solidaruchach (recenzja książki J. Główczyka, Kapitalizm po polsku)' (in Polish: 'The communist about the socialist (review of J. Główczyk, Capitalism in Polish)'), in: *Gazeta Wyborcza*, 9 February 1997.

Kowalik, T. (1998) 'Od oligarchicznego bogactwa do oligarchicznej demokracji' (in Polish: 'From oligarchic wealth to oligarchic democracy'), in: *Master of Business Administration*, no. 5–6.

Kowalik, T. (1998) 'Artykuł o książce Kornaia, Stabilizacja i wzrost w procesie transformacji', in: *Nowe Życie Gospodarcze*, no. 13.

Kowalik, T. (1998) 'Lepiej równiej' (in Polish: 'More equal is better'), in: *Polityka*, 18 April 1998.

Kowalik, T. (1998) 'Sygnały z Waszyngtonu' (in Polish: 'Signals from Washington'), in: *Przegląd Tygodniowy*, 9 September 1998.

Kowalik, T. (1999) 'Kaleckian crucial reform of capitalism and after', presentation at the international conference dedicated to the 100th birthday of Michał Kalecki, Polskie Towarzystwo Ekonomiczne, Warszawa.

Kowalik, T. (2000) 'Mity wolnego rynku' (in Polish: 'The myths of the free market'), in: *Przegląd Tygodniowy*, 25 September 2000.

Kowalik, T. (2001) 'Zachodnie państwo opiekuńcze obroniło się, co czeka Polskę?' (in Polish: 'The Western welfare state defended itelf, what is awaiting Poland?'), in: *Oświata i Wychowanie*, no. 3.

Kowalik, T. (2001) 'Społeczne aspekty transformacji a rola państwa' (in Polish: 'Social aspects of transformation and the role of the state'), in: *Gospodarka Narodowa*, no. 9.

Kowalik, T. (2001) 'W czyśćcu historii (na 80-lecie Włodzimierza Brusa)' (in Polish: 'In the purgatory of history (for the 80th birthday of Włodzimierz Brus)'), in: *Gazeta Wyborcza*, 25–26 August 2001.

Kowalik, T. (2001) 'Notas sobre la reforma Crucial do capitalismo de Kalecki e depois', in: Pomeranz, L., Miglioli, J. and G. T. Lima (eds) *Dinamica economica do capitalismo contemporaneo, Homenagem a M. Kalecki*, Universidade de Sao Paulo, and in English: Kowalik, T. (2004) 'Kaleckian crucial reform of capitalism and after', in: Sadowski, Z. L. and A. Szeworski (eds) *Kalecki's economics today*, Routledge, London.

Kowalik, T. (2001) 'Systemowe przesłanki' (in Polish: 'Systemic evidence'), in: *Nauka i Przyszłość*, September 2001.

Kowalik, T. (2001) 'O potrzebie radykalnych zmian w polityce gospodarczej i społecznej naszego kraju, wywiad Z. Słowika' (in Polish: 'About the need to change economic and social policies of our country, interview with Z. Słowika'), in: *Res Humana*, no. 1.

Kowalik, T. (2002) 'Joseph Stiglitz a polska transformacja' (in Polish: 'Joseph Stiglitz and the Polish transformation'), in: *Oświata i Wychowanie*, no. 1.

Kowalik, T. (2002) 'Mój rok osiemdziesiąty dziewiąty' (in Polish: 'My year 1989'), in: *Gazeta Wyborcza*, 23–24 March 2002.

Kowalik, T. (2002) 'Polska miała pecha' (in Polish: 'Poland had bad luck'), in: *Trybuna*, 12 April 2002.

Kowalik, T. (2002) 'System gospodarczy' (in Polish: 'Economic system'), entry in: *Encyklopedia Socjologii* (*Sociological encyclopaedia*), Tom 5, Oficyna Naukowa, Warszawa.

Kowalik, T. (2003) 'Accession to EU – yesterday, today, tomorrow', in: Conference proceedings from the conference *Improvement of economic policy co-ordination for employment and social cohesion in Europe*, Budapest University of Economic Sciences and Public Administration, Budapest.

Kowalik, T. (2003) 'Błędne przesłanki, błędne wnioski' (in Polish: 'Wrong assumptions, wrong conclusions'), in: *Rzeczpospolita*, 20 January 2003.

Kowalik, T. (2003) 'Polska transformacja a lewica (par uwag adresowanych do działaczy SLD)' (in Polish: 'The Polish transformation and the left (some remarks addressed to SLD members)'), in: *Kontrpropozycje*, no. 4/7.

Kowalik, T. (2003) 'Narodowe fundusze inwestycyjne – góra urodziła mysz, miesięcznik' (in Polish: 'National investment funds – the mountain gave birth to a mouse, a monthly story'), in: *Oświata i Wychowanie*, no. 4.

Kowalik, T. (2003) 'Mój przyjaciel Jerzy Hauser' (in Polish: 'My friend Jerzy Hauser'), in: *Przegląd*, 23 March 2003.

Kowalik, T. (2004) Globalizacja na rozdrożu' (in Polish: 'Globalisation at the crossroads'), in: *Bank i Kredyt*, no. 8.

Kowalik, T. (2004) 'Porozmawiajmy o kapitalizmie, rozmawia Przemysław Wielgosz' (in Polish: 'Let's talk about capitalism, interview with Przemysław Wielgosz'), in: *Trybuna*, 14–15 July 2004.

Kowalik, T. (2005) 'Antyetatyzm jako misja, polemiczny artykuł o książce: Janusz Beksiak redaktor i główny autor, Polska gospodarka w XX wieku, eseje historyczno-ekonomiczne, Łódź, 2003' (in Polish: 'Anti-statism as a mission, polemical article about Janusz Beksiak's book, The Polish economy in the 20th century, socio-historical essays, Łódź, 2003'), in: *Oświata i Wychowanie*, no. 1.

Kowalik, T. (2005) 'Bezdroża "Solidarności", wywiad przeprowadzony przez Andrzeja Zybałę' (in Polish: 'The sideways of "Solidarności", interview by Andrzej Zybał'), in: *Obywatel*, no. 5–25.

Kowalik, T. (2005) 'Trudne wybory po Sierpniu '80, rozmawiają Irena Dryll i Adam Cymer' (in Polish: 'Though choices after August '80, interview with Irena Dryll and Adam Cymer'), in: *Nowe Życie Gospodarcze*, no. 16.

Kowalik, T. (2005) 'Pracy i chleba' (in Polish: 'Work and bread'), in: *Trybuna*, 28 April 2005.

Kowalik, T. (2006) 'Jan Bossak, Systemy gospodarcze a globalna konkurencja (recenzja)' (in Polish: 'Jan Bossak, The economic system and global competition (book review)'), in: *Gospodarka Narodowa*, no. 11–12.

Kowalik, T. (2006) 'Bez buntu się nie obejdzie' (in Polish: 'There is no way without rebellion'), in: *Trybuna*, 2 February 2006.

Kowalik, T. (2006) 'Polish roots of and debates on R. Luxemburg's theories', presentation at the *International Conference on Rosa Luxemburg's Thought and Its Contemporary Value*, 20–22 March 2006, Wuhan University, China.

Kowalik, T. (2006) 'Wina i wiara Jacka Kuronia' (in Polish: 'Fault and faith of Jacek Kuroń'), in: *Le Monde Diplomatiques*, June.

Kowalik, T. (2006) 'Własność jako źródło nierówności' (in Polish: 'Property as source of inequality'), presentation at the interdisciplinary conference *Nierówności społeczne* (*Social inequalities*), 5–6 June 2006, Institute of Psychology of the Wrocław University, Wrocław.

Kowalik, T. (2006) 'Poland's sudden shift to the right', presentation at the *EuroMemorandum conference*, 30 September 2006, Bruxelles.

Kowalik, T. (2007) 'Miltona Friedmana droga na szczyty' (in Polish: 'Milton Friedman's way to the top'), in: *Oświata i Wychowanie*, February.

Kowalik, T. (2007) 'Chiny – Wielki sukces i nie mniejsze problemy' (in Polish: 'China – Great success and equally large problems'), in: *Le Monde Diplomatique*, February/2007.

Kowalik, T. (2007) 'Barwy Ochronne Donalda Tuska' (in Polish: 'Donald Tusk's protective mimicry'), in: *Le Monde Diplomatique*, December.

Kowalik, T. (2007) 'Polskie reformy (na marginesie książki W. Baki: Zmagania o reformę. Z dziennika politycznego 1980–1990)' (in Polish: 'Polish reforms (on the margins of W. Baka's book: The struggle for reform. Political diary 1980–1990)'), in: *Dziś*, no. 8.

Kowalik, T. (2007) 'Piotr Kozarzewski, Prywatyzacja w krajach postkomunistycznych (recenzja)' (in Polish: 'Piotr Kozarzewski, Privatisation in post-communist countries (book review)'), in: *Nowe Życie Gospodarcze* no. 30.

Kowalik, T. (2008) 'Szok zamiast terapii' (in Polish: 'Shock instead of therapy'), letter by the association 'Kuźnica', in: *Zdanie*, no. 1–2.

Kowalik, T. (2008) 'Dokąd zmierzają Chiny?' (in Polish: 'Where is China heading?'), in: *Dziś*, no. 3.

Kowalik, T. (2008) 'Kornai wśród skorpionów' (in Polish: 'Kornai amidst scorpions'), in: *Gazeta Wyborcza*, 18 October 2008.

Kowalik, T. (2009) 'Recenzja książki Jacka Tittenbruna, Z deszczu pod rynnę, Meandry polskiej prywatyzacji' (in Polish: 'Review of Jacek Tittenbrun's book, Out of the frying pan into the fire, Meanders of Polish privatisation'), in: *Nowe Książki*, January.

Kowalik, T. (2009) 'Kryzys oddalił naszą euroizację' (in Polish: 'The crisis has rolled back our euroisation'), in: *Kwartalnik Nauk o Przedsiębiorstwie*, no. 2.

Kowalik, T. (2009) 'Systemowe źródła obecnego kryzysu światowego' (in Polish: 'Systemic origins of the current global crisis'), in: *Master of Business Administration*, no. 5.

Kowalik, T. (2010) 'Konstytucyjna zasada sprawiedliwości społecznej' (in Polish: 'Constitutional principles of social justic'), presentation at the Constitutional Court, 9 March 2010, in: *Podstawowe założenia Konstytucji Rzeczpospolitej Polskiej*, Wydawnictwo Trybunału Konstytucyjnego, Warszawa.

Kowalik, T. (2010) 'Czy nadchodzi "cywilizacja nierówności"?' (in Polish: 'Is the "civilisation of inequality" approaching?'), in: *Res Humana*, no. 6.

Kowalik, T. (2010) 'Czy PRL był państwem polskim?' (in Polish: 'Was the Polish People's Republic a Polish state?'), in: *Kancelaria Prezydenta RP, Seminaria Lucieńskie 2008–2009*, Warszawa.

Index

The manufacturer's authorised representative in the EU is Springer Nature Customer Service Centre GmbH, Europaplatz 3, 69115 Heidelberg, Germany. If you have any concerns regarding our products, please contact ProductSafety@springernature.com

Printed and bound by CPI Group (UK) Ltd, Croydon, CR0 4YY

13/10/2026

02232481-0010